FREE Study Skills Videos/DVD Offer

Dear Customer,

Thank you for your purchase from Mometrix! We consider it an honor and a privilege that you have purchased our product and we want to ensure your satisfaction.

As part of our ongoing effort to meet the needs of test takers, we have developed a set of Study Skills Videos that we would like to give you for <u>FREE</u>. These videos cover our *best practices* for getting ready for your exam, from how to use our study materials to how to best prepare for the day of the test.

All that we ask is that you email us with feedback that would describe your experience so far with our product. Good, bad, or indifferent, we want to know what you think!

To get your FREE Study Skills Videos, you can use the **QR code** below, or send us an **email** at <u>studyvideos@mometrix.com</u> with *FREE VIDEOS* in the subject line and the following information in the body of the email:

- The name of the product you purchased.
- Your product rating on a scale of 1-5, with 5 being the highest rating.
- Your feedback. It can be long, short, or anything in between. We just want to know your impressions and experience so far with our product. (Good feedback might include how our study material met your needs and ways we might be able to make it even better. You could highlight features that you found helpful or features that you think we should add.)

If you have any questions or concerns, please don't hesitate to contact me directly.

Thanks again!

Sincerely,

Jay Willis
Vice President
<u>jay.willis@mometrix.com</u>
1-800-673-8175

PreACT Secrets

Study Guide

Your Key to Exam Success

Written and edited by the Mometrix College Admissions Test Team

Printed in the United States of America

This paper meets the requirements of ANSI/NISO Z39.48-1992 (Permanence of Paper).

Mometrix offers volume discount pricing to institutions. For more information or a price quote, please contact our sales department at sales@mometrix.com or 888-248-1219.

Mometrix Media LLC is not affiliated with or endorsed by any official testing organization. All organizational and test names are trademarks of their respective owners.

Paperback
ISBN 13: 978-1-5167-0746-1
ISBN 10: 1-5167-0746-X

Ebook
ISBN 13: 978-1-5167-0775-1
ISBN 10: 1-5167-0775-3

Hardback
ISBN 13: 978-1-5167-1157-4
ISBN 10: 1-5167-1157-2

DEAR FUTURE EXAM SUCCESS STORY

First of all, **THANK YOU** for purchasing Mometrix study materials!

Second, congratulations! You are one of the few determined test-takers who are committed to doing whatever it takes to excel on your exam. **You have come to the right place.** We developed these study materials with one goal in mind: to deliver you the information you need in a format that's concise and easy to use.

In addition to optimizing your guide for the content of the test, we've outlined our recommended steps for breaking down the preparation process into small, attainable goals so you can make sure you stay on track.

We've also analyzed the entire test-taking process, identifying the most common pitfalls and showing how you can overcome them and be ready for any curveball the test throws you.

Standardized testing is one of the biggest obstacles on your road to success, which only increases the importance of doing well in the high-pressure, high-stakes environment of test day. Your results on this test could have a significant impact on your future, and this guide provides the information and practical advice to help you achieve your full potential on test day.

Your success is our success

We would love to hear from you! If you would like to share the story of your exam success or if you have any questions or comments in regard to our products, please contact us at **800-673-8175** or **support@mometrix.com**.

Thanks again for your business and we wish you continued success!

Sincerely,
The Mometrix Test Preparation Team

> **Need more help? Check out our flashcards at:**
> **http://MometrixFlashcards.com/PreACT**

TABLE OF CONTENTS

Introduction

Thank you for purchasing this resource! You have made the choice to prepare yourself for a test that could have a huge impact on your future, and this guide is designed to help you be fully ready for test day. Obviously, it's important to have a solid understanding of the test material, but you also need to be prepared for the unique environment and stressors of the test, so that you can perform to the best of your abilities.

For this purpose, the first section that appears in this guide is the **Secret Keys**. We've devoted countless hours to meticulously researching what works and what doesn't, and we've boiled down our findings to the five most impactful steps you can take to improve your performance on the test. We start at the beginning with study planning and move through the preparation process, all the way to the testing strategies that will help you get the most out of what you know when you're finally sitting in front of the test.

We recommend that you start preparing for your test as far in advance as possible. However, if you've bought this guide as a last-minute study resource and only have a few days before your test, we recommend that you skip over the first two Secret Keys since they address a long-term study plan.

If you struggle with **test anxiety**, we strongly encourage you to check out our recommendations for how you can overcome it. Test anxiety is a formidable foe, but it can be beaten, and we want to make sure you have the tools you need to defeat it.

Secret Key #1 – Plan Big, Study Small

There's a lot riding on your performance. If you want to ace this test, you're going to need to keep your skills sharp and the material fresh in your mind. You need a plan that lets you review everything you need to know while still fitting in your schedule. We'll break this strategy down into three categories.

Information Organization

Start with the information you already have: the official test outline. From this, you can make a complete list of all the concepts you need to cover before the test. Organize these concepts into groups that can be studied together, and create a list of any related vocabulary you need to learn so you can brush up on any difficult terms. You'll want to keep this vocabulary list handy once you actually start studying since you may need to add to it along the way.

Time Management

Once you have your set of study concepts, decide how to spread them out over the time you have left before the test. Break your study plan into small, clear goals so you have a manageable task for each day and know exactly what you're doing. Then just focus on one small step at a time. When you manage your time this way, you don't need to spend hours at a time studying. Studying a small block of content for a short period each day helps you retain information better and avoid stressing over how much you have left to do. You can relax knowing that you have a plan to cover everything in time. In order for this strategy to be effective though, you have to start studying early and stick to your schedule. Avoid the exhaustion and futility that comes from last-minute cramming!

Study Environment

The environment you study in has a big impact on your learning. Studying in a coffee shop, while probably more enjoyable, is not likely to be as fruitful as studying in a quiet room. It's important to keep distractions to a minimum. You're only planning to study for a short block of time, so make the most of it. Don't pause to check your phone or get up to find a snack. It's also important to **avoid multitasking**. Research has consistently shown that multitasking will make your studying dramatically less effective. Your study area should also be comfortable and well-lit so you don't have the distraction of straining your eyes or sitting on an uncomfortable chair.

 The time of day you study is also important. You want to be rested and alert. Don't wait until just before bedtime. Study when you'll be most likely to comprehend and remember. Even better, if you know what time of day your test will be, set that time aside for study. That way your brain will be used to working on that subject at that specific time and you'll have a better chance of recalling information.

Finally, it can be helpful to team up with others who are studying for the same test. Your actual studying should be done in as isolated an environment as possible, but the work of organizing the information and setting up the study plan can be divided up. In between study sessions, you can discuss with your teammates the concepts that you're all studying and quiz each other on the details. Just be sure that your teammates are as serious about the test as you are. If you find that your study time is being replaced with social time, you might need to find a new team.

2

Secret Key #2 – Make Your Studying Count

You're devoting a lot of time and effort to preparing for this test, so you want to be absolutely certain it will pay off. This means doing more than just reading the content and hoping you can remember it on test day. It's important to make every minute of study count. There are two main areas you can focus on to make your studying count.

Retention

It doesn't matter how much time you study if you can't remember the material. You need to make sure you are retaining the concepts. To check your retention of the information you're learning, try recalling it at later times with minimal prompting. Try carrying around flashcards and glance at one or two from time to time or ask a friend who's also studying for the test to quiz you.

To enhance your retention, look for ways to put the information into practice so that you can apply it rather than simply recalling it. If you're using the information in practical ways, it will be much easier to remember. Similarly, it helps to solidify a concept in your mind if you're not only reading it to yourself but also explaining it to someone else. Ask a friend to let you teach them about a concept you're a little shaky on (or speak aloud to an imaginary audience if necessary). As you try to summarize, define, give examples, and answer your friend's questions, you'll understand the concepts better and they will stay with you longer. Finally, step back for a big picture view and ask yourself how each piece of information fits with the whole subject. When you link the different concepts together and see them working together as a whole, it's easier to remember the individual components.

Finally, practice showing your work on any multi-step problems, even if you're just studying. Writing out each step you take to solve a problem will help solidify the process in your mind, and you'll be more likely to remember it during the test.

Modality

Modality simply refers to the means or method by which you study. Choosing a study modality that fits your own individual learning style is crucial. No two people learn best in exactly the same way, so it's important to know your strengths and use them to your advantage.

For example, if you learn best by visualization, focus on visualizing a concept in your mind and draw an image or a diagram. Try color-coding your notes, illustrating them, or creating symbols that will trigger your mind to recall a learned concept. If you learn best by hearing or discussing information, find a study partner who learns the same way or read aloud to yourself. Think about how to put the information in your own words. Imagine that you are giving a lecture on the topic and record yourself so you can listen to it later.

For any learning style, flashcards can be helpful. Organize the information so you can take advantage of spare moments to review. Underline key words or phrases. Use different colors for different categories. Mnemonic devices (such as creating a short list in which every item starts with the same letter) can also help with retention. Find what works best for you and use it to store the information in your mind most effectively and easily.

3

Secret Key #3 – Practice the Right Way

Your success on test day depends not only on how many hours you put into preparing, but also on whether you prepared the right way. It's good to check along the way to see if your studying is paying off. One of the most effective ways to do this is by taking practice tests to evaluate your progress. Practice tests are useful because they show exactly where you need to improve. Every time you take a practice test, pay special attention to these three groups of questions:

- The questions you got wrong
- The questions you had to guess on, even if you guessed right
- The questions you found difficult or slow to work through

This will show you exactly what your weak areas are, and where you need to devote more study time. Ask yourself why each of these questions gave you trouble. Was it because you didn't understand the material? Was it because you didn't remember the vocabulary? Do you need more repetitions on this type of question to build speed and confidence? Dig into those questions and figure out how you can strengthen your weak areas as you go back to review the material.

 Additionally, many practice tests have a section explaining the answer choices. It can be tempting to read the explanation and think that you now have a good understanding of the concept. However, an explanation likely only covers part of the question's broader context. Even if the explanation makes perfect sense, **go back and investigate** every concept related to the question until you're positive you have a thorough understanding.

As you go along, keep in mind that the practice test is just that: practice. Memorizing these questions and answers will not be very helpful on the actual test because it is unlikely to have any of the same exact questions. If you only know the right answers to the sample questions, you won't be prepared for the real thing. **Study the concepts** until you understand them fully, and then you'll be able to answer any question that shows up on the test.

It's important to wait on the practice tests until you're ready. If you take a test on your first day of study, you may be overwhelmed by the amount of material covered and how much you need to learn. Work up to it gradually.

On test day, you'll need to be prepared for answering questions, managing your time, and using the test-taking strategies you've learned. It's a lot to balance, like a mental marathon that will have a big impact on your future. Like training for a marathon, you'll need to start slowly and work your way up. When test day arrives, you'll be ready.

Start with the strategies you've read in the first two Secret Keys—plan your course and study in the way that works best for you. If you have time, consider using multiple study resources to get different approaches to the same concepts. It can be helpful to see difficult concepts from more than one angle. Then find a good source for practice tests. Many times, the test website will suggest potential study resources or provide sample tests.

Practice Test Strategy

If you're able to find at least three practice tests, we recommend this strategy:

UNTIMED AND OPEN-BOOK PRACTICE

Take the first test with no time constraints and with your notes and study guide handy. Take your time and focus on applying the strategies you've learned.

TIMED AND OPEN-BOOK PRACTICE

Take the second practice test open-book as well, but set a timer and practice pacing yourself to finish in time.

TIMED AND CLOSED-BOOK PRACTICE

Take any other practice tests as if it were test day. Set a timer and put away your study materials. Sit at a table or desk in a quiet room, imagine yourself at the testing center, and answer questions as quickly and accurately as possible.

Keep repeating timed and closed-book tests on a regular basis until you run out of practice tests or it's time for the actual test. Your mind will be ready for the schedule and stress of test day, and you'll be able to focus on recalling the material you've learned.

Secret Key #4 – Pace Yourself

Once you're fully prepared for the material on the test, your biggest challenge on test day will be managing your time. Just knowing that the clock is ticking can make you panic even if you have plenty of time left. Work on pacing yourself so you can build confidence against the time constraints of the exam. Pacing is a difficult skill to master, especially in a high-pressure environment, so **practice is vital**.

Set time expectations for your pace based on how much time is available. For example, if a section has 60 questions and the time limit is 30 minutes, you know you have to average 30 seconds or less per question in order to answer them all. Although 30 seconds is the hard limit, set 25 seconds per question as your goal, so you reserve extra time to spend on harder questions. When you budget extra time for the harder questions, you no longer have any reason to stress when those questions take longer to answer.

Don't let this time expectation distract you from working through the test at a calm, steady pace, but keep it in mind so you don't spend too much time on any one question. Recognize that taking extra time on one question you don't understand may keep you from answering two that you do understand later in the test. If your time limit for a question is up and you're still not sure of the answer, mark it and move on, and come back to it later if the time and the test format allow. If the testing format doesn't allow you to return to earlier questions, just make an educated guess; then put it out of your mind and move on.

On the easier questions, be careful not to rush. It may seem wise to hurry through them so you have more time for the challenging ones, but it's not worth missing one if you know the concept and just didn't take the time to read the question fully. Work efficiently but make sure you understand the question and have looked at all of the answer choices, since more than one may seem right at first.

Even if you're paying attention to the time, you may find yourself a little behind at some point. You should speed up to get back on track, but do so wisely. Don't panic; just take a few seconds less on each question until you're caught up. Don't guess without thinking, but do look through the answer choices and eliminate any you know are wrong. If you can get down to two choices, it is often worthwhile to guess from those. Once you've chosen an answer, move on and don't dwell on any that you skipped or had to hurry through. If a question was taking too long, chances are it was one of the harder ones, so you weren't as likely to get it right anyway.

On the other hand, if you find yourself getting ahead of schedule, it may be beneficial to slow down a little. The more quickly you work, the more likely you are to make a careless mistake that will affect your score. You've budgeted time for each question, so don't be afraid to spend that time. Practice an efficient but careful pace to get the most out of the time you have.

Secret Key #5 – Have a Plan for Guessing

When you're taking the test, you may find yourself stuck on a question. Some of the answer choices seem better than others, but you don't see the one answer choice that is obviously correct. What do you do?

The scenario described above is very common, yet most test takers have not effectively prepared for it. Developing and practicing a plan for guessing may be one of the single most effective uses of your time as you get ready for the exam.

In developing your plan for guessing, there are three questions to address:

- When should you start the guessing process?
- How should you narrow down the choices?
- Which answer should you choose?

When to Start the Guessing Process

Unless your plan for guessing is to select C every time (which, despite its merits, is not what we recommend), you need to leave yourself enough time to apply your answer elimination strategies. Since you have a limited amount of time for each question, that means that if you're going to give yourself the best shot at guessing correctly, you have to decide quickly whether or not you will guess.

Of course, the best-case scenario is that you don't have to guess at all, so first, see if you can answer the question based on your knowledge of the subject and basic reasoning skills. Focus on the key words in the question and try to jog your memory of related topics. Give yourself a chance to bring the knowledge to mind, but once you realize that you don't have (or you can't access) the knowledge you need to answer the question, it's time to start the guessing process.

It's almost always better to start the guessing process too early than too late. It only takes a few seconds to remember something and answer the question from knowledge. Carefully eliminating wrong answer choices takes longer. Plus, going through the process of eliminating answer choices can actually help jog your memory.

Summary: Start the guessing process as soon as you decide that you can't answer the question based on your knowledge.

How to Narrow Down the Choices

The next chapter in this book (**Test-Taking Strategies**) includes a wide range of strategies for how to approach questions and how to look for answer choices to eliminate. You will definitely want to read those carefully, practice them, and figure out which ones work best for you. Here though, we're going to address a mindset rather than a particular strategy.

Your odds of guessing an answer correctly depend on how many options you are choosing from.

Number of options left	5	4	3	2	1
Odds of guessing correctly	20%	25%	33%	50%	100%

You can see from this chart just how valuable it is to be able to eliminate incorrect answers and make an educated guess, but there are two things that many test takers do that cause them to miss out on the benefits of guessing:

- Accidentally eliminating the correct answer
- Selecting an answer based on an impression

We'll look at the first one here, and the second one in the next section.

To avoid accidentally eliminating the correct answer, we recommend a thought exercise called **the $5 challenge**. In this challenge, you only eliminate an answer choice from contention if you are willing to bet $5 on it being wrong. Why $5? Five dollars is a small but not insignificant amount of money. It's an amount you could afford to lose but wouldn't want to throw away. And while losing

$5 once might not hurt too much, doing it twenty times will set you back $100. In the same way, each small decision you make—eliminating a choice here, guessing on a question there—won't by itself impact your score very much, but when you put them all together, they can make a big difference. By holding each answer choice elimination decision to a higher standard, you can reduce the risk of accidentally eliminating the correct answer.

The $5 challenge can also be applied in a positive sense: If you are willing to bet $5 that an answer choice *is* correct, go ahead and mark it as correct.

Summary: Only eliminate an answer choice if you are willing to bet $5 that it is wrong.

8

Which Answer to Choose

You're taking the test. You've run into a hard question and decided you'll have to guess. You've eliminated all the answer choices you're willing to bet $5 on. Now you have to pick an answer. Why do we even need to talk about this? Why can't you just pick whichever one you feel like when the time comes?

The answer to these questions is that if you don't come into the test with a plan, you'll rely on your impression to select an answer choice, and if you do that, you risk falling into a trap. The test writers know that everyone who takes their test will be guessing on some of the questions, so they intentionally write wrong answer choices to seem plausible. You still have to pick an answer though, and if the wrong answer choices are designed to look right, how can you ever be sure that you're not falling for their trap? The best solution we've found to this dilemma is to take the decision out of your hands entirely. Here is the process we recommend:

Once you've eliminated any choices that you are confident (willing to bet $5) are wrong, select the first remaining choice as your answer.

Whether you choose to select the first remaining choice, the second, or the last, the important thing is that you use some preselected standard. Using this approach guarantees that you will not be enticed into selecting an answer choice that looks right, because you are not basing your decision on how the answer choices look.

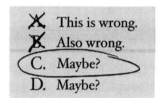

This is not meant to make you question your knowledge. Instead, it is to help you recognize the difference between your knowledge and your impressions. There's a huge difference between thinking an answer is right because of what you know, and thinking an answer is right because it looks or sounds like it should be right.

Summary: To ensure that your selection is appropriately random, make a predetermined selection from among all answer choices you have not eliminated.

Test-Taking Strategies

This section contains a list of test-taking strategies that you may find helpful as you work through the test. By taking what you know and applying logical thought, you can maximize your chances of answering any question correctly!

It is very important to realize that every question is different and every person is different: no single strategy will work on every question, and no single strategy will work for every person. That's why we've included all of them here, so you can try them out and determine which ones work best for different types of questions and which ones work best for you.

Question Strategies

☑ READ CAREFULLY

Read the question and the answer choices carefully. Don't miss the question because you misread the terms. You have plenty of time to read each question thoroughly and make sure you understand what is being asked. Yet a happy medium must be attained, so don't waste too much time. You must read carefully and efficiently.

☑ CONTEXTUAL CLUES

Look for contextual clues. If the question includes a word you are not familiar with, look at the immediate context for some indication of what the word might mean. Contextual clues can often give you all the information you need to decipher the meaning of an unfamiliar word. Even if you can't determine the meaning, you may be able to narrow down the possibilities enough to make a solid guess at the answer to the question.

☑ PREFIXES

If you're having trouble with a word in the question or answer choices, try dissecting it. Take advantage of every clue that the word might include. Prefixes can be a huge help. Usually, they allow you to determine a basic meaning. *Pre-* means before, *post-* means after, *pro-* is positive, *de-* is negative. From prefixes, you can get an idea of the general meaning of the word and try to put it into context.

☑ HEDGE WORDS

Watch out for critical hedge words, such as *likely, may, can, sometimes, often, almost, mostly, usually, generally, rarely,* and *sometimes*. Question writers insert these hedge phrases to cover every possibility. Often an answer choice will be wrong simply because it leaves no room for exception. Be on guard for answer choices that have definitive words such as *exactly* and *always*.

☑ SWITCHBACK WORDS

Stay alert for *switchbacks*. These are the words and phrases frequently used to alert you to shifts in thought. The most common switchback words are *but, although,* and *however*. Others include *nevertheless, on the other hand, even though, while, in spite of, despite,* and *regardless of*. Switchback words are important to catch because they can change the direction of the question or an answer choice.

10

⊘ FACE VALUE

When in doubt, use common sense. Accept the situation in the problem at face value. Don't read too much into it. These problems will not require you to make wild assumptions. If you have to go beyond creativity and warp time or space in order to have an answer choice fit the question, then you should move on and consider the other answer choices. These are normal problems rooted in reality. The applicable relationship or explanation may not be readily apparent, but it is there for you to figure out. Use your common sense to interpret anything that isn't clear.

Answer Choice Strategies

⊘ ANSWER SELECTION

The most thorough way to pick an answer choice is to identify and eliminate wrong answers until only one is left, then confirm it is the correct answer. Sometimes an answer choice may immediately seem right, but be careful. The test writers will usually put more than one reasonable answer choice on each question, so take a second to read all of them and make sure that the other choices are not equally obvious. As long as you have time left, it is better to read every answer choice than to pick the first one that looks right without checking the others.

⊘ ANSWER CHOICE FAMILIES

An answer choice family consists of two (in rare cases, three) answer choices that are very similar in construction and cannot all be true at the same time. If you see two answer choices that are direct opposites or parallels, one of them is usually the correct answer. For instance, if one answer choice says that quantity x increases and another either says that quantity x decreases (opposite) or says that quantity y increases (parallel), then those answer choices would fall into the same family. An answer choice that doesn't match the construction of the answer choice family is more likely to be incorrect. Most questions will not have answer choice families, but when they do appear, you should be prepared to recognize them.

⊘ ELIMINATE ANSWERS

Eliminate answer choices as soon as you realize they are wrong, but make sure you consider all possibilities. If you are eliminating answer choices and realize that the last one you are left with is also wrong, don't panic. Start over and consider each choice again. There may be something you missed the first time that you will realize on the second pass.

⊘ AVOID FACT TRAPS

Don't be distracted by an answer choice that is factually true but doesn't answer the question. You are looking for the choice that answers the question. Stay focused on what the question is asking for so you don't accidentally pick an answer that is true but incorrect. Always go back to the question and make sure the answer choice you've selected actually answers the question and is not merely a true statement.

⊘ EXTREME STATEMENTS

In general, you should avoid answers that put forth extreme actions as standard practice or proclaim controversial ideas as established fact. An answer choice that states the "process should be used in certain situations, if..." is much more likely to be correct than one that states the "process should be discontinued completely." The first is a calm rational statement and doesn't even make a definitive, uncompromising stance, using a hedge word *if* to provide wiggle room, whereas the second choice is far more extreme.

⊘ Benchmark

As you read through the answer choices and you come across one that seems to answer the question well, mentally select that answer choice. This is not your final answer, but it's the one that will help you evaluate the other answer choices. The one that you selected is your benchmark or standard for judging each of the other answer choices. Every other answer choice must be compared to your benchmark. That choice is correct until proven otherwise by another answer choice beating it. If you find a better answer, then that one becomes your new benchmark. Once you've decided that no other choice answers the question as well as your benchmark, you have your final answer.

⊘ Predict the Answer

Before you even start looking at the answer choices, it is often best to try to predict the answer. When you come up with the answer on your own, it is easier to avoid distractions and traps because you will know exactly what to look for. The right answer choice is unlikely to be word-for-word what you came up with, but it should be a close match. Even if you are confident that you have the right answer, you should still take the time to read each option before moving on.

General Strategies

⊘ Tough Questions

If you are stumped on a problem or it appears too hard or too difficult, don't waste time. Move on! Remember though, if you can quickly check for obviously incorrect answer choices, your chances of guessing correctly are greatly improved. Before you completely give up, at least try to knock out a couple of possible answers. Eliminate what you can and then guess at the remaining answer choices before moving on.

⊘ Check Your Work

Since you will probably not know every term listed and the answer to every question, it is important that you get credit for the ones that you do know. Don't miss any questions through careless mistakes. If at all possible, try to take a second to look back over your answer selection and make sure you've selected the correct answer choice and haven't made a costly careless mistake (such as marking an answer choice that you didn't mean to mark). This quick double check should more than pay for itself in caught mistakes for the time it costs.

⊘ Pace Yourself

It's easy to be overwhelmed when you're looking at a page full of questions; your mind is confused and full of random thoughts, and the clock is ticking down faster than you would like. Calm down and maintain the pace that you have set for yourself. Especially as you get down to the last few minutes of the test, don't let the small numbers on the clock make you panic. As long as you are on track by monitoring your pace, you are guaranteed to have time for each question.

⊘ Don't Rush

It is very easy to make errors when you are in a hurry. Maintaining a fast pace in answering questions is pointless if it makes you miss questions that you would have gotten right otherwise. Test writers like to include distracting information and wrong answers that seem right. Taking a little extra time to avoid careless mistakes can make all the difference in your test score. Find a pace that allows you to be confident in the answers that you select.

12

⏱ Keep Moving

Panicking will not help you pass the test, so do your best to stay calm and keep moving. Taking deep breaths and going through the answer elimination steps you practiced can help to break through a stress barrier and keep your pace.

Final Notes

The combination of a solid foundation of content knowledge and the confidence that comes from practicing your plan for applying that knowledge is the key to maximizing your performance on test day. As your foundation of content knowledge is built up and strengthened, you'll find that the strategies included in this chapter become more and more effective in helping you quickly sift through the distractions and traps of the test to isolate the correct answer.

Now that you're preparing to move forward into the test content chapters of this book, be sure to keep your goal in mind. As you read, think about how you will be able to apply this information on the test. If you've already seen sample questions for the test and you have an idea of the question format and style, try to come up with questions of your own that you can answer based on what you're reading. This will give you valuable practice applying your knowledge in the same ways you can expect to on test day.

Good luck and good studying!

The English Test

Overview

The English portion of the PreACT will have questions about underlined portions of text, with possible replacements as answer choices. Read the text four times, each time replacing the underlined portion with one of the choices. While reading the choices, read the sentence before, the sentence containing, and the sentence after the underlined portion. Sometimes an answer may not make sense until you read the following sentence and see how the two sentences flow together. Transitional words should create smooth, logical transitions and maintain a constant flow of text.

Some questions will be concerning sentence insertions. In those cases, do not look for the ones that simply restate what was in the previous sentence. New sentences should contain new information and new insights into the subject of the text. If asked for the paragraph to which a sentence would most naturally be added, find a key noun or word in that new sentence. Then, find the paragraph containing that exact word, or another word closely related to that key noun or word. That is the paragraph that should include the new sentence.

Some questions will ask what purpose a phrase fulfilled in a particular text. It depends upon the subject of the text. If the text is dramatic, then the phrase was probably used to show tension. If the text is comedic, then the phrase may have been there to relieve tension.

In related cases, you may be asked to provide a sentence that summarizes the text. Simple sentences, without wordy phrases, are usually best. If asked for a succinct answer, then the shorter the answer the more likely it is correct.

Topic Development

UNDERSTANDING THE ASSIGNMENT

For your exam, you will be given a prompt (i.e., a writing assignment) that needs your response within the time limit. However you feel about the prompt, you need to give an answer that addresses the entire prompt. Your response needs to be creative and informed. In other words, you need to keep the attention and interest of your audience. Most importantly, you need to show your readers that you know what you are talking about in your essay. As you consider the prompt, you may want to ask these questions to understand the assignment:

1. What specifically is the assignment asking you to do?
2. What information or knowledge is necessary to fulfill the assignment?
3. Are there other requirements for the assignment?
4. What is the purpose of the assignment?
5. Who is the intended audience?
6. What is the length of the assignment?

After you read the prompt, you need to determine what you know about the topic. You may think that you have very few ideas when you first read the prompt. However, you can use some strategies to think of ideas. These strategies include brainstorming, free writing, looping, and questioning.

PURPOSES OF WRITING

Before you begin writing your essay, you need to ask: *What is the main purpose of the proposed piece?* This may be focused or unclear. You should be clear about the purpose of your writing. Generally, purposes may be divided into three groups:

1. To educate or inform
2. To entertain
3. To persuade or convince

For your essay, you will be asked to persuade or inform; however, an assignment could ask for both. When you identify the major purpose of your prompt, you should consider if there are any secondary purposes. For example, the major purpose of a prompt may be to persuade your audience, and the secondary purpose would be to educate your audience.

A speaker's argument and claims need to be evaluated for their soundness and relevance. While it is tempting to believe everything that an excellent speaker tells you, it is because of that excellence that a listener should be critical of everything that is being said. While listening, critique what the person is saying. Determine if there is a clear delineation between evidence and theory.

Make sure to determine whether the speaker's arguments are logical or emotional, and make sure there is sufficient reasoning to support any claims.

Precise Language

When writing informational or explanatory texts it is of utmost importance to use precise language and domain-specific vocabulary to explain your main idea and supporting details. Generalized vocabulary will not help the audience grasp the points that you are attempting to make because they will not accurately reflect your main idea and supporting details. Domain-specific vocabulary is important to use because it will accurately describe or explain the ideas or processes that are central to your text. When you research a subject, make sure to familiarize yourself with any vocabulary that is involved in its explanation. Use context clues, dictionaries, or, if necessary, a technical dictionary to decode any words that you are not familiar with. Also, include definitions of domain-specific vocabulary in your text to enlighten readers.

Read the excerpt and analyze the language.

> At dawn, in a stuffy and smoky second-class car in which five people had already spent the night, a bulky woman in deep mourning was hoisted in—almost like a shapeless bundle. Behind her, puffing and moaning, followed her husband—a tiny man; thin and weakly, his face death-white, his eyes small and bright and looking shy and uneasy.

The language selected by the author is filled with fresh and precise words that describe and color the two passengers as well as the setting of the excerpt. The author describes the car as "stuffy and smoky," "second-class," and "in which five people had already spent the night." All this conjures up a dreary train car. The author describes the woman as "a shapeless bundle." Her husband is "tiny," "thin," and "weakly" with a "death-white" face. These words not only lend freshness to the writing, they also clearly depict what the people look like for the reader. This is the way that a writer can color his story and the characters in it.

Organization, Unity, and Cohesion

PRACTICE MAKES PREPARED WRITERS

Writing is a skill that continues to need development throughout a person's life. For some people, writing seems to be a natural gift. They rarely struggle with writer's block. When you read their papers, they have persuasive ideas. For others, writing is an intimidating task that they endure. As you practice, you can improve your skills and be better prepared for writing a time-sensitive essay.

A traditional and reliable way to prepare for the writing section is to read. When you read newspapers, magazines, and books, you learn about new ideas. You can read newspapers and magazines to become informed about issues that affect many people. As you think about those issues and ideas, you can take a position and form opinions. Try to develop these ideas and your opinions by sharing them with friends. After you develop your opinions, try writing them down as if you were going to spread your ideas beyond your friends.

Remember that you are practicing for more than an exam. Two of the most valuable skills in life are the abilities to **read critically** and to **write clearly**. When you work on evaluating the arguments of a passage and explain your thoughts well, you are developing skills that you will use for a lifetime. In the following pages, you will find strategies and tools that will prepare you to write better essays.

POINT OF VIEW

Point of view is the perspective from which writing occurs. There are several possibilities:

- *First person* is written so that the *I* of the story is a participant or observer.
- *Second person* is a device to draw the reader in more closely. It is really a variation or refinement of the first-person narrative.
- *Third person*, the most traditional form of point of view, is the omniscient narrator, in which the narrative voice, presumed to be the writer's, is presumed to know everything about the characters, plot, and action. Most novels use this point of view.

> **Review Video: <u>Point of View</u>**
> Visit mometrix.com/academy and enter code: 383336

BRAINSTORMING

Brainstorming is a technique that is used to find a creative approach to a subject. You can accomplish this by simple free-association with a topic. For example, with paper and pen, you write every thought that you have about the topic in a word or phrase. This is done without critical thinking. Everything that comes to your mind about the topic, you should put on your scratch paper. Then, you need to read the list over a few times. Next, you look for patterns, repetitions, and clusters of ideas. This allows a variety of fresh ideas to come as you think about the topic.

FREE WRITING

Free writing is a more structured form of brainstorming. The method involves a limited amount of time (e.g., 2 to 3 minutes) and writing everything that comes to mind about the topic in complete sentences. When time expires, you need to review everything that has been written down. Many of your sentences may make little or no sense, but the insights and observations that can come from free writing make this method a valuable approach. Usually, free writing results in a fuller expression of ideas than brainstorming because thoughts and associations are written in complete sentences. However, both techniques can be used to complement each other.

REVISIONS

A writer's choice of words is a signature of their style. Careful thought about the use of words can improve a piece of writing. A passage can be an exciting piece to read when attention is given to the use of specific nouns rather than general ones.

Example:

General: His kindness will never be forgotten.

Specific: His thoughtful gifts and bear hugs will never be forgotten.

Attention should also be given to the kind of verbs that are used in sentences. Active verbs (e.g., run, swim) should be about an action. Whenever possible, an active verb should replace a linking verb to provide clear examples for arguments and to strengthen a passage overall.

Example:

Passive: The winners were called to the stage by the judges.

Active: The judges called the winners to the stage.

Revising sentences is done to make writing more effective. Editing sentences is done to correct any errors. Sentences are the building blocks of writing, and they can be changed by paying attention to sentence length, sentence structure, and sentence openings.

You should add variety to sentence length, structure, and openings so that the essay does not seem boring or repetitive. A careful analysis of a piece of writing will expose these stylistic problems, and they can be corrected before you finish your essay. Changing up your sentence structure and sentence length can make your essay more inviting and appealing to readers.

> **Review Video: <u>Making Sentences More Distinct</u>**
> Visit mometrix.com/academy and enter code: 538557

RECURSIVE WRITING PROCESS

However you approach writing, you may find comfort in knowing that the revision process can occur in any order. The **recursive writing process** is not as difficult as the phrase may make it seem. Simply put, the recursive writing process means that the steps in the writing process occur in **no particular order**. For example, planning, drafting, and revising (all a part of the writing process) can all take place at about the same time and you may not notice that all three happen so close together. Truly, the writing process is a series of moving back and forth between planning, drafting, and revising followed by more planning, more drafting, and more revising until the writing is complete.

> **Review Video: <u>Recursive Writing Process</u>**
> Visit mometrix.com/academy and enter code: 951611

INTRODUCTION

An introduction announces the main point of the passage. Normally, the introduction ranges from 50 to 70 words (i.e., 3 or 4 sentences). The purpose of the introduction is to gain the reader's attention and conclude with the essay's main point. An introduction can begin with an interesting quote, question, or strong opinion that grabs the reader's attention. Your introduction should include a restatement of the prompt, a summary of the main points of your essay, and your position on the prompt (i.e., the thesis sentence/statement). Depending on the amount of available time, you may want to give more or less information on the main points of your essay. The important thing is to impress the audience with your thesis statement (i.e., your reason for writing the essay).

> **Review Video: Introduction**
> Visit mometrix.com/academy and enter code: 961328

THESIS STATEMENT

A thesis gives the main idea of the essay. A temporary thesis should be established early in the writing process because it will serve to keep the writer focused as ideas develop. This temporary thesis is subject to change as you continue to write.

The temporary thesis has two parts: a topic (i.e., the focus of your paper based on the prompt) and a comment. The comment makes an important point about the topic. A temporary thesis should be interesting and specific. Also, you need to limit the topic to a manageable scope. These three criteria are useful tools to measure the effectiveness of any temporary thesis:

1. Does the focus of my essay have enough interest to hold an audience?
2. Is the focus of my essay specific enough to generate interest?
3. Is the focus of my essay manageable for the time limit? Too broad? Too narrow?

The thesis should be a generalization rather than a fact because the thesis prepares readers for facts and details that support the thesis. The process of bringing the thesis into sharp focus may help in outlining major sections of the work. Once the thesis and introduction are complete, you can address the body of the work.

> **Review Video: Thesis Statements**
> Visit mometrix.com/academy and enter code: 691033

SUPPORTING THE THESIS

Throughout your essay, the thesis should be explained clearly and supported adequately by additional arguments. The thesis sentence needs to contain a clear statement of the purpose of your essay and a comment about the thesis. With the thesis statement, you have an opportunity to state what is noteworthy of this particular treatment of the prompt. Each sentence and paragraph should build on and support the thesis.

When you respond to the prompt, use parts of the passage to support your argument or defend your position. With supporting evidence from the passage, you strengthen your argument because readers can see your attention to the entire passage and your response to the details and facts within the passage. You can use facts, details, statistics, and direct quotations from the passage to uphold your position. Be sure to point out which information comes from the original passage and base your argument around that evidence.

PARAGRAPHS

Following the introduction, you will begin with body paragraphs. A paragraph should be unified around a main point. Normally, a good topic sentence summarizes the paragraph's main point. A topic sentence is a general sentence that gives an introduction to the paragraph. The sentences that follow are a support to the topic sentence. You may use the topic sentence as the final sentence to the paragraph if the earlier sentences give a clear explanation of the topic sentence. Overall, you need to stay true to the main point. This means that you need to remove unnecessary sentences that do not advance the main point.

The main point of a paragraph requires adequate development (i.e., a substantial paragraph that covers the main point). A paragraph of two or three sentences does not cover a main point. This is true when the main point of the paragraph gives strong support to the argument of the thesis. An occasional short paragraph is fine as a transitional device. However, you should aim to have six to seven sentences for each paragraph.

> **Review Video: Drafting Body Paragraphs**
> Visit mometrix.com/academy and enter code: 724590

METHODS OF DEVELOPING PARAGRAPHS

A common method of development in your essay can be done with **examples**. These examples are the supporting details to the main idea of a paragraph or passage. When you write about something that your audience may not understand, you can provide an example to show your point. When you write about something that is not easily accepted, you can give examples to prove your point.

Illustrations are extended examples that require several sentences. Well selected illustrations can be a great way to develop a point that may not be familiar to your audience. With a time limit, you may have enough time to use one illustration. So, be sure that you use one that connects well with your main argument.

Analogies make comparisons between items that appear to have nothing in common. Analogies are employed by writers to provoke fresh thoughts about a subject. They may be used to explain the unfamiliar, to clarify an abstract point, or to argue a point. Although analogies are effective literary devices, they should be used carefully in arguments. Two things may be alike in some respects but completely different in others.

Cause and effect is an excellent device used when the cause and effect are accepted as true. One way of using cause and effect is to state the effect in the topic sentence of a paragraph and add the causes in the body of the paragraph. With this method, your paragraphs can have structure which always strengthens writing.

TYPES OF PARAGRAPHS

A **paragraph of narration** tells a story or a part of a story. Normally, the sentences are arranged in chronological order (i.e., the order that the events happened). However, you can include flashbacks (i.e., beginning the story at an earlier time).

A **descriptive paragraph** makes a verbal portrait of a person, place, or thing. When you use specific details that appeal to one or more of the senses (i.e., sight, sound, smell, taste, and touch), you give your readers a sense of being present in the moment.

A **process paragraph** is related to time order (i.e., First, you open the bottle. Second, you pour the liquid, etc.). Usually, this describes a process or teaches readers how to perform a process.

Comparing two things draws attention to their similarities and indicates a number of differences. When you contrast, you focus only on differences. Both comparisons and contrasts may be used point-by-point or in following paragraphs.

Reasons for starting a new paragraph include:

1. To mark off the introduction and concluding paragraphs
2. To signal a shift to a new idea or topic
3. To indicate an important shift in time or place
4. To explain a point in additional detail
5. To highlight a comparison, contrast, or cause and effect relationship

CONCLUSION

A good conclusion should leave readers satisfied and provide a sense of completeness. Many conclusions state the thesis in different words and give a summary of the ideas in the body paragraphs. Some writers find ways to conclude in a dramatic fashion. They may conclude with a vivid image or a warning and remind readers of the main point. The conclusion can be a few sentences because the body of the text has made the case for the thesis. A conclusion can summarize the main points and offer advice or ask a question. You should never introduce new ideas or arguments in a conclusion. Also, you need to avoid vague and aimless endings. Instead, close with a clear and specific paragraph.

> **Review Video: <u>Drafting Conclusions</u>**
> Visit mometrix.com/academy and enter code: 209408

PARAGRAPH LENGTH

Most readers find that their comfort level for a paragraph is between 100 and 200 words. Shorter paragraphs cause too much starting and stopping, and give a choppy effect. Paragraphs that are too long often test the attention span of readers. Two notable exceptions to this rule exist. In scientific or scholarly papers, longer paragraphs suggest seriousness and depth. In journalistic writing, constraints are placed on paragraph size by the narrow columns in a newspaper format.

The first and last paragraphs of a text will usually be the introduction and conclusion. These special-purpose paragraphs are likely to be shorter than paragraphs in the body of the work. Paragraphs in the body of the essay follow the subject's outline; one paragraph per point in short essays and a group of paragraphs per point in longer works. Some ideas require more development than others, so it is good for a writer to remain flexible. A paragraph of excessive length may be divided, and shorter ones may be combined.

COHERENT PARAGRAPHS

A smooth flow of sentences and paragraphs without gaps, shifts, or bumps will lead to paragraph coherence. Ties between old and new information can be smoothed by several methods:

- Linking ideas clearly, from the topic sentence to the body of the paragraph, is essential for a smooth transition. The topic sentence states the main point, and this should be followed by specific details, examples, and illustrations that support the topic sentence. The support may be direct or indirect. In indirect support, the illustrations and examples may support a sentence that in turn supports the topic directly.
- The repetition of key words adds coherence to a paragraph. To avoid dull language, variations of the key words may be used.

- Parallel structures are often used within sentences to emphasize the similarity of ideas and connect sentences giving similar information.
- Maintaining a consistent verb tense throughout the paragraph helps. Shifting tenses affects the smooth flow of words and can disrupt the coherence of the paragraph.

Review Video: Methods to Obtain Coherence in Writing
Visit mometrix.com/academy and enter code: 831344

TRANSITIONS

Transitions are **bridges** between what has been read and what is about to be read. Transitions smooth the reader's path between sentences and inform the reader of major connections to new ideas forthcoming in the text. **Transitional phrases** should be used with care, selecting the appropriate phrase for a transition. **Tone** is another important consideration in using transitional phrases, and a good writer varies tone for different audiences. For example, in a scholarly essay, *in summary* would be preferable to the more informal *in short.*

When working with transitional words and phrases, writers usually find a natural flow that indicates when a transition is needed. In reading a draft of the text, it should become apparent where the flow is uneven or rough. At this point, the writer can add transitional elements during the revision process. Revising can also afford an opportunity to delete transitional devices that seem heavy handed or unnecessary.

Review Video: Connecting Sentences
Visit mometrix.com/academy and enter code: 948325

Transitional words and phrases are used to transition between paragraphs and also to transition within a single paragraph. Transitions assist the flow of ideas and help to unify an essay. A writer can use certain words to indicate that an example or summary is being presented. The following phrases, among others, can be used as this type of transition: *as a result, as I have said, for example, for instance, in any case, in any event, in brief, in conclusion, in fact, in other words, in short, on the whole,* and *to sum it up.*

Review Video: Transition Words
Visit mometrix.com/academy and enter code: 707563

TRANSITIONAL WORDS
LINK SIMILAR IDEAS

When a writer links ideas that are similar in nature, there are a variety of words and phrases he or she can choose, including but not limited to: *also, and, another, besides, equally important, further, furthermore, in addition, likewise, too, similarly, nor, of course,* and *for instance.*

LINK DISSIMILAR OR CONTRADICTORY IDEAS

Writers can link contradictory ideas in an essay by using, among others, the following words and phrases: *although, and yet, even if, conversely, but, however, otherwise, still, yet, instead, in spite of, nevertheless, on the contrary,* and *on the other hand.*

INDICATE CAUSE, PURPOSE, OR RESULT

Writers may need to indicate that one thing is the cause, purpose, or result of another thing. To show this relationship, writers can use, among others, the following linking words and phrases: *as, as a result, because, consequently, hence, for, for this reason, since, so, then, thus,* and *therefore.*

INDICATE TIME OR POSITION

Certain words can be used to indicate the time and position of one thing in relation to another. Writers can use, for example, the following terms to create a timeline of events in an essay: *above, across, afterward, before, beyond, eventually, meanwhile, next, presently, around, at once, at the present time, finally, first, here, second, thereafter,* and *upon.* These words can show the order or placement of items or ideas in an essay.

Knowledge of Language

CONTEXT CLUES

Learning new words is an important part of **comprehending** and **integrating** unfamiliar information. When a reader encounters a new word, he can stop and find it in the dictionary or the glossary of terms, but sometimes those reference tools aren't readily available or using them at the moment is impractical (e.g., during a test). Furthermore, most readers are usually not willing to take the time. Another way to determine the meaning of a word is by considering the **context** in which it is being used. These indirect learning hints are called **context clues**. They include definitions, descriptions, examples, and restatements. Because most words are learned by listening to conversations, people use this tool all the time even if they do it unconsciously. But to be effective in written text, context clues must be used judiciously because the unfamiliar word may have several subtle variations, and therefore the context clues could be misinterpreted.

Context refers to how a word is used in a sentence. Identifying context can help determine the definition of unknown words. There are different contextual clues such as definition, description, example, comparison, and contrast. The following are examples:

- Definition: the unknown word is clearly defined by the previous words. – "When he was painting, his instrument was a __." (paintbrush)
- Description: the unknown word is described by the previous words. – "I was hot, tired, and thirsty; I was __." (dehydrated)
- Example: the unknown word is part of a series of examples. – "Water, soda, and __ were the offered beverages." (coffee)
- Comparison: the unknown word is compared to another word. – "Barney is agreeable and happy like his __ parents." (positive)
- Contrast: the unknown word is contrasted with another word. – "I prefer cold weather to __ conditions." (hot)

> **Review Video: <u>Reading Comprehension: Using Context Clues</u>**
> Visit mometrix.com/academy and enter code: 613660

SYNONYMS AND ANTONYMS

When you understand how words relate to each other, you will discover more in a passage. This is explained by understanding **synonyms** (e.g., words that mean the same thing) and **antonyms** (e.g., words that mean the opposite of one another). As an example, *dry* and *arid* are synonyms, and *dry* and *wet* are antonyms. There are many pairs of words in English that can be considered synonyms, despite having slightly different definitions. For instance, the words *friendly* and *collegial* can both be used to describe a warm interpersonal relationship, and one would be correct to call them **synonyms**. However, *collegial* (kin to *colleague*) is often used in reference to professional or academic relationships, and *friendly* has no such connotation. If the difference between two words is too great, then they should not be called synonyms. *Hot* and *warm* are not synonyms because their meanings are too distinct. A good way to determine whether two words are synonyms is to substitute one word for the other word and verify that the meaning of the sentence has not changed. Substituting *warm* for *hot* in a sentence would convey a different meaning. Although warm and hot may seem close in meaning, warm generally means that the temperature is moderate, and hot generally means that the temperature is excessively high.

Antonyms are words with opposite meanings. *Light* and *dark*, *up* and *down*, *right* and *left*, *good* and *bad*: these are all sets of antonyms. Be careful to distinguish between antonyms and pairs of words

25

that are simply different. *Black* and *gray*, for instance, are not antonyms because gray is not the opposite of black. *Black* and *white*, on the other hand, are antonyms. Not every word has an antonym. For instance, many nouns do not: What would be the antonym of chair? During your exam, the questions related to antonyms are more likely to concern adjectives. You will recall that adjectives are words that describe a noun. Some common adjectives include *purple*, *fast*, *skinny*, and *sweet*. From those four adjectives, *purple* is the item that lacks a group of obvious antonyms.

Review Video: What are Synonyms and Antonyms?
Visit mometrix.com/academy and enter code: 105612

DESCRIPTION

Occasionally, you will be able to define an unfamiliar word by looking at the descriptive words in the context. Consider the following sentence: *Fred dragged the recalcitrant boy kicking and screaming up the stairs.* The words *dragged*, *kicking*, and *screaming* all suggest that the boy does not want to go up the stairs. The reader may assume that *recalcitrant* means something like unwilling or protesting. In this example, an unfamiliar adjective was identified.

Additionally, using description to define an unfamiliar noun is a common practice compared to unfamiliar adjectives, as in this sentence: *Don's wrinkled frown and constantly shaking fist identified him as a curmudgeon of the first order.* Don is described as having a *wrinkled frown and constantly shaking fist* suggesting that a *curmudgeon* must be a grumpy person. Contrasts do not always provide detailed information about the unfamiliar word, but they at least give the reader some clues.

When a word has more than one meaning, readers can have difficulty with determining how the word is being used in a given sentence. For instance, the verb *cleave*, can mean either *join* or *separate*. When readers come upon this word, they will have to select the definition that makes the most sense. Consider the following sentence: *Hermione's knife cleaved the bread cleanly.* Since, a knife cannot join bread together, the word must indicate separation.

A slightly more difficult example would be the sentence: *The birds cleaved together as they flew from the oak tree.* Immediately, the presence of the word *together* should suggest that in this sentence *cleave* is being used to mean *join*. Discovering the intent of a word with multiple meanings requires the same tricks as defining an unknown word: look for contextual clues and evaluate the substituted words.

Review Video: Determining Word Meanings
Visit mometrix.com/academy and enter code: 894894

LEVEL OF FORMALITY

The relationship between writer and reader is important in choosing a level of formality as most writing requires some degree of formality. Formal writing is for addressing a superior in a school or work environment. Business letters, textbooks, and newspapers use a moderate to high level of formality. Informal writing is appropriate for private letters, personal e-mails, and business correspondence between close associates.

For your exam, you will want to be aware of informal and formal writing. One way that this can be accomplished is to watch for shifts in point of view in the essay. For example, unless writers are using a personal example, they will rarely refer to themselves (e.g., "*I* think that *my* point is very clear.") to avoid being informal when they need to be formal. Also, be mindful of an author who addresses his or her audience directly in their writing (e.g., "Readers, *like you*, will understand this argument.") as this can be a sign of informal writing. Good writers understand the need to be consistent with their level of formality. Shifts in levels of formality or point of view can confuse readers and discount the message of an author's writing.

CLICHÉS

Clichés are phrases that have been overused to the point that the phrase has no importance or has lost the original meaning. The phrases have no originality and add very little to a passage. Therefore, most writers will avoid the use of clichés. Another option is to make changes to a cliché so that it is not predictable and empty of meaning.

Examples:

When life gives you lemons, make lemonade.

Every cloud has a silver lining.

JARGON

Jargon is a specialized vocabulary that is used among members of a trade or profession. Since jargon is understood by a small audience, writers tend to leave them to passages where certain readers will understand the vocabulary. Jargon includes exaggerated language that tries to impress rather than inform. Sentences filled with jargon are not precise and difficult to understand.

Examples:

"He is going to *toenail* these frames for us." (Toenail is construction jargon for nailing at an angle.)

"They brought in a *kip* of material today." (Kip refers to 1000 pounds in architecture and engineering.)

SLANG

Slang is an informal and sometimes private language that is understood by some individuals. Slang has some usefulness, but the language can have a small audience. So, most formal writing will not include this kind of language.

Examples:

"Yes, the event was a blast!" (In this sentence, *blast* means that the event was a great experience.)

"That attempt was an epic fail." (By *epic fail*, the speaker means that his or her attempt was not a success.)

COLLOQUIALISM

A colloquialism is a word or phrase that is found in informal writing. Unlike slang, colloquial language will be familiar to a greater range of people. Colloquial language can include some slang, but these are limited to contractions for the most part.

Examples:

"Can *y'all* come back another time?" (Y'all is a contraction of "you all" which has become a colloquialism.)

"Will you stop him from building this *castle in the air*?" (A "castle in the air" is an improbable or unlikely event.)

Foundations of Grammar

THE EIGHT PARTS OF SPEECH
NOUNS

When you talk about a person, place, thing, or idea, you are talking about **nouns**. The two main types of nouns are **common** and **proper** nouns. Also, nouns can be abstract (i.e., general) or concrete (i.e., specific).

Common nouns are the class or group of people, places, and things (Note: Do not capitalize common nouns). Examples of common nouns:

> *People*: boy, girl, worker, manager

> *Places*: school, bank, library, home

> *Things*: dog, cat, truck, car

Proper nouns are the names of a specific person, place, or thing (Note: Capitalize all proper nouns). Examples of proper nouns:

> *People*: Abraham Lincoln, George Washington, Martin Luther King, Jr.

> *Places*: Los Angeles, California / New York / Asia

> *Things*: Statue of Liberty, Earth*, Lincoln Memorial

> *Note: When you talk about the planet that we live on, you capitalize *Earth*. When you mean the dirt, rocks, or land, you lowercase *earth*.

General nouns are the names of conditions or ideas. **Specific nouns** name people, places, and things that are understood by using your senses.

General nouns:

> *Condition*: beauty, strength

> *Idea*: truth, peace

Specific nouns:

> *People*: baby, friend, father

> *Places*: town, park, city hall

> *Things*: rainbow, cough, apple, silk, gasoline

Collective nouns are the names for a person, place, or thing that may act as a whole. The following are examples of collective nouns: *class, company, dozen, group, herd, team,* and *public*.

PRONOUNS

Pronouns are words that are used to stand in for a noun. A pronoun may be classified as personal, intensive, relative, interrogative, demonstrative, indefinite, and reciprocal.

28

Personal: *Nominative* is the case for nouns and pronouns that are the subject of a sentence. *Objective* is the case for nouns and pronouns that are an object in a sentence. *Possessive* is the case for nouns and pronouns that show possession or ownership.

SINGULAR

	Nominative	Objective	Possessive
First Person	I	me	my, mine
Second Person	you	you	your, yours
Third Person	he, she, it	him, her, it	his, her, hers, its

PLURAL

	Nominative	Objective	Possessive
First Person	we	us	our, ours
Second Person	you	you	your, yours
Third Person	they	them	their, theirs

Intensive: I myself, you yourself, he himself, she herself, the (thing) itself, we ourselves, you yourselves, they themselves

Relative: which, who, whom, whose

Interrogative: what, which, who, whom, whose

Demonstrative: this, that, these, those

Indefinite: all, any, each, everyone, either/neither, one, some, several

Reciprocal: each other, one another

> **Review Video: Nouns and Pronouns**
> Visit mometrix.com/academy and enter code: 312073

VERBS

If you want to write a sentence, then you need a verb in your sentence. Without a verb, you have no sentence. The verb of a sentence explains action or being. In other words, the verb shows the subject's movement or the movement that has been done to the subject.

TRANSITIVE AND INTRANSITIVE VERBS

A transitive verb is a verb whose action (e.g., drive, run, jump) points to a receiver (e.g., car, dog, kangaroo). Intransitive verbs do not point to a receiver of an action. In other words, the action of the verb does not point to a subject or object.

Transitive: He plays the piano. | The piano was played by him.

Intransitive: He plays. | John writes well.

A dictionary will let you know whether a verb is transitive or intransitive. Some verbs can be transitive and intransitive.

29

ACTION VERBS AND LINKING VERBS

An action verb is a verb that shows what the subject is doing in a sentence. In other words, an action verb shows action. A sentence can be complete with one word: an action verb. Linking verbs are intransitive verbs that show a condition (i.e., the subject is described but does no action).

Linking verbs link the subject of a sentence to a noun or pronoun, or they link a subject with an adjective. You always need a verb if you want a complete sentence. However, linking verbs are not able to complete a sentence.

Common linking verbs include *appear, be, become, feel, grow, look, seem, smell, sound,* and *taste.* However, any verb that shows a condition and has a noun, pronoun, or adjective that describes the subject of a sentence is a linking verb.

Action: He sings. | Run! | Go! | I talk with him every day. | She reads.

Linking:

   Incorrect: I am.

   Correct: I am John. | I smell roses. | I feel tired.

Note: Some verbs are followed by words that look like prepositions, but they are a part of the verb and a part of the verb's meaning. These are known as phrasal verbs and examples include *call off, look up,* and *drop off.*

> **Review Video: <u>Action Verbs and Linking Verbs</u>**
> Visit mometrix.com/academy and enter code: 743142

VOICE

Transitive verbs come in active or passive voice. If the subject does an action or receives the action of the verb, then you will know whether a verb is active or passive. When the subject of the sentence is doing the action, the verb is **active voice**. When the subject receives the action, the verb is **passive voice**.

   Active: Jon drew the picture. (The subject *Jon* is doing the action of *drawing a picture.*)

   Passive: The picture is drawn by Jon. (The subject *picture* is receiving the action from Jon.)

VERB TENSES

A verb tense shows the different form of a verb to point to the time of an action. The present and past tense are shown by changing the verb's form. An action in the present *I talk* can change form for the past: *I talked.* However, for the other tenses, an auxiliary (i.e., helping) verb is needed to show the change in form. These helping verbs include *am, are, is* | *have, has, had* | *was, were, will* (or *shall*).

Present: I talk	Present perfect: I have talked
Past: I talked	Past perfect: I had talked
Future: I will talk	Future perfect: I will have talked

Present: The action happens at the current time.

Example: He *walks* to the store every morning.

To show that something is happening right now, use the progressive present tense: I *am walking*.

Past: The action happened in the past.

Example: He *walked* to the store an hour ago.

Future: The action is going to happen later.

Example: I *will walk* to the store tomorrow.

Present perfect: The action started in the past and continues into the present.

Example: I *have walked* to the store three times today.

Past perfect: The second action happened in the past. The first action came before the second.

Example: Before I walked to the store (Action 2), I *had walked* to the library (Action 1).

Future perfect: An action that uses the past and the future. In other words, the action is complete before a future moment.

Example: When she comes for the supplies (future moment), I *will have walked* to the store (action completed in the past).

CONJUGATING VERBS

When you need to change the form of a verb, you are **conjugating** a verb. The key parts of a verb are first person singular, present tense (dream); first person singular, past tense (dreamed); and the past participle (dreamed). Note: the past participle needs a helping verb to make a verb tense. For example, I *have dreamed* of this day. | I *am dreaming* of this day.

Present Tense: Active Voice

	Singular	**Plural**
First Person	I dream	We dream
Second Person	You dream	You dream
Third Person	He, she, it dreams	They dream

MOOD

There are three moods in English: the indicative, the imperative, and the subjunctive.

The **indicative mood** is used for facts, opinions, and questions.

Fact: You can do this.

Opinion: I think that you can do this.

Question: Do you know that you can do this?

The **imperative** is used for orders or requests.

Order: You are going to do this!

Request: Will you do this for me?

The **subjunctive mood** is for wishes and statements that go against fact.

Wish: I wish that I were going to do this.

Statement against fact: If I were you, I would do this. (This goes against fact because I am not you. You have the chance to do this, and I do not have the chance.)

The mood that causes trouble for most people is the subjunctive mood. If you have trouble with any of the moods, then be sure to practice.

ADJECTIVES

An adjective is a word that is used to modify a noun or pronoun. An adjective answers a question: *Which one? What kind of?* or *How many?* Usually, adjectives come before the words that they modify, but they may also come after a linking verb.

Which one? The *third* suit is my favorite.

What kind? This suit is *navy blue*.

How many? Can I look over the *four* neckties for the suit?

ARTICLES

Articles are adjectives that are used to mark nouns. There are only three: the **definite** (i.e., limited or fixed amount) article *the*, and the **indefinite** (i.e., no limit or fixed amount) articles *a* and *an*. Note: *An* comes before words that start with a vowel sound (i.e., vowels include *a, e, i, o, u*, and *y*). For example, "Are you going to get an **u**mbrella?"

Definite: I lost *the* bottle that belongs to me.

Indefinite: Does anyone have *a* bottle to share?

COMPARISON WITH ADJECTIVES

Some adjectives are relative and other adjectives are absolute. Adjectives that are **relative** can show the comparison between things. Adjectives that are **absolute** can show comparison. However, they show comparison in a different way. Let's say that you are reading two books. You think that one book is perfect, and the other book is not exactly perfect. It is not possible for the book to be more perfect than the other. Either you think that the book is perfect, or you think that the book is not perfect.

The adjectives that are relative will show the different **degrees** of something or someone to something else or someone else. The three degrees of adjectives include positive, comparative, and superlative.

The **positive** degree is the normal form of an adjective.

Example: This work is *difficult*. | She is *smart*.

The **comparative** degree compares one person or thing to another person or thing.

Example: This work is *more difficult* than your work. | She is *smarter* than me.

The **superlative** degree compares more than two people or things.

Example: This is the *most difficult* work of my life. | She is the *smartest* lady in school.

> **Review Video: What is an Adjective?**
> Visit mometrix.com/academy and enter code: 470154

ADVERBS

An adverb is a word that is used to **modify** a verb, adjective, or another adverb. Usually, adverbs answer one of these questions: *When?*, *Where?*, *How?*, and *Why?* . The negatives *not* and *never* are known as adverbs. Adverbs that modify adjectives or other adverbs **strengthen** or **weaken** the words that they modify.

Examples:

He walks quickly through the crowd.

The water flows smoothly on the rocks.

Note: While many adverbs end in *-ly*, you need to remember that not all adverbs end in *-ly*. Also, some words that end in *-ly* are adjectives, not adverbs. Some examples include: *early, friendly, holy, lonely, silly*, and *ugly*. To know if a word that ends in *-ly* is an adjective or adverb, you need to check your dictionary.

Examples:

He is *never* angry.

You talk *too* loudly.

COMPARISON WITH ADVERBS

The rules for comparing adverbs are the same as the rules for adjectives.

The **positive** degree is the standard form of an adverb.

Example: He arrives soon. | She speaks softly to her friends.

The **comparative** degree compares one person or thing to another person or thing.

Example: He arrives sooner than Sarah. | She speaks more softly than him.

The **superlative** degree compares more than two people or things.

Example: He arrives soonest of the group. | She speaks most softly of any of her friends.

> **Review Video: What is an Adverb?**
> Visit mometrix.com/academy and enter code: 713951

PREPOSITIONS

A preposition is a word placed before a noun or pronoun that shows the relationship between an object and another word in the sentence.

Common prepositions:

about	before	during	on	under
after	beneath	for	over	until
against	between	from	past	up
among	beyond	in	through	with
around	by	of	to	within
at	down	off	toward	without

Examples:

The napkin is *in* the drawer.

The Earth rotates *around* the Sun.

The needle is *beneath* the haystack.

Can you find me *among* the words?

> **Review Video: What is a Preposition?**
> Visit mometrix.com/academy and enter code: 946763

CONJUNCTIONS

Conjunctions join words, phrases, or clauses, and they show the connection between the joined pieces. **Coordinating** conjunctions connect equal parts of sentences. **Correlative** conjunctions show the connection between pairs. **Subordinating** conjunctions join subordinate (i.e., dependent) clauses with independent clauses.

COORDINATING CONJUNCTIONS

The coordinating conjunctions include: *and, but, yet, or, nor, for,* and *so*

Examples:

The rock was small, but it was heavy.

She drove in the night, and he drove in the day.

CORRELATIVE CONJUNCTIONS

The correlative conjunctions are: *either...or | neither...nor | not only...but also*

Examples:

Either you are coming *or* you are staying.

He ran *not only* three miles *but also* swam 200 yards.

> **Review Video: Coordinating and Correlative Conjunctions**
> Visit mometrix.com/academy and enter code: 390329

SUBORDINATING CONJUNCTIONS

Common subordinating conjunctions include:

after	since	whenever
although	so that	where
because	unless	wherever
before	until	whether
in order that	when	while

Examples:

I am hungry *because* I did not eat breakfast.

He went home *when* everyone left.

Review Video: <u>Subordinating Conjunctions</u>
Visit mometrix.com/academy and enter code: 958913

INTERJECTIONS

An interjection is a word for **exclamation** (i.e., great amount of feeling) that is used alone or as a piece to a sentence. Often, they are used at the beginning of a sentence for an **introduction**. Sometimes, they can be used in the middle of a sentence to show a **change** in thought or attitude.

Common Interjections: Hey! | Oh, | Ouch! | Please! | Wow!

Agreement and Sentence Structure

SUBJECTS AND PREDICATES

SUBJECTS

Every sentence has two things: a subject and a verb. The **subject** of a sentence names who or what the sentence is all about. The subject may be directly stated in a sentence, or the subject may be the implied *you*.

The **complete subject** includes the simple subject and all of its modifiers. To find the complete subject, ask *Who* or *What* and insert the verb to complete the question. The answer is the complete subject. To find the **simple subject**, remove all of the modifiers (adjectives, prepositional phrases, etc.) in the complete subject. Being able to locate the subject of a sentence helps with many problems, such as those involving sentence fragments and subject-verb agreement.

Examples:

The small red car is the one that he wants for Christmas.

(The complete subject is *the small red car.*)

The young artist is coming over for dinner.

(The complete subject is *the young artist.*)

> **Review Video: Subjects in English**
> Visit mometrix.com/academy and enter code: 444771

In **imperative** sentences, the verb's subject is understood (e.g., [You] Run to the store) but not actually present in the sentence. Normally, the subject comes before the verb. However, the subject comes after the verb in sentences that begin with *There are* or *There was.*

Direct:

John knows the way to the park.

(Who knows the way to the park? Answer: John)

The cookies need ten more minutes.

(What needs ten minutes? Answer: The cookies)

By five o' clock, Bill will need to leave.

(Who needs to leave? Answer: Bill)

Remember: The subject can come after the verb.

There are five letters on the table for him.

(What is on the table? Answer: Five letters)

There were coffee and doughnuts in the house.

(What was in the house? Answer: Coffee and doughnuts)

36

Implied:

> Go to the post office for me.

> (Who is going to the post office? Answer: You are.)

> Come and sit with me, please?

> (Who needs to come and sit? Answer: You do.)

PREDICATES

In a sentence, you always have a predicate and a subject. The subject tells what the sentence is about, and the **predicate** explains or describes the subject.

Think about the sentence: *He sings*. In this sentence, we have a subject (He) and a predicate (sings). This is all that is needed for a sentence to be complete. Would we like more information? Of course, we would like to know more. However, if this is all the information that you are given, you have a complete sentence.

Now, let's look at another sentence:

> *John and Jane sing on Tuesday nights at the dance hall.*

What is the subject of this sentence?

> **Answer**: John and Jane.

What is the predicate of this sentence?

> **Answer**: Everything else in the sentence (sing on Tuesday nights at the dance hall).

SUBJECT-VERB AGREEMENT

Verbs **agree** with their subjects in number. In other words, *singular* subjects need *singular* verbs. *Plural* subjects need *plural* verbs. Singular is for one person, place, or thing. Plural is for more than one person, place, or thing. Subjects and verbs must also agree in person: first, second, or third. The present tense ending *-s* is used on a verb if its subject is third person singular; otherwise, the verb takes no ending.

> **Review Video: Subject-Verb Agreement**
> Visit mometrix.com/academy and enter code: 479190

NUMBER AGREEMENT EXAMPLES:

> Single Subject and Verb: *Dan calls home.*

> (Dan is one person. So, the singular verb *calls* is needed.)

> Plural Subject and Verb: *Dan and Bob call home.*

> (More than one person needs the plural verb *call*.)

PERSON AGREEMENT EXAMPLES:

First Person: I *am* walking.

Second Person: You *are* walking.

Third Person: He *is* walking.

COMPLICATIONS WITH SUBJECT-VERB AGREEMENT

WORDS BETWEEN SUBJECT AND VERB

Words that come between the simple subject and the verb may serve as an effective distraction, but they have no bearing on subject-verb agreement.

Examples:

The joy of my life returns home tonight.

(**Singular Subject**: joy. **Singular Verb**: returns)

The phrase *of my life* does not influence the verb *returns*.

The question that still remains unanswered is "Who are you?"

(**Singular Subject**: question. **Singular Verb**: is)

Don't let the phrase "*that still remains…*" trouble you. The subject *question* goes with *is*.

COMPOUND SUBJECTS

A compound subject is formed when two or more nouns joined by *and*, *or*, or *nor* jointly act as the subject of the sentence.

JOINED BY AND

When a compound subject is joined by *and*, it is treated as a plural subject and requires a plural verb.

Examples:

You and Jon are invited to come to my house.

(**Plural Subject**: You and Jon. **Plural Verb**: are)

The pencil and paper belong to me.

(**Plural Subject**: pencil and paper. **Plural Verb**: belong)

JOINED BY OR/NOR

For a compound subject joined by *or* or *nor*, the verb must agree in number with the part of the subject that is closest to the verb (italicized in the examples below).

Examples:

Today or *tomorrow is* the day.

(**Subject**: Today / tomorrow. **Verb**: is)

Stan or *Phil wants* to read the book.

(**Subject**: Stan / Phil. **Verb**: wants)

Neither the books nor the *pen is* on the desk.

(**Subject**: Books / Pen. **Verb**: is)

Either the blanket or *pillows arrive* this afternoon.

(**Subject**: Blanket / Pillows. **Verb**: arrive)

INDEFINITE PRONOUNS AS SUBJECT

An indefinite pronoun is a pronoun that does not refer to a specific noun. Indefinite pronouns may be only singular, be only plural, or change depending on how they are used.

ALWAYS SINGULAR

Pronouns such as *each*, *either*, *everybody*, *anybody*, *somebody*, and *nobody* are always singular.

Examples:

Each of the runners *has* a different bib number.

(**Singular Subject**: Each. **Singular Verb**: has)

Is either of you ready for the game?

(**Singular Subject**: Either. **Singular Verb**: is)

Note: The words *each* and *either* can also be used as adjectives (e.g., *each* person is unique). When one of these adjectives modifies the subject of a sentence, it is always a singular subject.

Everybody grows a day older every day.

(**Singular Subject**: Everybody. **Singular Verb**: grows)

Anybody is welcome to bring a tent.

(**Singular Subject**: Anybody. **Singular Verb**: is)

ALWAYS PLURAL

Pronouns such as *both*, *several*, and *many* are always plural.

Examples:

Both of the siblings *were* too tired to argue.

(**Plural Subject**: Both. **Plural Verb**: were)

Many have tried, but none have succeeded.

(**Plural Subject**: Many. **Plural Verb**: have tried)

DEPEND ON CONTEXT

Pronouns such as *some, any, all, none, more,* and *most* can be either singular or plural depending on what they are representing in the context of the sentence.

Examples:

All of my dog's food *was* still there in his bowl

(**Singular Subject**: All. **Singular Verb**: was)

By the end of the night, *all* of my guests *were* already excited about coming to my next party.

(**Plural Subject**: All. **Plural Verb**: were)

OTHER CASES INVOLVING PLURAL OR IRREGULAR FORM

Some nouns are **singular in meaning but plural in form**: news, mathematics, physics, and economics.

The *news is* coming on now.

Mathematics is my favorite class.

Some nouns are plural in form and meaning, and have **no singular equivalent**: scissors and pants.

Do these *pants come* with a shirt?

The *scissors are* for my project.

Mathematical operations are **irregular** in their construction, but are normally considered to be **singular in meaning**.

One plus one is two.

Three times three is nine.

Note: Look to your **dictionary** for help when you aren't sure whether a noun with a plural form has a singular or plural meaning.

COMPLEMENTS

A complement is a noun, pronoun, or adjective that is used to give more information about the subject or verb in the sentence.

DIRECT OBJECTS

A direct object is a noun or pronoun that takes or receives the **action** of a verb. (Remember: a complete sentence does not need a direct object, so not all sentences will have them. A sentence needs only a subject and a verb.) When you are looking for a direct object, find the verb and ask *who* or *what.*

Examples:

I took the blanket. (Who or what did I take? *The blanket*)

Jane read books. (Who or what does Jane read? *Books*)

INDIRECT OBJECTS

An indirect object is a word or group of words that show how an action had an **influence** on someone or something. If there is an indirect object in a sentence, then you always have a direct object in the sentence. When you are looking for the indirect object, find the verb and ask *to/for whom or what*.

Examples:

We taught the old dog a new trick.

(To/For Whom or What was taught? *The old dog*)

I gave them a math lesson.

(To/For Whom or What was given? *Them*)

> **Review Video: Direct and Indirect Objects**
> Visit mometrix.com/academy and enter code: 817385

PREDICATE NOMINATIVES AND PREDICATE ADJECTIVES

As we looked at previously, verbs may be classified as either action verbs or linking verbs. A linking verb is so named because it links the subject to words in the predicate that describe or define the subject. These words are called predicate nominatives (if nouns or pronouns) or predicate adjectives (if adjectives).

Examples:

My father is a *lawyer*.

(Father is the **subject**. Lawyer is the **predicate nominative**.)

Your mother is *patient*.

(Mother is the **subject**. Patient is the **predicate adjective**.)

PRONOUN USAGE

The **antecedent** is the noun that has been replaced by a pronoun. A pronoun and its antecedent **agree** when they have the same number (singular or plural) and gender (male, female, or neuter).

Examples:

Singular agreement: *John* came into town, and *he* played for us.

(The word *he* replaces *John*.)

Plural agreement: *John and Rick* came into town, and *they* played for us.

(The word *they* replaces *John and Rick*.)

To determine which is the correct pronoun to use in a compound subject or object, try each pronoun **alone** in place of the compound in the sentence. Your knowledge of pronouns will tell you which one is correct.

Example:

Bob and (I, me) will be going.

Test: (1) *I will be going* or (2) *Me will be going*. The second choice cannot be correct because *me* cannot be used as the subject of a sentence. Instead, *me* is used as an object.

Answer: Bob and I will be going.

When a pronoun is used with a noun immediately following (as in "we boys"), try the sentence **without the added noun**.

Example:

(We/Us) boys played football last year.

Test: (1) *We played football last ye*ar or (2) *Us played football last year*. Again, the second choice cannot be correct because *us* cannot be used as a subject of a sentence. Instead, *us* is used as an object.

Answer: We boys played football last year.

Review Video: <u>Pronoun Usage</u>
Visit mometrix.com/academy and enter code: 666500

A pronoun should point clearly to the **antecedent**. Here is how a pronoun reference can be unhelpful if it is not directly stated or puzzling.

Unhelpful: Ron and Jim went to the store, and *he* bought soda.

(Who bought soda? Ron or Jim?)

Helpful: Jim went to the store, and *he* bought soda.

(The sentence is clear. Jim bought the soda.)

Some pronouns change their form by their placement in a sentence. A pronoun that is a subject in a sentence comes in the **subjective case**. Pronouns that serve as objects appear in the **objective case**. Finally, the pronouns that are used as possessives appear in the **possessive case**.

Examples:

Subjective case: *He* is coming to the show.

(The pronoun *He* is the subject of the sentence.)

Objective case: Josh drove *him* to the airport.

(The pronoun *him* is the object of the sentence.)

Possessive case: The flowers are *mine*.

(The pronoun *mine* shows ownership of the flowers.)

The word *who* is a subjective-case pronoun that can be used as a **subject**. The word *whom* is an objective-case pronoun that can be used as an **object**. The words *who* and *whom* are common in subordinate clauses or in questions.

Examples:

Subject: He knows who wants to come.

(*Who* is the subject of the verb *wants*.)

Object: He knows the man whom we want at the party.

(*Whom* is the object of *we want*.)

CLAUSES

A clause is a group of words that contains both a subject and a predicate (verb). There are two types of clauses: independent and dependent. An **independent clause** contains a complete thought, while a **dependent (or subordinate) clause** does not. A dependent clause includes a subject and a verb, and may also contain objects or complements, but it cannot stand as a complete thought without being joined to an independent clause. Dependent clauses function within sentences as adjectives, adverbs, or nouns.

Example:

Independent Clause: I am running

Dependent Clause: because I want to stay in shape

The clause *I am running* is an independent clause: it has a subject and a verb, and it gives a complete thought. The clause *because I want to stay in shape* is a dependent clause: it has a subject and a verb, but it does not express a complete thought. It adds detail to the independent clause to which it is attached.

Combined: I am running because I want to stay in shape.

> **Review Video: What is a Clause?**
> Visit mometrix.com/academy and enter code: 940170

TYPES OF DEPENDENT CLAUSES
ADJECTIVE CLAUSES

An **adjective clause** is a dependent clause that modifies a noun or a pronoun. Adjective clauses begin with a relative pronoun (*who, whose, whom, which,* and *that*) or a relative adverb (*where, when,* and *why*).

Also, adjective clauses come after the noun that the clause needs to explain or rename. This is done to have a clear connection to the independent clause.

Examples:

I learned the reason *why I won the award.*

This is the place *where I started my first job.*

An adjective clause can be an essential or nonessential clause. An essential clause is very important to the sentence. **Essential clauses** explain or define a person or thing. **Nonessential clauses** give more information about a person or thing but are not necessary to define them. Nonessential clauses are set off with commas while essential clauses are not.

> **Review Video: Adjective Clauses and Phrases**
> Visit mometrix.com/academy and enter code: 520888

Examples:

Essential: A person *who works hard at first* can often rest later in life.

Nonessential: Neil Armstrong, *who walked on the moon*, is my hero.

ADVERB CLAUSES

An **adverb clause** is a dependent clause that modifies a verb, adjective, or adverb. In sentences with multiple dependent clauses, adverb clauses are usually placed immediately before or after the independent clause. An adverb clause is introduced with words such as *after, although, as, before, because, if, since, so, unless, when, where*, and *while*.

Examples:

When you walked outside, I called the manager.

I will go with you *unless you want to stay.*

NOUN CLAUSES

A **noun clause** is a dependent clause that can be used as a subject, object, or complement. Noun clauses begin with words such as *how, that, what, whether, which, who,* and *why*. These words can also come with an adjective clause. Unless the noun clause is being used as the subject of the sentence, it should come after the verb of the independent clause.

Examples:

The real mystery is *how you avoided serious injury.*

What you learn from each other depends on your honesty with others.

SUBORDINATION

When two related ideas are not of equal importance, the ideal way to combine them is to make the more important idea an independent clause, and the less important idea a dependent or subordinate clause. This is called **subordination**.

Example:

> **Separate ideas**: The team had a perfect regular season. The team lost the championship.

> **Subordinated**: Despite having a perfect regular season, *the team lost the championship.*

PHRASES

A phrase is a group of words that functions as a single part of speech, usually a noun, adjective, or adverb. A phrase is not a complete thought, but it adds **detail** or **explanation** to a sentence, or **renames** something within the sentence.

PREPOSITIONAL PHRASES

One of the most common types of phrases is the prepositional phrase. A **prepositional phrase** begins with a preposition and ends with a noun or pronoun that is the object of the preposition. Normally, the prepositional phrase functions as an **adjective** or an **adverb** within the sentence.

Examples:

> The picnic is *on the blanket.*

> I am sick *with a fever* today.

> *Among the many flowers*, John found a four-leaf clover.

VERBAL PHRASES

A verbal is a word or phrase that is formed from a verb but does not function as a verb. Depending on its particular form, it may be used as a noun, adjective, or adverb. A verbal does **not** replace a verb in a sentence.

Examples:

> Correct: *Walk* a mile daily.

> (*Walk* is the verb of this sentence. The subject is the implied *you*.)

> Incorrect: *To walk* a mile.

> (*To walk* is a type of verbal. This is not a sentence since there is no functional verb)

There are three types of verbals: **participles**, **gerunds**, and **infinitives**. Each type of verbal has a corresponding **phrase** that consists of the verbal itself along with any complements or modifiers.

PARTICIPLES

A **participle** is a type of verbal that always functions as an adjective. The present participle always ends with -*ing*. Past participles end with -*d, -ed, -n,* or -*t.*

> Examples: Verb: *dance* | Present Participle: *dancing* | Past Participle: *danced*

Participial phrases most often come right before or right after the noun or pronoun that they modify.

Examples:

Shipwrecked on an island, the boys started to fish for food.

Having been seated for five hours, we got out of the car to stretch our legs.

Praised for their work, the group accepted the first-place trophy.

GERUNDS

A **gerund** is a type of verbal that always functions as a noun. Like present participles, gerunds always end with *-ing*, but they can be easily distinguished from one another by the part of speech they represent (participles always function as adjectives). Since a gerund or gerund phrase always functions as a noun, it can be used as the subject of a sentence, the predicate nominative, or the object of a verb or preposition.

Examples:

We want to be known for *teaching the poor*. (Object of preposition)

Coaching this team is the best job of my life. (Subject)

We like *practicing our songs* in the basement. (Object of verb)

INFINITIVES

An **infinitive** is a type of verbal that can function as a noun, an adjective, or an adverb. An infinitive is made of the word *to* + the basic form of the verb. As with all other types of verbal phrases, an infinitive phrase includes the verbal itself and all of its complements or modifiers.

Examples:

To join the team is my goal in life. (Noun)

The animals have enough food *to eat for the night*. (Adjective)

People lift weights *to exercise their muscles*. (Adverb)

> **Review Video: Verbals**
> Visit mometrix.com/academy and enter code: 915480

APPOSITIVE PHRASES

An **appositive** is a word or phrase that is used to explain or rename nouns or pronouns. Noun phrases, gerund phrases, and infinitive phrases can all be used as appositives.

Examples:

Terriers, *hunters at heart*, have been dressed up to look like lap dogs.

(The noun phrase *hunters at heart* renames the noun *terriers*.)

His plan, *to save and invest his money*, was proven as a safe approach.

(The infinitive phrase explains what the plan is.)

Appositive phrases can be **essential** or **nonessential**. An appositive phrase is essential if the person, place, or thing being described or renamed is too general for its meaning to be understood without the appositive.

Examples:

> **Essential**: Two Founding Fathers George Washington and Thomas Jefferson served as presidents.

> **Nonessential**: George Washington and Thomas Jefferson, two Founding Fathers, served as presidents.

ABSOLUTE PHRASES

An absolute phrase is a phrase that consists of **a noun followed by a participle**. An absolute phrase provides **context** to what is being described in the sentence, but it does not modify or explain any particular word; it is essentially independent.

Examples:

> *The alarm ringing*, he pushed the snooze button.

> *The music paused*, she continued to dance through the crowd.

Note: Absolute phrases can be confusing, so don't be discouraged if you have a difficult time with them.

PARALLELISM

When multiple items or ideas are presented in a sentence in series, such as in a list, the items or ideas must be stated in grammatically equivalent ways. In other words, if one idea is stated in gerund form, the second cannot be stated in infinitive form. For example, to write, *I enjoy reading and to study* would be incorrect. An infinitive and a gerund are not equivalent. Instead, you should write *I enjoy reading and studying*. In lists of more than two, it can be harder to keep everything straight, but all items in a list must be parallel.

Example:

> **Incorrect**: He stopped at the office, grocery store, and the pharmacy before heading home.

> The first and third items in the list of places include the article *the*, so the second item needs it as well.

> **Correct**: He stopped at the office, *the* grocery store, and the pharmacy before heading home.

Example:

> **Incorrect**: While vacationing in Europe, she went biking, skiing, and climbed mountains.

> The first and second items in the list are gerunds, so the third item must be as well.

> **Correct**: While vacationing in Europe, she went biking, skiing, and *mountain climbing*.

SENTENCE PURPOSE

There are four types of sentences: declarative, imperative, interrogative, and exclamatory.

A **declarative** sentence states a fact and ends with a period.

> Example: *The football game starts at seven o'clock.*

An **imperative** sentence tells someone to do something and generally ends with a period. (An urgent command might end with an exclamation point instead.)

> Example: *Don't forget to buy your ticket.*

An **interrogative** sentence asks a question and ends with a question mark.

> Example: *Are you going to the game on Friday?*

An **exclamatory** sentence shows strong emotion and ends with an exclamation point.

> Example: *I can't believe we won the game!*

SENTENCE STRUCTURE

Sentences are classified by structure based on the type and number of clauses present. The four classifications of sentence structure are the following:

Simple: A simple sentence has one independent clause with no dependent clauses. A simple sentence may have **compound elements** (i.e., compound subject or verb).

Examples:

> Judy *watered* the lawn. (single <u>subject</u>, single *verb*)
>
> Judy and Alan *watered* the lawn. (compound <u>subject</u>, single *verb*)
>
> Judy *watered* the lawn and *pulled* weeds. (single <u>subject</u>, compound *verb*)
>
> Judy and Alan *watered* the lawn and *pulled* weeds. (compound <u>subject</u>, compound *verb*)

Compound: A compound sentence has two or more <u>independent clauses</u> with no dependent clauses. Usually, the independent clauses are joined with a comma and a coordinating conjunction or with a semicolon.

Examples:

> <u>The time has come</u>, and <u>we are ready</u>.
>
> <u>I woke up at dawn</u>; <u>the sun was just coming up</u>.

Complex: A complex sentence has one <u>independent clause</u> and at least one *dependent clause.*

Examples:

> *Although he had the flu,* <u>Harry went to work</u>.
>
> <u>Marcia got married</u> *after she finished college.*

48

Compound-Complex: A compound-complex sentence has at least two <u>independent clauses</u> and at least one *dependent clause.*

Examples:

<u>John is my friend</u> *who went to India,* and <u>he brought back souvenirs.</u>

<u>You may not realize this,</u> but <u>we heard the music</u> *that you played last night.*

> **Review Video: <u>Sentence Structure</u>**
> Visit mometrix.com/academy and enter code: 700478

SENTENCE FRAGMENTS

Usually when the term *sentence fragment* comes up, it is because you have to decide whether or not a group of words is a complete sentence, and if it's not a complete sentence, you're about to have to fix it. Recall that a group of words must contain at least one **independent clause** in order to be considered a sentence. If it doesn't contain even one independent clause, it would be called a **sentence fragment**. (If it contains two or more independent clauses that are not joined correctly, it would be called a run-on sentence.)

The process to use for **repairing** a sentence fragment depends on what type of fragment it is. If the fragment is a dependent clause, it can sometimes be as simple as removing a subordinating word (e.g., when, because, if) from the beginning of the fragment. Alternatively, a dependent clause can be incorporated into a closely related neighboring sentence. If the fragment is missing some required part, like a subject or a verb, the fix might be as simple as adding it in.

Examples:

Fragment: Because he wanted to sail the Mediterranean.

Removed subordinating word: He wanted to sail the Mediterranean.

Combined with another sentence: Because he wanted to sail the Mediterranean, he booked a Greek island cruise.

RUN-ON SENTENCES

Run-on sentences consist of multiple independent clauses that have not been joined together properly. Run-on sentences can be corrected in several different ways:

Join clauses properly: This can be done with a comma and coordinating conjunction, with a semicolon, or with a colon or dash if the second clause is explaining something in the first.

Example:

Incorrect: I went on the trip, we visited lots of castles.

Corrected: I went on the trip, and we visited lots of castles.

Split into separate sentences: This correction is most effective when the independent clauses are very long or when they are not closely related.

Example:

> **Incorrect**: The drive to New York takes ten hours, my uncle lives in Boston.

> **Corrected**: The drive to New York takes ten hours. My uncle lives in Boston.

Make one clause dependent: This is the easiest way to make the sentence correct and more interesting at the same time. It's often as simple as adding a subordinating word between the two clauses

Example:

> **Incorrect**: I finally made it to the store and I bought some eggs.

> **Corrected**: When I finally made it to the store, I bought some eggs.

Reduce to one clause with a compound verb: If both clauses have the same subject, remove the subject from the second clause, and you now have just one clause with a compound verb.

Example:

> **Incorrect**: The drive to New York takes ten hours, it makes me very tired.

> **Corrected**: The drive to New York takes ten hours and makes me very tired.

Note: While these are the simplest ways to correct a run-on sentence, often the best way is to completely reorganize the thoughts in the sentence and rewrite it.

> **Review Video: Fragments and Run-on Sentences**
> Visit mometrix.com/academy and enter code: 541989

DANGLING AND MISPLACED MODIFIERS
DANGLING MODIFIERS
A dangling modifier is a dependent clause or verbal phrase that does not have a **clear logical connection** to a word in the sentence.

Example:

> **Dangling**: *Reading each magazine article*, the stories caught my attention.

> The word *stories* cannot be modified by *Reading each magazine article*. People can read, but stories cannot read. Therefore, the subject of the sentence must be a person.

> **Corrected**: Reading each magazine article, *I* was entertained by the stories.

Example:

> **Dangling**: Ever since childhood, my grandparents have visited me for Christmas.

> The speaker in this sentence can't have been visited by her grandparents when *they* were children, since she wouldn't have been born yet. Either the modifier should be **clarified** or the sentence should be **rearranged** to specify whose childhood is being referenced.

> **Clarified**: Ever since I was a child, my grandparents have visited for Christmas.

Rearranged: Ever since childhood, I have enjoyed my grandparents visiting for Christmas.

MISPLACED MODIFIERS

Because modifiers are grammatically versatile, they can be put in many different places within the structure of a sentence. The danger of this versatility is that a modifier can accidentally be placed where it is modifying the wrong word or where it is not clear which word it is modifying.

Example:

Misplaced: She read the book to a crowd *that was filled with beautiful pictures.*

The book was filled with beautiful pictures, not the crowd.

Corrected: She read the book *that was filled with beautiful pictures* to a crowd.

Example:

Ambiguous: Derek saw a bus nearly hit a man *on his way to work.*

Was Derek on his way to work? Or was the other man?

Derek: *On his way to work*, Derek saw a bus nearly hit a man.

The other man: Derek saw a bus nearly hit a man *who was on his way to work.*

SPLIT INFINITIVES

A split infinitive occurs when a modifying word comes between the word *to* and the verb that pairs with *to*.

Example: To *clearly* explain vs. *To explain* clearly | To *softly* sing vs. *To sing* softly

Though considered improper by some, split infinitives may provide better clarity and simplicity in some cases than the alternatives. As such, avoiding them should not be considered a universal rule.

DOUBLE NEGATIVES

Standard English allows **two negatives** only when a **positive** meaning is intended. For example, *The team was not displeased with their performance.* Double negatives to emphasize negation are not used in standard English.

Negative modifiers (e.g., never, no, and not) should not be paired with other negative modifiers or negative words (e.g., none, nobody, nothing, or neither). The modifiers *hardly, barely*, and *scarcely* are considered negatives in standard English, so they should not be used with other negatives.

Punctuation

END PUNCTUATION

PERIODS

Use a period to end all sentences except direct questions, exclamations.

DECLARATIVE SENTENCE

A declarative sentence gives information or makes a statement.

> Examples: I can fly a kite. | The plane left two hours ago.

IMPERATIVE SENTENCE

An imperative sentence gives an order or command.

> Examples: You are coming with me. | Bring me that note.

PERIODS FOR ABBREVIATIONS

> Examples: 3 P.M. | 2 A.M. | Mr. Jones | Mrs. Stevens | Dr. Smith | Bill Jr. | Pennsylvania Ave.

Note: an abbreviation is a shortened form of a word or phrase.

QUESTION MARKS

Question marks should be used following a direct question. A polite request can be followed by a period instead of a question mark.

> **Direct Question**: What is for lunch today? | How are you? | Why is that the answer?

> **Polite Requests**: Can you please send me the item tomorrow. | Will you please walk with me on the track.

EXCLAMATION MARKS

Exclamation marks are used after a word group or sentence that shows much feeling or has special importance. Exclamation marks should not be overused. They are saved for proper **exclamatory interjections**.

> Example: We're going to the finals! | You have a beautiful car! | That's crazy!

COMMAS

The comma is a punctuation mark that can help you understand connections in a sentence. Not every sentence needs a comma. However, if a sentence needs a comma, you need to put it in the right place. A comma in the wrong place (or an absent comma) will make a sentence's meaning unclear. These are some of the rules for commas:

1. Use a comma **before a coordinating conjunction** joining independent clauses
   Example: Bob caught three fish, and I caught two fish.

2. Use a comma after an introductory phrase or an adverbial clause
   Examples:
   After the final out, we went to a restaurant to celebrate.
   Studying the stars, I was surprised at the beauty of the sky.

3. Use a comma between items in a series.

   Example: I will bring the turkey, the pie, and the coffee.

4. Use a comma **between coordinate adjectives** not joined with *and*

   Incorrect: The kind, brown dog followed me home.
   Correct: The *kind, loyal* dog followed me home.
   Not all adjectives are **coordinate** (i.e., equal or parallel). There are two simple ways to know if your adjectives are coordinate. One, you can join the adjectives with *and*: *The kind and loyal dog.* Two, you can change the order of the adjectives: *The loyal, kind dog.*

5. Use commas for **interjections** and **after *yes* and *no*** responses

   Examples:

   > **Interjection**: Oh, I had no idea. | Wow, you know how to play this game.
   > **Yes and No**: *Yes,* I heard you. | *No,* I cannot come tomorrow.

6. Use commas to separate nonessential modifiers and nonessential appositives

   Examples:

   > **Nonessential Modifier**: John Frank, who is coaching the team, was promoted today.
   > **Nonessential Appositive**: Thomas Edison, an American inventor, was born in Ohio.

7. Use commas to set off nouns of direct address, interrogative tags, and contrast

   Examples:

   > **Direct Address**: You, *John,* are my only hope in this moment.
   > **Interrogative Tag**: This is the last time, *correct?*
   > **Contrast**: You are my friend, *not my enemy.*

8. Use commas with dates, addresses, geographical names, and titles

   Examples:

   > **Date**: *July 4, 1776,* is an important date to remember.
   > **Address**: He is meeting me at *456 Delaware Avenue, Washington, D.C.,* tomorrow morning.
   > **Geographical Name**: *Paris, France,* is my favorite city.
   > **Title**: John Smith, *Ph. D.,* will be visiting your class today.

9. Use commas to **separate expressions like *he said* and *she said*** if they come between a sentence of a quote

   Examples:

   > "I want you to know," he began, "that I always wanted the best for you."
   > "You can start," Jane said, "with an apology."

> **Review Video: When To Use a Comma**
> Visit mometrix.com/academy and enter code: 786797

SEMICOLONS

The semicolon is used to connect major sentence pieces of equal value. Some rules for semicolons include:

1. Use a semicolon **between closely connected independent clauses** that are not connected with a coordinating conjunction.

   Examples:

   > She is outside; we are inside.
   > You are right; we should go with your plan.

2. Use a semicolon **between independent clauses linked with a transitional word.**

   Examples:

   > I think that we can agree on this; *however,* I am not sure about my friends.
   > You are looking in the wrong places; *therefore,* you will not find what you need.

3. Use a semicolon **between items in a series that has internal punctuation.**

   Example: I have visited New York, New York; Augusta, Maine; and Baltimore, Maryland.

   > **Review Video: How to Use Semicolons**
   > Visit mometrix.com/academy and enter code: 370605

COLONS

The colon is used to call attention to the words that follow it. A colon must come after a **complete independent clause**. The rules for colons are as follows:

1. Use a colon after an independent clause to **make a list**

   Example: I want to learn many languages: Spanish, German, and Italian.

2. Use a colon for **explanations** or to **give a quote**

   Examples:

   > **Quote**: He started with an idea: "We are able to do more than we imagine."
   > **Explanation**: There is one thing that stands out on your resume: responsibility.

3. Use a colon **after the greeting in a formal letter**, to **show hours and minutes**, and to **separate a title and subtitle**

   Examples:

   > **Greeting in a formal letter**: Dear Sir: | To Whom It May Concern:
   > **Time**: It is 3:14 P.M.
   > **Title**: The essay is titled "America: A Short Introduction to a Modern Country"

PARENTHESES

Parentheses are used for additional information. Also, they can be used to put labels for letters or numbers in a series. Parentheses should be not be used very often. If they are overused, parentheses can be a distraction instead of a help.

Examples:

Extra Information: The rattlesnake (see Image 2) is a dangerous snake of North and South America.

Series: Include in the email (1) your name, (2) your address, and (3) your question for the author.

QUOTATION MARKS

Use quotation marks to close off **direct quotations** of a person's spoken or written words. Do not use quotation marks around indirect quotations. An indirect quotation gives someone's message without using the person's exact words. Use **single quotation marks** to close off a quotation inside a quotation.

Direct Quote: Nancy said, "I am waiting for Henry to arrive."

Indirect Quote: Henry said that he is going to be late to the meeting.

Quote inside a Quote: The teacher asked, "Has everyone read 'The Gift of the Magi'?"

Quotation marks should be used around the titles of **short works**: newspaper and magazine articles, poems, short stories, songs, television episodes, radio programs, and subdivisions of books or web sites.

Examples:

"Rip van Winkle" (short story by Washington Irving)

"O Captain! My Captain!" (poem by Walt Whitman)

Although it is not standard usage, quotation marks are sometimes used to highlight **irony**, or the use of words to mean something other than their dictionary definition. This type of usage should be employed sparingly, if at all.

Examples:

The boss warned Frank that he was walking on "thin ice."

(Frank is not walking on real ice. Instead, Frank is being warned to avoid mistakes.)

The teacher thanked the young man for his "honesty."

(In this example, the quotation marks around *honesty* show that the teacher does not believe the young man's explanation.)

> **Review Video: Quotation Marks**
> Visit mometrix.com/academy and enter code: 884918

Periods and commas are put **inside** quotation marks. Colons and semicolons are put **outside** the quotation marks. Question marks and exclamation points are placed inside quotation marks when they are part of a quote. When the question or exclamation mark goes with the whole sentence, the mark is left outside of the quotation marks.

Examples:

> *Period and comma*: We read "The Gift of the Magi," "The Skylight Room," and "The Cactus."

> *Semicolon*: They watched "The Nutcracker"; then, they went home.

> *Exclamation mark that is a part of a quote*: The crowd cheered, "Victory!"

> *Question mark that goes with the whole sentence*: Is your favorite short story "The Tell-Tale Heart"?

APOSTROPHES

An apostrophe is used to show **possession** or the **deletion of letters in contractions**. An apostrophe is not needed with the possessive pronouns *his, hers, its, ours, theirs, whose*, and *yours*.

> **Singular Nouns**: David's car | a book's theme | my brother's board game

> **Plural Nouns with -*s***: the scissors' handle | boys' basketball

> **Plural Nouns without -*s***: Men's department | the people's adventure

HYPHENS

Hyphens are used to **separate compound words**. Use hyphens in the following cases:

1. **Compound numbers** between 21 and 99 when written out in words
   Example: This team needs *twenty-five* points to win the game.

2. **Written-out fractions** that are used as **adjectives**
   Correct: The recipe says that we need a *three-fourths* cup of butter.
   Incorrect: *One-fourth* of the road is under construction.

3. Compound words used as **adjectives that come before a noun**
   Correct: The *well-fed* dog took a nap.
   Incorrect: The dog was *well-fed* for his nap.

4. Compound words that would be **hard to read** or **easily confused with other words**
   Examples: Semi-irresponsible | Anti-itch | Re-sort

Note: This is not a complete set of the rules for hyphens. A dictionary is the best tool for knowing if a compound word needs a hyphen.

DASHES

Dashes are used to show a **break** or a **change in thought** in a sentence or to act as parentheses in a sentence. When typing, use two hyphens to make a dash. Do not put a space before or after the dash. The following are the rules for dashes:

1. To set off **parenthetical statements** or an **appositive with internal punctuation**

   Example: The three trees—oak, pine, and magnolia—are coming on a truck tomorrow.

2. To show a **break or change in tone or thought**

   Example: The first question—how silly of me—does not have a correct answer.

ELLIPSIS MARKS

The ellipsis mark has three periods (...) to show when **words have been removed** from a quotation. If a full sentence or more is removed from a quoted passage, you need to use four periods to show the removed text and the end punctuation mark. The ellipsis mark should not be used at the beginning of a quotation. The ellipsis mark should also not be used at the end of a quotation unless some words have been deleted from the end of the final sentence.

Example:

"Then he picked up the groceries...paid for them...later he went home."

BRACKETS

There are two main reasons to use brackets:

1. When **placing parentheses inside of parentheses**

   Example: The hero of this story, Paul Revere (a silversmith and industrialist [see Ch. 4]), rode through towns of Massachusetts to warn of advancing British troops.

2. When adding **clarification or detail** to a quotation that is **not part of the quotation**

   Example:

   The father explained, "My children are planning to attend my alma mater [State University]."

Common Errors

WORD CONFUSION
WHICH, THAT, AND WHO
The words *which*, *that*, and *who* can act as **relative pronouns** to help clarify or describe a noun.

Which is used for things only.

> Example: Andrew's car, *which is old and rusty*, broke down last week.

That is used for people or things. *That* is usually informal when used to describe people.

> Example: Is this the only book *that Louis L'Amour wrote?*

> Example: Is Louis L'Amour the author *that wrote Western novels?*

Who is used for people or for animals that have a name.

> Example: Mozart was the composer *who wrote those operas.*

> Example: John's dog, *who is called Max,* is large and fierce.

HOMOPHONES
Homophones are words that sound alike (or similar), but they have different **spellings** and **definitions**.

TO, TOO, AND TWO
To can be an adverb or a preposition for showing direction, purpose, and relationship. See your dictionary for the many other ways use *to* in a sentence.

> Examples: I went to the store. | I want to go with you.

Too is an adverb that means *also, as well, very, or more than enough*.

> Examples: I can walk a mile too. | You have eaten too much.

Two is the second number in the series of numbers (e.g., one (1), two, (2), three (3)...)

> Example: You have two minutes left.

THERE, THEIR, AND THEY'RE
There can be an adjective, adverb, or pronoun. Often, *there* is used to show a place or to start a sentence.

> Examples: I went there yesterday. | There is something in his pocket.

Their is a pronoun that is used to show ownership.

> Examples: He is their father. | This is their fourth apology this week.

They're is a contraction of *they are*.

> Example: Did you know that they're in town?

KNEW AND NEW

Knew is the past tense of *know*.

> Example: I knew the answer.

New is an adjective that means something is current, has not been used, or modern.

> Example: This is my new phone.

THEN AND THAN

Then is an adverb that indicates sequence or order:

> Example: I'm going to run to the library and then come home.

Than is special-purpose word used only for comparisons:

> Example: Susie likes chips better than candy.

ITS AND IT'S

Its is a pronoun that shows ownership.

> Example: The guitar is in its case.

It's is a contraction of *it is*.

> Example: It's an honor and a privilege to meet you.

Note: The *h* in honor is silent, so the sound of the vowel *o* must have the article *an*.

YOUR AND YOU'RE

Your is a pronoun that shows ownership.

> Example: This is your moment to shine.

You're is a contraction of *you are*.

> Example: Yes, you're correct.

AFFECT AND EFFECT

There are two main reasons that **affect** and **effect** are so often confused: 1) both words can be used as either a noun or a verb, and 2) unlike most homophones, their usage and meanings are closely related to each other. Here is a quick rundown of the four usage options:

Affect (n): feeling, emotion, or mood that is displayed

> Example: The patient had a flat *affect*. (i.e., his face showed little or no emotion)

Affect (v): to alter, to change, to influence

> Example: The sunshine *affects* the plant's growth.

Effect (n): a result, a consequence

> Example: What *effect* will this weather have on our schedule?

Effect (v): to bring about, to cause to be

> Example: These new rules will *effect* order in the office.

The noun form of *affect* is rarely used outside of technical medical descriptions, so if a noun form is needed on the test, you can safely select *effect*. The verb form of *effect* is not as rare as the noun form of *affect*, but it's still not all that likely to show up on your test. If you need a verb and you can't decide which to use based on the definitions, choosing *affect* is your best bet.

HOMOGRAPHS

Homographs are words that share the same spelling, and they have multiple meanings. To figure out which meaning is being used, you should be looking for context clues. The context clues give hints to the meaning of the word. For example, the word *spot* has many meanings. It can mean "a place" or "a stain or blot." In the sentence "After my lunch, I saw a spot on my shirt," the word *spot* means "a stain or blot." The context clues of "After my lunch…" and "on my shirt" guide you to this decision.

BANK

> (noun): an establishment where money is held for savings or lending

> (verb): to collect or pile up

CONTENT

> (noun): the topics that will be addressed within a book

> (adjective): pleased or satisfied

FINE

> (noun): an amount of money that acts a penalty for an offense

> (adjective): very small or thin

INCENSE

> (noun): a material that is burned in religious settings and makes a pleasant aroma

> (verb): to frustrate or anger

LEAD

> (noun): the first or highest position

> (verb): to direct a person or group of followers

OBJECT

> (noun): a lifeless item that can be held and observed

> (verb): to disagree

PRODUCE

> (noun): fruits and vegetables

> (verb): to make or create something

REFUSE

(noun): garbage or debris that has been thrown away

(verb): to not allow

SUBJECT

(noun): an area of study

(verb): to force or subdue

TEAR

(noun): a fluid secreted by the eyes

(verb): to separate or pull apart

The Math Test

Number and Quantity

Numbers are the basic building blocks of mathematics. Specific features of numbers are identified by the following terms:

Integer – any positive or negative whole number, including zero. Integers do not include fractions $\left(\frac{1}{3}\right)$, decimals (0.56), or mixed numbers $\left(7\frac{3}{4}\right)$.

Prime number – any whole number greater than 1 that has only two factors, itself and 1; that is, a number that can be divided evenly only by 1 and itself.

Composite number – any whole number greater than 1 that has more than two different factors; in other words, any whole number that is not a prime number. For example: The composite number 8 has the factors of 1, 2, 4, and 8.

Even number – any integer that can be divided by 2 without leaving a remainder. For example: 2, 4, 6, 8, and so on.

Odd number – any integer that cannot be divided evenly by 2. For example: 3, 5, 7, 9, and so on.

Decimal number – any number that uses a decimal point to show the part of the number that is less than one. Example: 1.234.

Decimal point – a symbol used to separate the ones place from the tenths place in decimals or dollars from cents in currency.

Decimal place – the position of a number to the right of the decimal point. In the decimal 0.123, the 1 is in the first place to the right of the decimal point, indicating tenths; the 2 is in the second place, indicating hundredths; and the 3 is in the third place, indicating thousandths.

The decimal, or base 10, system is a number system that uses ten different digits (0, 1, 2, 3, 4, 5, 6, 7, 8, 9). An example of a number system that uses something other than ten digits is the binary, or base 2, number system, used by computers, which uses only the numbers 0 and 1. It is thought that the decimal system originated because people had only their 10 fingers for counting.

Rational numbers include all integers, decimals, and fractions. Any terminating or repeating decimal number is a rational number.

Irrational numbers cannot be written as fractions or decimals because the number of decimal places is infinite and there is no recurring pattern of digits within the number. For example, pi (π)

62

begins with 3.141592 and continues without terminating or repeating, so pi is an irrational number.

Real numbers are the set of all rational and irrational numbers.

> **Review Video: Classification of Numbers**
> Visit mometrix.com/academy and enter code: 461071
>
> **Review Video: Rational and Irrational Numbers**
> Visit mometrix.com/academy and enter code: 280645
>
> **Review Video: Prime and Composite Numbers**
> Visit mometrix.com/academy and enter code: 565581

PLACE VALUE

Write the place value of each digit in the following number: 14,059.826

1: ten thousands

4: thousands

0: hundreds

5: tens

9: ones

8: tenths

2: hundredths

6: thousandths

WRITING NUMBERS IN WORD FORM

Example 1

Write each number in words.

29: twenty-nine

478: four hundred seventy-eight

9,435: nine thousand four hundred thirty-five

98,542: ninety-eight thousand five hundred forty-two

302876: three hundred two thousand eight hundred seventy-six

Example 2

Write each decimal in words.

0.06: six hundredths

0.6: six tenths

6.0: six

0.009: nine thousandths;

0.113: one hundred thirteen thousandths;

0.901: nine hundred and one thousandths

THE NUMBER LINE

A number line is a graph to see the distance between numbers. Basically, this graph shows the relationship between numbers. So a number line may have a point for zero and may show negative numbers on the left side of the line. Any positive numbers are placed on the right side of the line. For example, consider the points labeled on the following number line:

We can use the dashed lines on the number line to identify each point. Each dashed line between two whole numbers is $\frac{1}{4}$. The line halfway between two numbers is $\frac{1}{2}$.

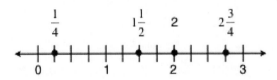

> **Review Video: The Number Line**
> Visit mometrix.com/academy and enter code: 816439

RATIONAL NUMBERS FROM LEAST TO GREATEST

Example

Order the following rational numbers from least to greatest: 0.55, 17%, $\sqrt{25}$, $\frac{64}{4}$, $\frac{25}{50}$, 3.

Recall that the term *rational* simply means that the number can be expressed as a ratio or fraction. The set of rational numbers includes integers and decimals. Notice that each of the numbers in the problem can be written as a decimal or integer:

$17\% = 0.17$

$\sqrt{25} = 5$

$\frac{64}{4} = 16$

$\frac{25}{50} = \frac{1}{2} = 0.5$

So, the answer is 17%, $\frac{25}{50}$, 0.55, 3, $\sqrt{25}$, $\frac{64}{4}$.

RATIONAL NUMBERS FROM GREATEST TO LEAST

<u>Example</u>

Order the following rational numbers from greatest to least: $0.3, 27\%, \sqrt{100}, \frac{72}{9}, \frac{1}{9}, 4.5$

Recall that the term *rational* simply means that the number can be expressed as a ratio or fraction. The set of rational numbers includes integers and decimals. Notice that each of the numbers in the problem can be written as a decimal or integer:

$27\% = 0.27$

$\sqrt{100} = 10$

$\frac{72}{9} = 8$

$\frac{1}{9} \approx 0.11$

So, the answer is $\sqrt{100}, \frac{72}{9}, 4.5, 0.3, 27\%, \frac{1}{9}$.

FRACTIONS

A fraction is a number that is expressed as one integer written above another integer, with a dividing line between them $\left(\frac{x}{y}\right)$. It represents the quotient of the two numbers "x divided by y." It can also be thought of as x out of y equal parts.

The top number of a fraction is called the numerator, and it represents the number of parts under consideration. The 1 in $\frac{1}{4}$ means that 1 part out of the whole is being considered in the calculation. The bottom number of a fraction is called the denominator, and it represents the total number of equal parts. The 4 in $\frac{1}{4}$ means that the whole consists of 4 equal parts. A fraction cannot have a denominator of zero; this is referred to as "undefined."

> **Review Video: Overview of Fractions**
> Visit mometrix.com/academy and enter code: 262335

Fractions can be manipulated, without changing the value of the fraction, by multiplying or dividing (but not adding or subtracting) both the numerator and denominator by the same number. If you divide both numbers by a common factor, you are reducing or simplifying the fraction. Two fractions that have the same value, but are expressed differently are known as equivalent fractions.

For example, $\frac{2}{10}, \frac{3}{15}, \frac{4}{20}$, and $\frac{5}{25}$ are all equivalent fractions. They can also all be reduced or simplified to $\frac{1}{5}$.

PROPER FRACTIONS AND MIXED NUMBERS

A fraction whose denominator is greater than its numerator is known as a proper fraction, while a fraction whose numerator is greater than its denominator is known as an improper fraction. Proper fractions have values less than one and improper fractions have values greater than one.

> **Review Video: Proper and Improper Fractions and Mixed Numbers**
> Visit mometrix.com/academy and enter code: 211077

A mixed number is a number that contains both an integer and a fraction. Any improper fraction can be rewritten as a mixed number. Example: $\frac{8}{3} = \frac{6}{3} + \frac{2}{3} = 2 + \frac{2}{3} = 2\frac{2}{3}$. Similarly, any mixed number can be rewritten as an improper fraction. Example: $1\frac{3}{5} = 1 + \frac{3}{5} = \frac{5}{5} + \frac{3}{5} = \frac{8}{5}$.

COMMON DENOMINATORS WITH FRACTIONS

When two fractions are manipulated so that they have the same denominator, this is known as finding a common denominator. The number chosen to be that common denominator should be the least common multiple of the two original denominators. Example: $\frac{3}{4}$ and $\frac{5}{6}$; the least common multiple of 4 and 6 is 12. Manipulating to achieve the common denominator: $\frac{3}{4} = \frac{9}{12}; \frac{5}{6} = \frac{10}{12}$.

DECIMALS
DECIMAL ILLUSTRATION

Use a model to represent the decimal: 0.24. Write 0.24 as a fraction.

The decimal 0.24 is twenty four hundredths. One possible model to represent this fraction is to draw 100 pennies, since each penny is worth 1 one hundredth of a dollar. Draw one hundred circles to represent one hundred pennies. Shade 24 of the pennies to represent the decimal twenty-four hundredths.

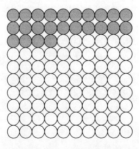

To write the decimal as a fraction, write a fraction: $\frac{\text{\# shaded spaces}}{\text{\# total spaces}}$. The number of shaded spaces is 24, and the total number of spaces is 100, so as a fraction 0.24 equals $\frac{24}{100}$. This fraction can then be reduced to $\frac{6}{25}$.

> **Review Video: Decimals**
> Visit mometrix.com/academy and enter code: 837268

PERCENTAGES

Percentages can be thought of as fractions that are based on a whole of 100; that is, one whole is equal to 100%. The word percent means "per hundred." Fractions can be expressed as percents by finding equivalent fractions with a denomination of 100. Example: $\frac{7}{10} = \frac{70}{100} = 70\%$; $\frac{1}{4} = \frac{25}{100} = 25\%$.

To express a percentage as a fraction, divide the percentage number by 100 and reduce the fraction to its simplest possible terms. Example: $60\% = \frac{60}{100} = \frac{3}{5}$; $96\% = \frac{96}{100} = \frac{24}{25}$.

> **Review Video: Computation with Percentages**
> Visit mometrix.com/academy and enter code: 693099

CONVERTING PERCENTS, FRACTIONS, AND DECIMALS

Converting decimals to percentages and percentages to decimals is as simple as moving the decimal point. To convert from a decimal to a percent, move the decimal point two places to the right. To convert from a percent to a decimal, move it two places to the left. Example: $0.23 = 23\%$; $5.34 = 534\%$; $0.007 = 0.7\%$; $700\% = 7.00$; $86\% = 0.86$; $0.15\% = 0.0015$.

It may be helpful to remember that the percentage number will always be larger than the equivalent decimal number.

Example 1

15% can be written as a fraction and as a decimal. 15% written as a fraction is $\frac{15}{100}$ which equals $\frac{3}{20}$. 15% written as a decimal is 0.15.

To convert a percent to a fraction, follow these steps:

1) Write the percent over 100 because percent means "per one hundred." So, 15% can be written as $\frac{15}{100}$.

2) Fractions should be written in simplest form, which means that the numbers in the numerator and denominator should be reduced if possible. Both 15 and 100 can be divided by 5.

3) Therefore, $\frac{15 \div 5}{100 \div 5} = \frac{3}{20}$.

To convert a percent to a decimal, follow these steps:

1) Write the percent over 100 because percent means "per one hundred." So, 15% can be written as $\frac{15}{100}$.

2) 15 divided by 100 equals 0.15, so 15% = 0.15. In other words, when converting from a percent to a decimal, drop the percent sign and move the decimal two places to the left.

Example 2

Write 24.36% as a fraction and then as a decimal. Explain how you made these conversions.

24.36% written as a fraction is $\frac{24.36}{100}$, or $\frac{2436}{10,000}$, which reduces to $\frac{609}{2500}$. 24.36% written as a decimal is 0.2436. Recall that dividing by 100 moves the decimal two places to the left.

Review Video: <u>Converting Percentages to Decimals and Fractions</u>

Visit mometrix.com/academy and enter code: 287297

Example 3

Convert $\frac{4}{5}$ to a decimal and to a percent.

To convert a fraction to a decimal, simply divide the numerator by the denominator in the fraction. The numerator is the top number in the fraction and the denominator is the bottom number in a fraction. So $\frac{4}{5} = 4 \div 5 = 0.80 = 0.8$.

Percent means "per hundred." $\frac{4 \times 20}{5 \times 20} = \frac{80}{100} = 80\%$.

Example 4

Convert $3\frac{2}{5}$ to a decimal and to a percent.

The mixed number $3\frac{2}{5}$ has a whole number and a fractional part. The fractional part $\frac{2}{5}$ can be written as a decimal by dividing 5 into 2, which gives 0.4. Adding the whole to the part gives 3.4. Alternatively, note that $3\frac{2}{5} = 3\frac{4}{10} = 3.4$

To change a decimal to a percent, multiply it by 100.
$3.4(100) = 340\%$. Notice that this percentage is greater than 100%. This makes sense because the original mixed number $3\frac{2}{5}$ is greater than 1.

Review Video: <u>Converting Fractions to Percentages and Decimals</u>

Visit mometrix.com/academy and enter code: 306233

OPERATIONS

There are four basic mathematical operations:

ADDITION AND SUBTRACTION

Addition increases the value of one quantity by the value of another quantity. Example: $2 + 4 = 6$; $8 + 9 = 17$. The result is called the sum. With addition, the order does not matter. $4 + 2 = 2 + 4$.

Subtraction is the opposite operation to addition; it decreases the value of one quantity by the value of another quantity. Example: $6 - 4 = 2$; $17 - 8 = 9$. The result is called the difference. Note that with subtraction, the order does matter. $6 - 4 \neq 4 - 6$.

MULTIPLICATION AND DIVISION

Multiplication can be thought of as repeated addition. One number tells how many times to add the other number to itself. Example: 3×2 (three times two) $= 2 + 2 + 2 = 6$. With multiplication, the order does not matter. $2 \times 3 = 3 \times 2$ or $3 + 3 = 2 + 2 + 2$.

Division is the opposite operation to multiplication; one number tells us how many parts to divide the other number into. Example: $20 \div 4 = 5$; if 20 is split into 4 equal parts, each part is 5. With division, the order of the numbers does matter. $20 \div 4 \neq 4 \div 20$.

ORDER OF OPERATIONS

The **order of operations** is a set of rules that dictates the order in which we must perform each operation in an expression so that we will evaluate it accurately. If we have an expression that includes multiple different operations, the order of operations tells us which operations to do first. The most common mnemonic for the order of operations is **PEMDAS**, or "Please Excuse My Dear Aunt Sally." PEMDAS stands for parentheses, exponents, multiplication, division, addition, and subtraction. It is important to understand that multiplication and division have equal precedence, as do addition and subtraction, so those pairs of operations are simply worked from left to right in order.

Example: Evaluate the expression $5 + 20 \div 4 \times (2 + 3)^2 - 6$ using the correct order of operations.

- **P:** Perform the operations inside the parentheses: $(2 + 3) = 5$
- **E:** Simplify the exponents: $(5)^2 = 5 \times 5 = 25$
  - The expression now looks like this: $5 + 20 \div 4 \times 25 - 6$
- **MD:** Perform multiplication and division from left to right: $20 \div 4 = 5$; then $5 \times 25 = 125$
  - The expression now looks like this: $5 + 125 - 6$
- **AS:** Perform addition and subtraction from left to right: $5 + 125 = 130$; then $130 - 6 = 124$

> **Review Video: <u>Order of Operations</u>**
> Visit mometrix.com/academy and enter code: 259675

PARENTHESES

Parentheses are used to designate which operations should be done first when there are multiple operations. Example: $4 - (2 + 1) = 1$; the parentheses tell us that we must add 2 and 1, and then subtract the sum from 4, rather than subtracting 2 from 4 and then adding 1 (this would give us an answer of 3).

EXPONENTS

An exponent is a superscript number placed next to another number at the top right. It indicates how many times the base number is to be multiplied by itself. Exponents provide a shorthand way to write what would be a longer mathematical expression. Example: $a^2 = a \times a$; $2^4 = 2 \times 2 \times 2 \times 2$. A number with an exponent of 2 is said to be "squared," while a number with an exponent of 3 is said to be "cubed." The value of a number raised to an exponent is called its power. So, 8^4 is read as "8 to the 4th power," or "8 raised to the power of 4." A negative exponent is the same as the reciprocal of a positive exponent. Example: $a^{-2} = \frac{1}{a^2}$.

ABSOLUTE VALUE

A precursor to working with negative numbers is understanding what **absolute values** are. A number's absolute value is simply the distance away from zero a number is on the number line. The absolute value of a number is always positive and is written $|x|$. For example, the absolute value of 3, written as $|3|$, is 3 because the distance between 0 and 3 on a number line is three units. Likewise, the absolute value of –3, written as $|-3|$, is 3 because the distance between 0 and –3 on a number line is three units. So $|3| = |-3|$.

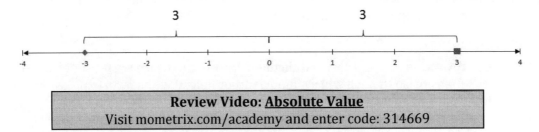

> **Review Video: Absolute Value**
> Visit mometrix.com/academy and enter code: 314669

OPERATIONS WITH POSITIVE AND NEGATIVE NUMBERS

ADDITION

When adding signed numbers, if the signs are the same simply add the absolute values of the addends and apply the original sign to the sum. For example, $(+4) + (+8) = +12$ and $(-4) + (-8) = -12$. When the original signs are different, take the absolute values of the addends and subtract the smaller value from the larger value, then apply the original sign of the larger value to the difference. For instance, $(+4) + (-8) = -4$ and $(-4) + (+8) = +4$.

SUBTRACTION

For subtracting signed numbers, change the sign of the number after the minus symbol and then follow the same rules used for addition. For example, $(+4) - (+8) = (+4) + (-8) = -4$.

MULTIPLICATION

If the signs are the same the product is positive when multiplying signed numbers. For example, $(+4) \times (+8) = +32$ and $(-4) \times (-8) = +32$. If the signs are opposite, the product is negative. For example, $(+4) \times (-8) = -32$ and $(-4) \times (+8) = -32$. When more than two factors are multiplied together, the sign of the product is determined by how many negative factors are present. If there are an odd number of negative factors then the product is negative, whereas an even number of negative factors indicates a positive product. For instance, $(+4) \times (-8) \times (-2) = +64$ and $(-4) \times (-8) \times (-2) = -64$.

DIVISION

The rules for dividing signed numbers are similar to multiplying signed numbers. If the dividend and divisor have the same sign, the quotient is positive. If the dividend and divisor have opposite signs, the quotient is negative. For example, $(-4) \div (+8) = -0.5$.

OPERATIONS WITH DECIMALS

ADDING AND SUBTRACTING DECIMALS

When adding and subtracting decimals, the decimal points must always be aligned. Adding decimals is just like adding regular whole numbers. Example: $4.5 + 2 = 6.5$.

If the problem-solver does not properly align the decimal points, an incorrect answer of 4.7 may result. An easy way to add decimals is to align all of the decimal points in a vertical column visually. This will allow you to see exactly where the decimal should be placed in the final answer. Begin adding from right to left. Add each column in turn, making sure to carry the number to the left if a column adds up to more than 9. The same rules apply to the subtraction of decimals.

> **Review Video: Adding and Subtracting Decimals**
> Visit mometrix.com/academy and enter code: 381101

MULTIPLYING DECIMALS

A simple multiplication problem has two components: a multiplicand and a multiplier. When multiplying decimals, work as though the numbers were whole rather than decimals. Once the final product is calculated, count the number of places to the right of the decimal in both the multiplicand and the multiplier. Then, count that number of places from the right of the product and place the decimal in that position.

For example, 12.3×2.56 has three places to the right of the respective decimals. Multiply 123×256 to get 31488. Now, beginning on the right, count three places to the left and insert the decimal. The final product will be 31.488.

> **Review Video: Multiplying Decimals**
> Visit mometrix.com/academy and enter code: 731574

DIVIDING DECIMALS

Every division problem has a divisor and a dividend. The dividend is the number that is being divided. In the problem $14 \div 7$, 14 is the dividend and 7 is the divisor. In a division problem with decimals, the divisor must be converted into a whole number. Begin by moving the decimal in the divisor to the right until a whole number is created. Next, move the decimal in the dividend the same number of spaces to the right. For example, 4.9 into 24.5 would become 49 into 245. The decimal was moved one space to the right to create a whole number in the divisor, and then the same was done for the dividend. Once the whole numbers are created, the problem is carried out normally: $245 \div 49 = 5$.

> **Review Video: Dividing Decimals**
> Visit mometrix.com/academy and enter code: 560690

OPERATIONS WITH FRACTIONS

ADDING AND SUBTRACTING FRACTIONS

If two fractions have a common denominator, they can be added or subtracted simply by adding or subtracting the two numerators and retaining the same denominator. Example: $\frac{1}{2} + \frac{1}{4} = \frac{2}{4} + \frac{1}{4} = \frac{3}{4}$.

If the two fractions do not already have the same denominator, one or both of them must be manipulated to achieve a common denominator before they can be added or subtracted.

> **Review Video: Adding and Subtracting Fractions**
> Visit mometrix.com/academy and enter code: 378080

MULTIPLYING FRACTIONS

Two fractions can be multiplied by multiplying the two numerators to find the new numerator and the two denominators to find the new denominator. Example: $\frac{1}{3} \times \frac{2}{3} = \frac{1 \times 2}{3 \times 3} = \frac{2}{9}$.

> **Review Video: Multiplying and Dividing Fractions**
> Visit mometrix.com/academy and enter code: 473632

DIVIDING FRACTIONS

Two fractions can be divided by flipping the numerator and denominator of the second fraction and then proceeding as though it were a multiplication. Example: $\frac{2}{3} \div \frac{3}{4} = \frac{2}{3} \times \frac{4}{3} = \frac{8}{9}$.

FACTORS AND MULTIPLES

Factors are numbers that are multiplied together to obtain a product. For example, in the equation $2 \times 3 = 6$, the numbers 2 and 3 are factors. A prime number has only two factors (1 and itself), but other numbers can have many factors.

> **Review Video: Factors**
> Visit mometrix.com/academy and enter code: 920086

A common factor is a number that divides exactly into two or more other numbers. For example, the factors of 12 are 1, 2, 3, 4, 6, and 12, while the factors of 15 are 1, 3, 5, and 15. The common factors of 12 and 15 are 1 and 3.

A prime factor is also a prime number. Therefore, the prime factors of 12 are 2 and 3. For 15, the prime factors are 3 and 5.

> **Review Video: Prime Factorization**
> Visit mometrix.com/academy and enter code: 760669

The greatest common factor (GCF) is the largest number that is a factor of two or more numbers. For example, the factors of 15 are 1, 3, 5, and 15; the factors of 35 are 1, 5, 7, and 35. Therefore, the greatest common factor of 15 and 35 is 5.

> **Review Video: Greatest Common Factor and Least Common Multiple**
> Visit mometrix.com/academy and enter code: 838699

The least common multiple (LCM) is the smallest number that is a multiple of two or more numbers. For example, the multiples of 3 include 3, 6, 9, 12, 15, etc.; the multiples of 5 include 5, 10, 15, 20, etc. Therefore, the least common multiple of 3 and 5 is 15.

RATIOS

A ratio is a comparison of two quantities in a particular order. Example: If there are 14 computers in a lab, and the class has 20 students, there is a student to computer ratio of 20 to 14, commonly written as 20:14.

Two more comparisons used frequently in algebra are ratios and proportions. A *Ratio* is a comparison of two quantities, expressed in a number of different ways. Ratios can be listed as "a to b", "a:b", or "a/b". Examples of ratios are miles per hour (miles/hour), meters per second (meters/second), miles per gallon (miles/gallon), etc.

PROPORTIONS AND CROSS PRODUCTS

A proportion is a relationship between two quantities that dictates how one changes when the other changes. A direct proportion describes a relationship in which a quantity increases by a set amount for every increase in the other quantity, or decreases by that same amount for every decrease in the other quantity. Example: For every 1 sheet cake, 18 people can be served cake. The number of sheet cakes, and the number of people that can be served from them is directly proportional.

A statement of two equal ratios is a *Proportion*, such as $\frac{m}{b} = \frac{w}{z}$. If Fred travels 2 miles in 1 hour and Jane travels 4 miles in 2 hours, their speeds are said to be proportional because $\frac{2}{1} = \frac{4}{2}$. In a proportion, the product of the numerator of the first ratio and the denominator of the second ratio is equal to the product of the denominator of the first ratio and the numerator of the second ratio. Using the previous example, we see that $m \times z = b \times w$, thus $2 \times 2 = 1 \times 4$.

An **inverse proportion** is a relationship in which an increase in one quantity is accompanied by a decrease in the other, or vice versa. Example: the time required for a car trip decreases as the speed increases, and increases as the speed decreases, so the time required is inversely proportional to the speed of the car.

ROOTS AND SQUARE ROOTS

A root, such as a square root, is another way of writing a fractional exponent. Instead of using a superscript, roots use the radical symbol ($\sqrt{}$) to indicate the operation. A radical will have a number underneath the bar, and may sometimes have a number in the upper left: $\sqrt[n]{a}$, read as "the nth root of a."

The relationship between radical notation and exponent notation can be described by this equation: $\sqrt[n]{a} = a^{1/n}$. The two special cases of n = 2 and n = 3 are called square roots and cube roots. If there is no number to the upper left, it is understood to be a square root (n = 2). Nearly all of the roots you encounter will be square roots. A square root is the same as a number raised to the one-half power. When we say that a is the square root of b (a = $\sqrt{b}$), we mean that a multiplied by itself equals b: (a × a = b).

A perfect square is a number that has an integer for its square root. There are 10 perfect squares from 1 to 100: 1, 4, 9, 16, 25, 36, 49, 64, 81, 100 (the squares of integers 1 through 10).

COEFFICIENTS AND THE DISTRIBUTIVE PROPERTY

COEFFICIENTS

A coefficient is a number or symbol that is multiplied by a variable. For example, in the expression 2(ab), the number 2 is the coefficient of (ab). The expression can be written in other ways to have a different coefficient. For example, the expression can be 2a(b). This means that 2a is the coefficient of (b).

DISTRIBUTIVE PROPERTY

The distributive property can be used to multiply each addend in parentheses. Then, the products are added to reach the result. The formula for the distributive property looks like this: a(b+c) = ab+ac.

Example: 6(2+4)

First, multiply 6 and 2. The answer is 12.

Then, multiply 6 and 4. The answer is 24.

Last, we add 12 and 24. The final answer is 36.

> **Review Video: Commutative, Associative, and Distributive Property**
> Visit mometrix.com/academy and enter code: 483176

OTHER PROPERTIES

Below is a list of the field properties of number systems for quick reference.

- Subtraction:
  - $a - b = a + (-b)$
- Additive Identity:
  - $a + 0 = a$
  - $0 + a = a$
- Additive Inverse:
  - $a + (-a) = 0$
  - $(-a) + a = 0$
- Associative:
  - $(a + b) + c = a + (b + c)$ for addition
  - $(ab)c = a(bc)$ for multiplication

- Closure:
  - $a + b$ is a real number for addition
  - ab is a real number for multiplication
- Commutative:
  - $a + b = b + a$ for addition
  - $ab = ba$ for multiplication
- Distributive:
  - $a(b + c) = ab + ac$
  - $(a + b)c = ac + bc$
- Multiplicative Identity:
  - $a \cdot 1 = a$
  - $1 \cdot a = a$
- Multiplicative Inverse:
  - $a \cdot a^{-1} = 1$
  - $a^{-1} \cdot a = 1$
- Division:
  - $a \div b = \dfrac{a}{b} = a \cdot b^{-1} = a \cdot \dfrac{1}{b}$

SCIENTIFIC NOTATION

Scientific notation is a way of writing long numbers in a shorter form. The form $a \times 10^n$ is used in scientific notation. This form means that a is greater than or equal to 1 but less than 10. Also, n is the number of places the decimal must move to get from the original number to a.

Example: The number 230,400,000 is long to write. To see this value in scientific notation, place a decimal point between the first and second numbers. This includes all digits through the last non-zero digit ($a = 2.304$).

To find the correct power of 10, count the number of places the decimal point had to move ($n = 8$). The number is positive if the decimal moved to the left. Thus, the number is negative if it moved to the right. So, 230,400,000 can be written as 2.304×10^8.

Now, let's look at the number 0.00002304. We have the same value for a. However, this time the decimal moved 5 places to the right ($n = -5$). So, 0.00002304 can be written as 2.304×10^{-5}. This notation makes it easy to compare very large or very small numbers. By comparing exponents, you can see that 3.28×10^4 is smaller than 1.51×10^5 because 4 is less than 5.

> **Review Video: Scientific Notation**
> Visit mometrix.com/academy and enter code: 976454

ADDITION AND SUBTRACTION

To add and subtract numbers in scientific notation, you need the numbers to have the same power of 10. Next, you can add the constants. Then, you can use the power of 10 with the result.

If the constant is greater than 10 or less than 1, you need to move the decimal place. For constants less than 1, the decimal is moved to the right. For constants greater than 10, the decimal is moved to the left. Also, the power of 10 needs to change as you move the decimal place.

Example 1

In the problem $(4.8 \times 10^4) + (2.2 \times 10^4)$, the numbers have the same power of 10. So, add 4.8 and 2.2. So, you have 7 as the result. Now, the number can be written as (7×10^4).

Example 2

In the problem $(3.1 \times 10^8) - (2.4 \times 10^8)$, the numbers have the same power of 10. So, subtract 3.1 and 2.4, and you'll have 0.7 as the result. Remember that you cannot have a constant that is less than 1. So, you need to move the decimal place one time to the right: (7×10^8). Also, the power of 10 has to change. Now, the number can be written as (7×10^{-1}).

The power of 10 is -1 because we moved the decimal place one time to the right. Now you have $(7 \times 10^{-1}) \times 10^8$. The reason is that we still have the power of 10 as 8. Now, you can add the -1 to the +8 for an answer of (7×10^7).

Example 3

In the problem $(5.3 \times 10^6) + (2.7 \times 10^7)$, the numbers do not have the same power of 10. So, you need one of the terms to have the same power. So, take (5.3×10^6) and change it to (0.53×10^7). Now, you can add 0.53 and 2.7. So, the number can be written as (3.23×10^7).

MULTIPLICATION

In the problem $(2.4 \times 10^3) \times (5.7 \times 10^5)$, you need to multiply 2.4 and 5.7. Then, you need to add the powers of 10 which are 3 and 5 for this example. So, you have (13.68×10^8). Remember that this cannot be an answer for scientific notation. The 13.68 for a constant is higher than 10. So, move the decimal to the left one time and change the exponent. Now, you have (1.368×10^9) as the answer.

DIVISION

In the problem $(5.6 \times 10^6) \div (2.3 \times 10^2)$, you need to divide 5.6 and 2.3. Then, you need to subtract the powers of 10 which are 6 and 2 for this example. So, you have (2.43×10^4).

Algebra

MATRICES
MATRIX BASICS

A **matrix** (plural: matrices) is a rectangular array of numbers or variables, often called **elements**, which are arranged in columns and rows. A matrix is generally represented by a capital letter, with its elements represented by the corresponding lowercase letter with two subscripts indicating the row and column of the element. For example, n_{ab} represents the element in row a column b of matrix N.

$$N = \begin{bmatrix} n_{11} & n_{12} & n_{13} \\ n_{21} & n_{22} & n_{23} \end{bmatrix}$$

A matrix can be described in terms of the number of rows and columns it contains in the format $a \times b$, where a is the number of rows and b is the number of columns. The matrix shown above is a 2×3 matrix. Any $a \times b$ matrix where $a = b$ is a square matrix.

ADDITION AND SUBTRACTION WITH MATRICES

There are two categories of basic operations with regard to matrices: operations between a matrix and a scalar, and operations between two matrices.

SCALAR OPERATIONS

A scalar being added to a matrix is treated as though it were being added to each element of the matrix:

$$M + 4 = \begin{bmatrix} m_{11} + 4 & m_{12} + 4 \\ m_{21} + 4 & m_{22} + 4 \end{bmatrix}$$

The same is true for the other three operations. Subtraction:

$$M - 4 = \begin{bmatrix} m_{11} - 4 & m_{12} - 4 \\ m_{21} - 4 & m_{22} - 4 \end{bmatrix}$$

MATRIX ADDITION AND SUBTRACTION

All four of the basic operations can be used with operations between matrices (although division is usually discarded in favor of multiplication by the inverse), but there are restrictions on the situations in which they can be used. Matrices that meet all the qualifications for a given operation are called **conformable matrices**. However, conformability is specific to the operation; two matrices that are conformable for addition are not necessarily conformable for multiplication.

For two matrices to be conformable for addition or subtraction, they must be of the same dimension; otherwise the operation is not defined. If matrix M is a 3×2 matrix and matrix N is a 2×3 matrix, the operations $M + N$ and $M - N$ are meaningless. If matrices M and N are the same size, the operation is as simple as adding or subtracting all of the corresponding elements:

$$\begin{bmatrix} m_{11} & m_{12} \\ m_{21} & m_{22} \end{bmatrix} + \begin{bmatrix} n_{11} & n_{12} \\ n_{21} & n_{22} \end{bmatrix} = \begin{bmatrix} m_{11} + n_{11} & m_{12} + n_{12} \\ m_{21} + n_{21} & m_{22} + n_{22} \end{bmatrix}$$

$$\begin{bmatrix} m_{11} & m_{12} \\ m_{21} & m_{22} \end{bmatrix} - \begin{bmatrix} n_{11} & n_{12} \\ n_{21} & n_{22} \end{bmatrix} = \begin{bmatrix} m_{11} - n_{11} & m_{12} - n_{12} \\ m_{21} - n_{21} & m_{22} - n_{22} \end{bmatrix}$$

The result of addition or subtraction is a matrix of the same dimension as the two original matrices involved in the operation.

POLYNOMIAL ALGEBRA

Equations are made up of monomials and polynomials. A *Monomial* is a single constant, variable, or product of constants and variables, such as 7, x, $2x$, or $x^3 y$. There will never be addition or subtraction symbols in a monomial. Like monomials have like variables, but they may have different coefficients. *Polynomials* are algebraic expressions which use addition and subtraction to combine two or more monomials. Two terms make a binomial; three terms make a trinomial; etc. The *Degree of a Monomial* is the sum of the exponents of the variables. The *Degree of a Polynomial* is the highest degree of any individual term.

ADD POLYNOMIALS

To add polynomials, you need to add like terms. These terms have the same variable part. An example is $4x^2$ and $3x^2$ have x^2 terms. To find the sum of like terms, find the sum of the coefficients.

Then, keep the same variable part. You can use the distributive property to distribute the plus sign to each term of the polynomial. For example:

$(4x^2 - 5x + 7) + (3x^2 + 2x + 1) =$

$(4x^2 - 5x + 7) + 3x^2 + 2x + 1 =$

$(4x^2 + 3x^2) + (-5x + 2x) + (7 + 1) =$

$7x^2 - 3x + 8$

SUBTRACT POLYNOMIALS

To subtract polynomials, you need to subtract like terms. To find the difference of like terms, find the difference of the coefficients. Then, keep the same variable part. You can use the distributive property to distribute the minus sign to each term of the polynomial. For example:

$$(-2x^2 - x + 5) - (3x^2 - 4x + 1) =$$

$$(-2x^2 - x + 5) - 3x^2 + 4x - 1 =$$

$$(-2x^2 - 3x^2) + (-x + 4x) + (5 - 1) =$$

$$-5x^2 + 3x + 4$$

MULTIPLY POLYNOMIALS

To multiply two binomials, follow the *FOIL* method. FOIL stands for:

- First: Multiply the first term of each binomial
- Outer: Multiply the outer terms of each binomial
- Inner: Multiply the inner terms of each binomial
- Last: Multiply the last term of each binomial

Using FOIL $(Ax + By)(Cx + Dy) = ACx^2 + ADxy + BCxy + BDy^2$.

Example: $(3x + 6)(4x - 2)$

First: $3x \times 4x = 12x^2$

Outer: $3x \times -2 = -6x$ | Current Expression: $12x^2 - 6x$

Inner: $6 \times 4x = 24x$ | Current Expression: $12x^2 - 6x + 24x$

Last: $6 \times -2 = -12$ | Final Expression: $12x^2 - 6x + 24x - 12$

Now, combine like terms. For this example, that is $-6x + 24x$. Then, the expression looks like: $12x^2 + 18x - 12$. Each number is a multiple of 6. So, the expression becomes $6(2x^2 + 3x - 2)$, and the polynomial has been expanded.

DIVIDE POLYNOMIALS

To divide polynomials, start with placing the terms of each polynomial in order of one variable. You may put them in ascending or descending order. Also, be consistent with both polynomials. To get the first term of the quotient, divide the first term of the dividend by the first term of the divisor.

Next, multiply the first term of the quotient by the entire divisor. Then, subtract that product from the dividend and repeat for the following terms.

You want to end with a remainder of zero or a remainder with a degree that is less than the degree of the divisor. If the quotient has a remainder, write the answer as a mixed expression in the form: quotient $+ \frac{\text{remainder}}{\text{divisor}}$.

Example: Divide $4x^5 + 3x^2 - x$ by x

$$\frac{4x^5}{x} + \frac{3x^2}{x} - \frac{x}{x} = 4x^4 + 3x - 1$$

Below are patterns of some special products to remember: *perfect trinomial squares*, the *difference between two squares*, the *sum and difference of two cubes*, and *perfect cubes*.

- Perfect Trinomial Squares: $x^2 + 2xy + y^2 = (x + y)^2$ or $x^2 - 2xy + y^2 = (x - y)^2$
- Difference between Two Squares: $x^2 - y^2 = (x + y)(x - y)$
- Sum of Two Cubes: $x^3 + y^3 = (x + y)(x^2 - xy + y^2)$
  Note: the second factor is NOT the same as a perfect trinomial square. So, do not try to factor it further.
- Difference between Two Cubes: $x^3 - y^3 = (x - y)(x^2 + xy + y^2)$
  Again, the second factor is NOT the same as a perfect trinomial square.
- Perfect Cubes: $x^3 + 3x^2y + 3xy^2 + y^3 = (x + y)^3$ and $x^3 - 3x^2y + 3xy^2 - y^3 = (x - y)^3$

FACTOR A POLYNOMIAL

1. Check for a common monomial factor.
2. Factor out the greatest common monomial factor
3. Look for patterns of special products: differences of two squares, the sum or difference of two cubes for binomial factors, or perfect trinomial squares for trinomial factors.

Example

Solve the equation 2x² – 5x – 12 = 0 by factoring.

The expression 2x² – 5x – 12 splits into two factors of the form (2x + a)(x + b). To find *a* and *b*, you must find two factors of -12 that sum to -5 after one of them is doubled.

-12 can be factored in the following ways: 1 and -12 | 2 and -6 | 3 and -4 |

4 and -3 | 6 and -2 | 12 and -1.

Of these factors, only 3 and -4 will sum to -5 after we double one of them. Since -4 is the factor that must be doubled, it should go in position *b*, where it will be multiplied by 2x when the FOIL method is used. The factored expression is (2x + 3)(x - 4). So, you are left with (2x + 3)(x - 4) = 0.

By the zero product property, each value of *x* that will make one of the factors equal zero is a solution to this equation. The first factor equals zero when *x* = -1.5, and the second factor equals zero when x = 4. So, those are the solutions.

Note: The factor may be a trinomial but not a perfect trinomial square. So, look for a factorable form: $x^2 + (a + b)x + ab = (x + a)(x + b)$

or $(ac)x^2 + (ad + bc)x + bd = (ax + b)(cx + d)$

Some factors may have four terms. So, look for groups to factor. After you have found the factors, write the original polynomial as the product of all the factors. Make sure that all of the polynomial factors are prime. Monomial factors may be prime or composite. Check your work by multiplying the factors to make sure you get the original polynomial.

> **Review Video: Polynomials**
> Visit mometrix.com/academy and enter code: 305005

RATIONAL EXPRESSIONS

Rational Expressions are fractions with polynomials in the numerator and the denominator. The value of the polynomial in the denominator cannot be equal to zero.

ADD OR SUBTRACT WITH RATIONAL EXPRESSIONS

1. Find the common denominator.
2. Rewrite each fraction as an equivalent fraction with the common denominator
3. Add or subtract the numerators to get the numerator of the answer
4. Keep the common denominator as the denominator of the answer

MULTIPLICATION WITH RATIONAL EXPRESSIONS

1. Factor each polynomial and cancel like factors. These are the factors that are in the numerator and the denominator.
2. Multiply all remaining factors in the numerator to get the numerator of the product
3. Multiply the remaining factors in the denominator to get the denominator of the product
4. Remember: cancel entire factors, not individual terms

DIVISION WITH RATIONAL EXPRESSIONS

1. Take the reciprocal of the divisor. This is the rational expression that you are dividing by.
2. Multiply by the dividend.

SOLVING QUADRATIC EQUATIONS

The *Quadratic Formula* is used to solve quadratic equations when other methods are more difficult. To use the quadratic formula to solve a quadratic equation, begin by rewriting the equation in standard form $ax^2 + bx + c = 0$, where a, b, and c are coefficients. Once you have identified the values of the coefficients, substitute those values into the quadratic formula $= \frac{-b \pm \sqrt{b^2 - 4ac}}{2a}$. Evaluate the equation and simplify the expression.

Again, check each root by substituting into the original equation. In the quadratic formula, the portion of the formula under the radical $(b^2 - 4ac)$ is called the *Discriminant*. If the discriminant is zero, there is only one root: zero. If the discriminant is positive, there are two different real roots. If the discriminant is negative, there are no real roots.

> **Review Video: Using the Quadratic Formula**
> Visit mometrix.com/academy and enter code: 163102

To solve a quadratic equation by *Factoring*, begin by rewriting the equation in standard form, if necessary. Factor the side with the variable then set each of the factors equal to zero and solve the resulting linear equations. Check your answers by substituting the roots you found into the original equation. If, when writing the equation in standard form, you have an equation in the form $x^2 + c =$

0 or $x^2 - c = 0$, set $x^2 = -c$ or $x^2 = c$ and take the square root of c. If $c = 0$, the only real root is zero. If c is positive, there are two real roots—the positive and negative square root values. If c is negative, there are no real roots because you cannot take the square root of a negative number.

To solve a quadratic equation by *Completing the Square*, rewrite the equation so that all terms containing the variable are on the left side of the equal sign, and all the constants are on the right side of the equal sign. Make sure the coefficient of the squared term is 1. If there is a coefficient with the squared term, divide each term on both sides of the equal side by that number. Next, work with the coefficient of the single-variable term. Square half of this coefficient, and add that value to both sides. Now you can factor the left side (the side containing the variable) as the square of a binomial. $x^2 + 2ax + a^2 = C \Rightarrow (x + a)^2 = C$, where x is the variable, and a and C are constants. Take the square root of both sides and solve for the variable. Substitute the value of the variable in the original problem to check your work.

INEQUALITIES

In algebra and higher areas of math, you will work with problems that do not equal each other. The statement comparing such expressions with symbols such as < (less than) or > (greater than) is called an *Inequality*.

One way to remember these symbols is to see that the sign for "less than" looks like an L for *Less*. *The terms less than or equal to, at most,* or *no more than* are for the symbol ≤. Also, the terms *greater than or equal to, at least,* and *no less than* are for the symbol ≥.

> **Review Video: Equations and Inequalities**
> Visit mometrix.com/academy and enter code: 869843

GRAPHING AND SOLVING INEQUALITIES

Solving inequalities can be done with the same rules as for solving equations. However, when multiplying or dividing by a negative number, the direction of the inequality sign must be flipped or reversed.

Example 1

An example of an inequality is $7x > 5$. To solve for x, divide both sides by 7, and the solution is $x > \frac{5}{7}$. Graphs of the solution set of inequalities are given on a number line. Open circles are used to show that an expression approaches a number. However, the open circle points out that it is not equal to that number.

Example 2

Graph $10 > -2x + 4$.

In order to graph the inequality $10 > -2x + 4$, you need to solve for x. The opposite of addition is subtraction. So, subtract 4 from both sides. This gives you $6 > -2x$.

Next, the opposite of multiplication is division. So, divide both sides by −2. Don't forget to flip the inequality symbol because you are dividing by a negative number. Now, you have $-3 < x$. You can rewrite this as $x > -3$.

To graph an inequality, you make a number line. Then, put a circle around the value that is being compared to x. If you are graphing a *greater than* or *less than* inequality, the circle remains open.

81

This stands for all of the values except −3. If the inequality is *greater than or equal to* or *less than or equal to*, you draw a closed circle around the value. This would stand for all of the values including the number.

Finally, look over the values that the solution stands for. Then, shade the number line in the needed direction. This example calls for graphing all of the values greater than −3. This is all of the numbers to the right of −3. So, you shade this area on the number line.

OTHER INEQUALITIES

Conditional Inequalities are those with certain values for the variable that will make the condition true. So, other values for the variable where the condition will be false. *Absolute Inequalities* can have any real number as the value for the variable to make the condition true. So, there is no real number value for the variable that will make the condition false.

Double Inequalities are when two inequality statements are part of the same variable expression. An example of this is $-c < ax + b < c$.

IMPORTANT CONCEPTS

SUBSTITUTE AN INTEGER

POLYNOMIAL EXPRESSIONS

Solve the expression $(x^2+4)+(3x^2+4x+2)$, when x=5.

First, substitute in 5 for each occurrence of 'x': $(5^2 + 4) + (3(5)^2 + 4(5) + 2) =$

Second, solve for the parentheses: $(25 + 4) + (75 + 20 + 2) =$

Third, add the totals: $29 + 97 = 126$

LINEAR EXPRESSIONS

Solve the expression $(x - 4) + (4x + 10)$, when x=6.

First, put in 6 for every x: $(6 - 4) + (4(6) + 10)$

Second, solve the parentheses: $(2) + (34) =$

Third, add 2 and 34: $(2) + (34) = 36$

RATIONAL EXPRESSIONS

Solve the expression: $\frac{x+7}{10-x}$, when x=9

First, put in 9 for every x: $\frac{9+7}{10-9}$

Second, solve the numerator and the denominator: $\frac{16}{1}$

Third, divide 16 and 1: $\frac{16}{1} = 16$.

WRITING AN EXPRESSION FROM WORD-TO-SYMBOL

To write an expression, you must first put variables with the unknown values in the problem. Then, translate the words and phrases into expressions that have numbers and symbols.

INEQUALITIES

To write out an inequality, you may need to translate a sentence into an inequality. This translation is putting the words into symbols. When translating, choose a variable to stand for the unknown value. Then, change the words or phrases into symbols. For example, the sum of 2 and a number is at most 12. So, you would write: $2 + b \leq 12$.

Example: A farm sells vegetables and dairy products. One third of the sales from dairy products plus half of the sales from vegetables should be greater than the monthly payment (P) for the farm.

Let d stand for the sales from dairy products. Let v stand for the sales from vegetables. One third of the sales from dairy products is the expression $\frac{d}{3}$. One half of the sales from vegetables is the expression $\frac{v}{2}$. The sum of these expressions should be greater than the monthly payment for the farm. An inequality for this is $\frac{d}{3} + \frac{v}{2} > P$.

> **Review Video: <u>Solving Inequalities Using All Four Basic Operations</u>**
> Visit mometrix.com/academy and enter code: 401111

RATIONAL EXPRESSIONS

John and Luke play basketball every week. John can make 5 free throws per minute faster than Luke can make three-point shots. On one day, John made 30 free throws in the same time that it took Luke to make 20 three-point shots. So, how fast are Luke and John scoring points?

First, set up what you know. You know that John made 30 free throws, and he had a rate of 5 free throws per minute faster than Luke's three-point shots: $\frac{30}{x+5}$. The x is for Luke's speed. Also, you know that Luke made 20 three-point shots in the same amount of time that John scored his free throws: $\frac{20}{x}$. So, we can set up proportions because their times are equal.

$$\frac{30}{x+5} = \frac{20}{x}$$

Cross factor the proportion: $30x = 20(x + 5)$

Then distribute the 20 across the values in the parentheses: $30x = 20x + 100$

Now you can subtract 20x from both sides of the equation, and you are left with: $10x = 100$

Divide both sides by 10: $\frac{10x}{10} = \frac{100}{10}$

Now you are left with: $x = 10$. So Luke's speed was 10 three-point shots per minute and John's speed was 15 free throws per minute.

POLYNOMIAL EXPRESSIONS

Fred buys some CDs for $12 each. He also buys two DVDs. The total that Fred spent is $60. Write an equation that shows the connection between the number of CDs and the average cost of a DVD.

Let c stand for the number of CDs that Fred buys. Also, let d stand for the average cost of one of the DVDs that Fred buys. The expression $12c$ gives the cost of the CDs and the expression $2d$ gives the cost of the DVDs. So the equation $12c + 2d = 60$ states the number of CDs and the average cost of a DVD.

SOLVE EQUATIONS IN ONE VARIABLE

MANIPULATING EQUATIONS

Sometimes you will have variables missing in equations. So, you need to find the missing variable. To do this, you need to remember one important thing: whatever you do to one side of an equation, you need to do to the other side. If you subtract 100 from one side of an equation, you need to subtract 100 from the other side of the equation. This will allow you to change the form of the equation to find missing values.

<u>Example</u>

Ray earns $10 an hour. This can be given with the expression $10x$, where x is equal to the number of hours that Ray works. This is the independent variable. The independent variable is the amount that can change. The money that Ray earns is in y hours. So, you would write the equation: $10x = y$. The variable y is the dependent variable. This depends on x and cannot be changed. Now, let's say that Ray makes $360. How many hours did he work to make $360?

$$10x = 360$$

Now, you want to know how many hours that Ray worked. So, you want to get x by itself. To do that, you can divide both sides of the equation by 10.

$$\frac{10x}{10} = \frac{360}{10}$$

So, you have: $x = 36$. Now, you know that Ray worked 36 hours to make $360.

SOLVING ONE VARIABLE LINEAR EQUATIONS

Another way to write an equation is $ax + b = 0$ where $a \neq 0$. This is known as a *One Variable Linear Equation*. A solution to an equation is called a *Root*.

Example: $5x + 10 = 0$

If we solve for x, the solution is $x = -2$. In other words, the root of the equation is -2.

The first step is to subtract 10 from both sides. This gives $5x = -10$.

Next, divide both sides by the coefficient of the variable. For this example, that is 5. So, you should have $x = -2$. You can make sure that you have the correct answer by placing -2 back into the original equation. So, the equation now looks like this: $(5)(-2) + 10 = -10 + 10 = 0$.

Review Video: Mathematical Operations
Visit mometrix.com/academy and enter code: 208095

The *Solution Set* is the set of all solutions to an equation. In the last example, the solution set would be -2. If there were more solutions, then they would also be included in the solution set. Usually, there are more solutions in multivariable equations. When an equation has no true solutions, this is known as an *Empty Set*. Equations with identical solution sets are *Equivalent Equations*. An *Identity* is a term whose value or determinant is equal to 1.

To solve a *Radical Equation*, start by placing the radical term on one side of the equation by itself. Then, move all other terms to the other side of the equation. Look at the index of the radical symbol. Remember, if no number is given, then you have a square root. Raise both sides of the equation to the power equal to the index of the radical. Solve the equation as you would a normal polynomial equation. When you have found the roots, you must check them in the original problem to remove any remaining roots.

SYSTEMS OF EQUATIONS

Systems of Equations are a set of simultaneous equations that all use the same variables. A solution to a system of equations must be true for each equation in the system. *Consistent Systems* are those with at least one solution. *Inconsistent Systems* are systems of equations that have no solution.

Review Video: Solving Systems of Linear Equations
Visit mometrix.com/academy and enter code: 746745

To solve a system of linear equations by **substitution**, start with the easier equation and solve for one of the variables. Express this variable in terms of the other variable. Substitute this expression in the other equation and solve for the other variable. The solution should be expressed in the form (x, y). Substitute the values into both of the original equations to check your answer. Consider the following system of equations:

$$x + 6y = 15$$
$$3x - 12y = 18$$

Solving the first equation for x: $x = 15 - 6y$

Substitute this value in place of x in the second equation, and solve for y:

$$3(15 - 6y) - 12y = 18$$
$$45 - 18y - 12y = 18$$
$$30y = 27$$
$$y = \frac{27}{30} = \frac{9}{10} = 0.9$$

Plug this value for y back into the first equation to solve for x:

$$x = 15 - 6(0.9) = 15 - 5.4 = 9.6$$

Check both equations if you have time:

$$9.6 + 6(0.9) = 15 \qquad 3(9.6) - 12(0.9) = 18$$
$$9.6 + 5.4 = 15 \qquad 28.8 - 10.8 = 18$$
$$15 = 15 \qquad 18 = 18$$

Therefore, the solution is (9.6, 0.9).

> **Review Video: The Substitution Method**
> Visit mometrix.com/academy and enter code: 565151

To solve a system of equations using *elimination* or *addition*, begin by rewriting both equations in standard form $Ax + By = C$. Check to see if the coefficients of one pair of like variables add to zero. If not, multiply one or both of the equations by a non-zero number to make one set of like variables add to zero. Add the two equations to solve for one of the variables. Substitute this value into one of the original equations to solve for the other variable. Check your work by substituting into the other equation. Next we will solve the same problem as above, but using the addition method.

Solve the system using substitution:

$$x + 6y = 15$$

$$3x - 12y = 18$$

For practice we will multiply the first equation by 6 and the second equation by -2 to get rid of the x variables.

$$6x + 36y = 90$$

$$-6x + 24y = -36$$

Add the equations together to get $60y = 54$. Thus, $y = \frac{54}{60} = \frac{9}{10} = 0.9$.

Plug the value for y back in to either of the original equations to get the value for x.

$$x + 6(0.9) = 15$$

$$x = 15 - 5.4 = 9.6$$

Now check both equations

$$9.6 + 6(0.9) = 9.6 + 5.4 = 15$$

$$3(9.6) - 12(0.9) = 28.8 - 10.8 = 18$$

Therefore, the solution is (9.6, 0.9).

> **Review Video: <u>Substitution and Elimination for Solving Linear Systems</u>**
> Visit mometrix.com/academy and enter code: 958611
>
> **Review Video: <u>Linear Equations Basics</u>**
> Visit mometrix.com/academy and enter code: 793005

Functions

FUNCTION NOTATION

Equations use numbers to show the equality of two expressions. These equations use the variables x and y. Equation notation is written in "$y =$" form. With an equation, you can find values for x and y by putting in a value for x and solving for y. These values are given as ordered pairs in a table of values. Then, the ordered pairs can be used as coordinates to graph the equation. An equation is a function if there is a relationship between x and y. The relationship is that for every x-value, there is only one y-value. This can be decided from a graph using the vertical line test.

Function notation is written in the "$f(x)$" form. The notation y and $f(x)$ are basically the same. The y refers to an equation. The $f(x)$ refers to a function. Knowing that an equation is a function can give you more information about its graph. Functions use equations to show relationships between quantities. All functions have equations. However, not all equations are functions.

DETERMINING A FUNCTION

You can decide if an equation is a function by putting in different values into the equation for x. These values are called input values. All possible input values are known as the domain. The result of putting these values into the equation is called the output or range. You can show and organize these numbers in a data table.

A data table has the values for x and y which you can list as coordinates. For a function to exist, the table cannot have any repeating x-values that go with different y-values. If each x-coordinate has one y-coordinate, the table has a function. However, there can be repeating y-values that go with different x-values. An example of this is when the function has an exponent. For example, $x^2 = y$. So, $2^2 = 4$, and $(-2)^2 = 4$.

For example, look at the following graphs.

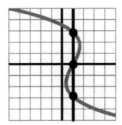 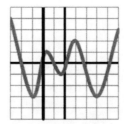

The vertical line test is used to decide if a graph has a function. The test says that if you pass a vertical line anywhere along the graph, then the line will only pass through the graph at one point. If it passes through the graph at more than one point, it is not considered a function. The vertical line in the image on the left intersects the graph in three points. So, the graph on the left is *not* a function. On the right, it does not matter where you place the vertical line. The line will never intersect more than one point. So, the graph on the right is a function.

FINDING THE DOMAIN OF THE FUNCTION

A function is given in the table below. How can you find the domain of the function?

x	0	3	2	1	8	10	6	7
$f(x)$	2	8	6	8	2	3	4	5

The *domain* of a function $f(x)$ is the set of all input values for a function. It is simple to find the domain of a function with this table. The reason is that every point in the function (i.e., every input-output pair) is given to you.

To find the domain, list all the x values. So, you have {0, 3, 2, 1, 8, 10, 6, 7}. Or, you can put them in ascending order: {0, 1, 2, 3, 6, 7, 8, 10}. You do not have to put the values in ascending order. However, this does make the set easier to read.

Note that you don't have to worry about an input value being repeated. By definition of a function, no input value can go with more than one output value.

FINDING THE DOMAIN OF A FUNCTION FROM A GRAPH

The domain of a function can be seen from the graph by looking for the values of x. Basically, if a vertical line drawn through the graph at a x value intercepts the graph of the function, then the function is defined at that point. If a vertical line intercepts the function no matter where it is drawn, then the domain is all real numbers.

SPECIAL CASES

Sometimes the full graph of a function cannot be displayed. So, the vertical line test cannot always be used. An asymptote is a line that a curve is always moving towards. Yet the curve never meets the line. Usually, if a function has an asymptote, it will be displayed on the graph as a dashed line. A function is never defined at a vertical asymptote.

If $f(x)$ is limited at the endpoint of the interval, then the endpoint is drawn as a filled circle to show that it is part of the function. Or, there is an empty circle to show that is not part of the function. The graph on the left has a domain of $[-1, \infty)$. The graph on the right has a domain of $(-1, \infty)$.

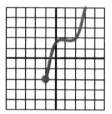 

FINDING THE RANGE OF A FUNCTION

A function is given in the table below. How can you find the range of the function?

x	-1	4	2	1	0	3	8	6
$f(x)$	3	0	3	−1	−1	2	4	6

The *range* of a function $f(x)$ is the set of all possible output values of the function. In other words, it includes every possible value of $f(x)$ for all values of x in the function's domain. It's easy to find the range with the table above. The reason is that every point in the function (i.e., every input-output pair) is given to you.

To find the range, you can list all the values of $f(x)$. For this example, that would be {3, 0, 3, −1, −1, 2, 4, 6}. Some of these values come up more than once. This is allowed for a function.

Each value of x must be matched to one value of $f(x)$. However, the opposite is not true. So, you don't need to list each value more than once. Now, the range is {3, 0, –1, 2, 4, 6}. You do not have to put the values in increasing order. However, this does make the set easier to read.

FUNCTION AND RELATION

When expressing functional relationships, the variables x and y are used. These values are written as the coordinates (x, y). The x-value is the independent variable. The y-value is the dependent variable. A relation is a set of data where there is not one y-value for each x-value in the data set. This means that there can be two of the same x-values that go with different y-values.

A relation is simply a relationship between the x and y-values in each coordinate. This does not apply to the relationship between the values of x and y in the data set. A function is a relation where one quantity depends on the other. For example, the amount of money that you make depends on the number of hours that you work. In a function, each x-value in the data set has one y-value. The reason is that the y-value depends on the x-value.

GRAPHING A FUNCTION

To graph a function, make a table of values based on the equation from the problem. Choose x-values for the table. Then, put them into the equation to find the matching y-values. There need to be at least 2 x-values for linear functions and more for quadratic.

Use each x and y value as a coordinate pair. Then, put these points on the coordinate grid. Next, connect the points with a line. The graph of a function will show a relationship among the coordinates so there are no two y-values for each x-value. Also, use the vertical line test to decide if a graph has a function.

> **Review Video: How to Graph a Function**
> Visit mometrix.com/academy and enter code: 492785

GRAPHS OF LINEAR AND QUADRATIC FUNCTIONS

Linear functions are in the form $y = x$. When they are graphed, they make a straight line. To graph a function, you need to find at least two points on the line. Choose values for x and put them into the equation. If $y = x$, then $0 = 0, 1 = 1, 2 = 2$, and so on. This means that the coordinates $(0, 0), (1, 1)$, and $(2, 2)$ are on the line.

> **Review Video: Graphing Linear Equations**
> Visit mometrix.com/academy and enter code: 479576
>
> **Review Video: Graphing Linear Functions**
> Visit mometrix.com/academy and enter code: 699478

Quadratic functions are written as $y = x^2$. When graphed, they make a u-shaped parabola. Every x-value is squared (i.e., multiplied by itself). After multiplying, you will find that the coordinates $(-2, 4), (1, 1)$, and $(2, 4)$ are on the parabola. The graphs go forever in both directions. So, they have an unending number of points. These graphs are called the parent functions of linear and quadratic equations. The reason is that they are the most basic in their family of functions. The equations do not have any coefficients or constants.

Example

You drive 12 miles to school and keep a constant speed until you come to traffic at 7:40 am. When the traffic clears, you return to your original speed until you get to school. Explain what the graph of this function would look like.

First, think about the variables that are part of this situation. You are comparing the miles that you travel to school, and the time that it takes you to get there. On the graph, the line that is made by this relationship stands for the speed that you travel. The graph should have the correct labels and scales. So, the independent variable (e.g., the time) goes on the x-axis. The dependent variable (e.g., the distance) goes on the y-axis.

If you keep a constant speed, the graph would show a diagonal line increasing from zero. When you are stopped in traffic at 7:40 am, the distance is not increasing. However, the time is increasing. So, you would see the line going horizontally for an amount of time. When the traffic clears, the line would again increase diagonally. This would stand for the return of the speed. You can use the graph to look at trends in the data to predict future events.

WRITING A FUNCTION RULE USING A TABLE

With a set of data, place the matching x and y-values into a table. Then, review the relationship between them. Think about what you can do to each x-value to have the matching y-value. Try adding or subtracting different numbers to and from x. Then, try multiplying or dividing different numbers to and from x.

If none of these operations give you the y-value, try combining the operations. When you find a rule that works for one pair, make sure to try it with each set of ordered pairs in the table. If the same operation or combination of operations takes care of each set of coordinates, then the table has a function. Then, the rule is used to write the equation of the function in "$y =$" form.

Example

What does the statement $f(x) = x^2 + 1$ mean?

This kind of statement defines a certain function. The statement tells how to match up each point in the domain with a point in the range. The possible values of x are part of the domain. Usually, this can be thought to have all real numbers unless you are told that it does not. Or, you are told that there are some points that make the expression on the right side of the equation undefined. Then, each value of x is matched with a value of $f(x)$ (or y) that may not be unique. All the values of $f(x)$ that are matched to values of x are part of the range.

The statement $f(x) = x^2 + 1$ defines a function where each real number x is matched to the number $x^2 + 1$. For example, $x = 0$ means that $f(0) = 0^2 + 1 = 1$. Also, $= 1$ $f(1) = 1^2 + 1 = 2$. Now, this will continue for each real number. Note that $f(x)$ in this example can never be less than 1. So, the range of this function is $[1, \infty)$.

RELATIVE MAXIMUM AND RELATIVE MINIMUM

A *relative maximum* of a function is a point where the function has a higher value than any other point that is near it. In other words, a relative maximum is a point (x, y). Let's say that we choose an acceptable small interval around x. Then, $f(x) > f(c)$ for any other point within the interval (c).

A relative minimum is just the opposite. This is a point where the function has a *lower* value than any other point that is near it. In other words, a point (x, y). Let's say that we choose an acceptable small interval around x. Then, $f(x) < f(c)$ for any other point within the interval (c).

A function may have many relative maxima* and relative minima*. However, it may have none. A linear function like $y = x$ has no relative maxima or minima. Now, $y = \sin(x)$ has an unending amount of relative maxima and minima.

*Note that *maxima* is plural for maximum. Also, *minima* is plural for minimum.

FINDING A RELATIVE MAXIMUM OR MINIMUM FROM A GRAPH

At a relative maximum, the graph goes from increasing to decreasing. This makes a "peak" on the graph. Also, at a relative minimum, the graph goes from decreasing to increasing. This makes a "trough". On the graph below, the points A and C are relative maxima. The point B is a relative minimum.

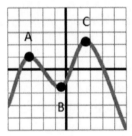

Note that point A is a relative maximum. However, this is not an absolute maximum. Also, this function has a higher value at point C. Now, point B is a relative minimum. However, this is not an absolute minimum. Also, the function has a lower value at the left and right ends of the graph than at point B. Point C is a relative and an absolute maximum. The reason is that at no place on the graph is there a function that has a higher value than at point C.

PERIODIC FUNCTIONS

A function is *periodic* if there is a repetition of the same shape. In other words, a periodic function is unchanged if it is moved some distance left or right on the graph. The distance that it has to be moved is called the function's *period* (P). A function $f(x)$ is periodic if $f(x + P) = f(x)$ for all x. Note that if this is true for P, then it's also true for all multiples of P. However, the function's period is known as the smallest possible value of P that the relation holds.

SYMMETRICAL FUNCTIONS

A function is symmetrical if it does not change with certain kinds of transformations. There are many kinds of transformations and symmetries. For functions, the type of transformation that is considered is reflection. Two important pieces are reflections through the y-axis and reflections through the origin on a coordinate plane.

If the mirror image (i.e., reflection) of a function is the same through the y-axis, then the function is symmetrical. This can be written as $f(x) = f(-x)$. This function is known to be *even*. A function can be symmetrical with reflection through the origin. The function needs to stay the same when each point is reflected to the other side of the origin. This can be written as $f(x) = -f(-x)$. This function is known to be *odd*.

A periodic function is also symmetrical. This may not be with reflection. However, this can be done with *translation*. The function is unchanged when translated (i.e., moved) horizontally by a distance that is equal to the function's period.

FUNCTION'S END BEHAVIOR

A function's *end behavior* is its tendency or activity at the extreme right and left sides of the graph. In other words, this is what happens to the function as x moves towards positive or negative ∞. There are three main possibilities.

First, $f(x)$ increases without limit (i.e., $f(x)$ goes to infinity). Second, $f(x)$ decreases without limit (i.e., $f(x)$ goes to negative infinity). Third, $f(x)$ tends toward some finite value (i.e., a horizontal asymptote). The behavior may be different at the two sides. For example, while $f(x) = x^2$ goes to ∞ on both sides, $g(x) = x^3$ goes to ∞ on the right side and to $-\infty$ on the left. Also, $h(x) = e^{-x}$ goes to ∞ on the left and approaches the horizontal asymptote $y = 0$ on the right.

COMPARING PROPERTIES OF FUNCTIONS

Example 1

One function is represented algebraically and one graphically. Which has the larger maximum?

You can compare two functions that are given in different ways by changing them to the same way of being presented. If one function is given algebraically and the other graphically, you can graph the first function on the same axis as the second. This allows you to see the comparison of their maxima. So, you can know which one goes farther in the positive y direction.

Also, you can compare their maxima without changing them to the same way of being presented. For example, you can find the maximum of each function and compare them. A function that be expressed algebraically is one that you can find the maximum analytically (e.g., a quadratic function). So, you can compare that value directly with the maximum estimated from the graphed function by looking at the y coordinate of its highest peak.

Example 2

One function is given algebraically and the other in a verbal description. How can you know which has the larger maximum?

You can compare two functions in different formats by changing the functions to the same format. One of the functions may be given in the form of a verbal description. So, you can write an algebraic expression to stand for the described relationship.

For example, you're told that a function is for the area of a rectangular field. Also, the total distance around three sides is 40 meters. So, you write $l + 2w = 40$.

Also, you can write the relationship between the area and the width in algebraic form as $A = l \cdot w = (40 - 2w)w$. Or, using the more familiar f and x, $f(x) = (40 - 2x)x = -2x^2 + 40x$. Now, completing the square gives you $f(x) = -2(x - 10)^2 + 200$. This function has a maximum when

93

$x = 10$ where $f(x) = 200$. Also, you can find the maximum of the other function that is given in algebraic form. Now, we can compare the maxima directly.

Example 3

One function is given graphically and one in a table. How you can find which has the larger y intercept?

You can compare two functions in different formats by changing the functions to the same format. If one of the functions is given as a table, you can graph that function. Then, compare it to the graph. As another way, you can find the values of the graphed function at the *x* values given in the table. Then, you can give both functions in table format.

Sometimes you can compare properties of the functions without changing them to the same format. When you need to find the *y* intercept, then this isn't difficult. Note that this way assumes that the *y* intercept of the second function is given in the table.

Also, you can find the *y* intercept of the graphed function by finding where the graph crosses the *y*-axis. Then, find the *y* intercept of the table function. Look for which value of the function matches with a *x* value of 0. Then, compare these values.

Writing Recursively Defined Functions

A recursively defined function is generally a *sequence*; that is, its domain consists of a subset of the integers (usually, though not always, the positive integers). Furthermore, the value of the function for a given value of *x* must be defined in terms of its value for smaller values of *x*. Often this means $f(x)$ is defined in terms of $f(x-1)$, though it may also be defined in terms of even smaller values. Finally, we need to have $f(x_0)$ explicitly defined for the smallest value or values of x_0 to give us a starting point.

For example, consider the following relationship: A pile of stones starts with three stones, and then every day its size is doubled and then one stone is removed. On day one, then, the size of the pile is $f(1) = 3$. On day *x* thereafter, we have the relationship $f(x) = 2f(x-1) - 1$. This is a valid recursive definition.

Situations Modeled by Arithmetic Sequences

An arithmetic sequence is a good model for any situation that involves a quantity that increases at equal intervals by a constant difference. That is, if the quantity is only defined relative to the positive integers (or technically at any other discrete, evenly spaced intervals), and the difference between the quantity corresponding to any two consecutive integers is the same, then it can be modeled by an arithmetic sequence.

Consider, for instance, the following situation: a large jar initially contains five marbles, and every day three more marbles are added to it. This fits the criteria described above: the quantity is defined relative to the positive integers (number of days), and the difference between the quantity corresponding to consecutive integers (the number of marbles on consecutive days) is constant (three). We can model this situation by the arithmetic sequence $f(n) = 5 + 3(n-1)$.

Review Video: Arithmetic Sequence
Visit mometrix.com/academy and enter code: 676885

SITUATIONS MODELED BY GEOMETRIC SEQUENCES

A geometric sequence is a good model for any situation that involves a quantity that increases at fixed intervals by a fixed ratio. That is, if the quantity is only defined relative to the positive integers (or technically at any other discrete, evenly spaced intervals), and the ratio of the quantity corresponding to any two consecutive integers is the same, then it can be modeled by a geometric sequence.

Consider, for instance, the following situation: the score for completing level one of a video game is 100, and the score for completing each level afterward is double the score for the previous level. This fits the criteria described above: the quantity is defined relative to the positive integers (levels), and the ratio between the quantity corresponding to consecutive integers (the scores for completing two consecutive levels) is constant (two). We can model this situation by the geometric sequence $f(n) = 100 \cdot 2^{n-1}$.

IDENTIFYING THE ZEROS OF FUNCTIONS AND POLYNOMIAL

LINEAR FACTORS OF A QUADRATIC EXPRESSION AND THE ZEROS OF A RELATED FUNCTION

Example: $(x - a)$ and $(x - b)$

If the linear factors of a quadratic expression are $(x - a)$ and $(x - b)$, then the quadratic function can be written as $y = k(x - a)(x - b)$, where k is a nonzero constant. The zeros of this function are the values of x for which $y = 0$. Direct substitution of a or b for x makes the value of y equal to 0, so $x = a$ and $x = b$ are zeros of the quadratic function. Note that the value of k may affect the shape or direction of the graph of the function, but not the x-intercepts (the zeros of the function).

FINDING THE ZEROS OF A FUNCTION

Example: $y = 4x^2 - 10x$

The zeros of the function $y = 4x^2 - 10x$ are the values of x for which $y = 0$. To find the zeros, factor the right side of the equation, and set $y = 0$:

$$y = 4x^2 - 10x$$

$$y = 2x(2x - 5)$$

$$0 = 2x(2x - 5)$$

Next, since a product is only equal to zero if at least one of the terms is zero, set the linear factors of the function $2x$ and $(2x - 5)$ equal to 0:

$$2x = 0 \qquad 2x - 5 = 0$$

$$x = 0 \qquad 2x = 5$$

$$x = \frac{5}{2}$$

The zeros of the function $y = 4x^2 - 10x$ are $x = 0$ and $x = \frac{5}{2}$.

ZEROS OF A QUADRATIC FUNCTION

Give an <u>Example</u> of a Quadratic Function with Zeros x = 1 and x = –3

If a is a zero of a quadratic function, then $(x – a)$ is a factor of the quadratic expression that defines the function. Therefore $(x – 1)$ and $(x + 3)$ are both factors of the quadratic function. Quadratic functions with these zeros therefore have the form $y = k(x – 1)(x + 3)$. The reason that this is just a form, and not a unique function, is because multiplying the two binomial factors by any nonzero constant results in another quadratic function with the same zeros. For example, the functions $y = –5(x – 1)(x + 3)$ and $y = 7(x – 1)$

$(x + 3)$ have zeros $x = 1$ and $x = –3$.

FACTOR A QUADRATIC EXPRESSION TO FIND THE ZEROS OF A FUNCTION

<u>Example</u>: Find the x-intercepts of y = 9x² – 6x + 1.

The x-intercepts of $y = 9x^2 – 6x + 1$ are the zeros of the function. These can be determined by first factoring the quadratic expression $9x^2 – 6x + 1$: $9x^2 - 6x + 1 = (3x - 1)(3x - 1) = (3x - 1)^2$

The expression is a perfect square trinomial. Because the two factors are the same, there is only one x-intercept of the function. Set the factor equal to 0:

$$3x - 1 = 0$$

$$3x = 1$$

$$x = \frac{1}{3}$$

The x-intercept of $y = 9x^2 – 6x + 1$ is therefore $x = \frac{1}{3}$.

ZEROS OF A POLYNOMIAL WITH CUBICS AND HIGHER POLYNOMIALS

We can find the zeros of a polynomial by factoring it. Cubics and higher polynomials can be difficult to factor, but there are special cases that can be readily factored. In the first sample polynomial here, for instance, $x^3 - 3x^2 - 4x$, it's clear that every term of the polynomial is divisible by x. We can therefore factor out the x to get $x(x^2 - 3x - 4)$. This now leaves a quadratic factor, which can be further factored to yield $x(x + 1)(x - 4)$. The zeros of the polynomial are therefore 0, –1, and 4.

GRAPHING A POLYNOMIAL

To graph a polynomial, like most other functions, there are a few key characteristics we can observe. First, we can observe the end behavior, which depends only on the largest order term. To find the y intercept, we evaluate the function at $x = 0$. To find the x intercepts, the points where the polynomial equals zero, is a little harder, but often we can factor the function and set each factor equal to zero. Depending on the polynomial, there may be other characteristics we can find, such as the local maxima and minima.

<u>Example</u>: $\frac{1}{4}x^4 - \frac{9}{4}x^2$

Since the highest order term has an even order and a positive coefficient, the polynomial goes to positive infinity at both ends. The y intercept is at $\frac{1}{4}(0^4) - \frac{9}{4}(0^2) = 0$. We can factor the polynomial as $\frac{1}{4}x^4 - \frac{9}{4}x^2 = \frac{1}{4}x^2(x^2 - 9) = \frac{1}{4}x^2(x+3)(x-3)$, so it has x intercepts at $x = 0, 3$, and -3. Its graph looks like this:

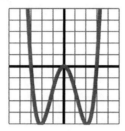

RATE OF CHANGE OF A FUNCTION
TABLE

The function's average rate of change over the interval $[x_1, x_2]$ can be calculated as $\frac{f(x_2)-f(x_1)}{x_2-x_1}$. For the sample table, for instance, if we want to determine the function's rate of change during the entire interval represented in the table, then $x_1 = 0$ and $x_2 = 16$. By reference to the table, $f(x_1) = f(0) = -100$, and $f(x_2) = f(16) = 100$. Thus, the function's rate of change is equal to $\frac{100-(-100)}{16-0} = \frac{200}{16} = 12.5$.

x	0	2	4	6	8	10	12	14	16
$f(x)$	-100	-54	-26	-10	0	10	26	54	100

If on the other hand we only want to find the rate of change between 0 and 4, then $x_1 = 0, x_2 = 4$, $f(x_1) = f(0) = -100$, and $f(x_2) = f(4) = -26$. The rate of change is then $\frac{-26-(-100)}{4-0} = \frac{74}{4} = 18.5$. If we are asked for the rate of change in the interval $[6, 10]$, then $x_1 = 6, x_2 = 10, f(x_1) = f(6) = -10$, and $f(x_2) = f(10) = 10$. The rate of change is then $\frac{10-(-10)}{10-6} = \frac{20}{4} = 5$.

ALGEBRAIC

The function's average rate of change over the interval $[x_1, x_2]$ can be calculated as $\frac{f(x_2)-f(x_1)}{x_2-x_1}$. Example: $f(x) = x^2 + 1$. Find the function's average rate of change between 0 and 10. So, $x_1 = 0$ and $x_2 = 10$.

To find $f(x_1)$ and $f(x_2)$, we simply evaluate the function at these two points: $f(x_1) = f(0) = 0^2 + 1 = 1$, and $f(x_2) = f(10) = 10^2 + 1 = 101$. The function's average rate of change in this interval is therefore $\frac{101-1}{10-0} = \frac{100}{10} = 10$.

If we're asked to find the function's average rate of change over the interval $[-4, 2]$, then $x_1 = -4$, $x_2 = 2, f(x_1) = f(-4) = (-4)^2 + 1 = 17$, and $f(x_2) = f(2) = 2^2 + 1 = 5$. The average rate of change is therefore $\frac{5-17}{2-(-4)} = \frac{-12}{6} = -2$. If we're asked to find the average rate of change over the interval $[-5, 5]$, then $x_1 = -5, x_2 = 5, f(x_1) = f(-5) = (-5)^2 + 1 = 26$, and $f(x_2) = f(5) = 5^2 + 1 = 26$. The average rate of change is therefore $\frac{26-26}{5-(-5)} = \frac{0}{10} = 0$.

ESTIMATE FROM A GRAPH

To estimate the average rate of change over an interval for a function given graphically, then, we have to estimate the coordinates of the endpoints of the desired interval and then put the appropriate values into that expression and carry out the calculation.

For example, consider the sample function over the entire interval shown on the graph, $[-5,5]$. At the left end is passes through the point $(-5,-5)$, and at the right end $(5,5)$; the average rate of change is therefore $\frac{f(5)-f(-5)}{5-(-5)} = \frac{5-(-5)}{10} = \frac{10}{10} = 1$. If we instead consider the interval $[-2,0]$, the left endpoint is about $(-2,1)$ and the right about $(0,-2)$; the average rate of change over the interval $[-2,0]$ is then $\frac{f(0)-f(-2)}{0-(-2)} = \frac{-2-1}{2} = \frac{-3}{2} = -\frac{3}{2}$. The average rate of change over the interval $[-5,0]$ is $\frac{f(0)-f(-5)}{0-(-5)} = \frac{-2-(-5)}{5} = \frac{3}{5}$.

Geometry

LINES AND PLANES

A point is a fixed location in space; has no size or dimensions; commonly represented by a dot.

A line is a set of points that extends infinitely in two opposite directions. It has length, but no width or depth. A line can be defined by any two distinct points that it contains. A line segment is a portion of a line that has definite endpoints. A ray is a portion of a line that extends from a single point on that line in one direction along the line. It has a definite beginning, but no ending.

A **plane** is a two-dimensional flat surface defined by three non-collinear points. A plane extends an infinite distance in all directions in those two dimensions. It contains an infinite number of points, parallel lines and segments, intersecting lines and segments, as well as parallel or intersecting rays. A plane will never contain a three-dimensional figure or skew lines, which are lines that don't intersect and are not parallel. Two given planes are either parallel or they intersect at a line. A plane may intersect a circular conic surface to form **conic sections**, such as a parabola, hyperbola, circle or ellipse.

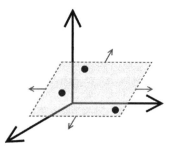

> **Review Video: Lines and Planes**
> Visit mometrix.com/academy and enter code: 554267

Perpendicular lines are lines that intersect at right angles. They are represented by the symbol ⊥. The shortest distance from a line to a point not on the line is a perpendicular segment from the point to the line.

Parallel lines are lines in the same plane that have no points in common and never meet. It is possible for lines to be in different planes, have no points in common, and never meet, but they are not parallel because they are in different planes.

A bisector is a line or line segment that divides another line segment into two equal lengths. A perpendicular bisector of a line segment is composed of points that are equidistant from the endpoints of the segment it is dividing.

Intersecting lines are lines that have exactly one point in common. Concurrent lines are multiple lines that intersect at a single point.

A transversal is a line that intersects at least two other lines, which may or may not be parallel to one another. A transversal that intersects parallel lines is a common occurrence in geometry.

COORDINATE PLANE

When algebraic functions and equations are shown graphically, they are usually shown on a *Cartesian Coordinate Plane*. The Cartesian coordinate plane consists of two number lines placed perpendicular to each other, and intersecting at the zero point, also known as the origin. The horizontal number line is known as the *x*-axis, with positive values to the right of the origin, and negative values to the left of the origin. The vertical number line is known as the *y*-axis, with positive values above the origin, and negative values below the origin.

Any point on the plane can be identified by an ordered pair in the form (*x,y*), called coordinates. The *x*-value of the coordinate is called the abscissa, and the *y*-value of the coordinate is called the ordinate. The two number lines divide the plane into four quadrants: I, II, III, and IV.

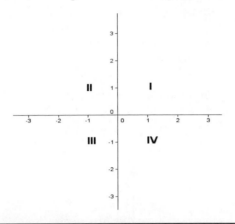

> **Review Video: Cartesian Coordinate Plane and Graphing**
> Visit mometrix.com/academy and enter code: 115173

Before learning the different forms equations can be written in, it is important to understand some terminology. A ratio of the change in the vertical distance to the change in horizontal distance is called the *Slope*. On a graph with two points, (x_1, y_1) and (x_2, y_2), the slope is represented by the formula $= \frac{y_2 - y_1}{x_2 - x_1}$; $x_1 \neq x_2$. If the value of the slope is positive, the line slopes upward from left to right. If the value of the slope is negative, the line slopes downward from left to right. If the *y*-coordinates are the same for both points, the slope is 0 and the line is a *Horizontal Line*. If the *x*-coordinates are the same for both points, there is no slope and the line is a *Vertical Line*. Two or more lines that have equal slopes are *Parallel Lines*. *Perpendicular Lines* have slopes that are negative reciprocals of each other, such as $\frac{a}{b}$ and $\frac{-b}{a}$.

As mentioned previously, equations can be written many ways. Below is a list of the many forms equations can take.

- Standard Form: $Ax + By = C$; the slope is $\frac{-A}{B}$ and the y-intercept is $\frac{C}{B}$
- *Slope Intercept Form*: $y = mx + b$, where *m* is the slope and *b* is the *y*-intercept
- Point-Slope Form: $y - y_1 = m(x - x_1)$, where m is the slope and (x_1, y_1) is a point on the line
- Two-Point Form: $\frac{y - y_1}{x - x_1} = \frac{y_2 - y_1}{x_2 - x_1}$, where (x_1, y_1) and (x_2, y_2) are two points on the given line
- *Intercept Form*: $\frac{x}{x_1} + \frac{y}{y_1} = 1$, where $(x_1, 0)$ is the point at which a line intersects the *x*-axis, and $(0, y_1)$ is the point at which the same line intersects the *y*-axis

CALCULATIONS USING POINTS

Sometimes you need to perform calculations using only points on a graph as input data. Using points, you can determine what the midpoint and distance are. If you know the equation for a line you can calculate the distance between the line and the point.

To find the *Midpoint* of two points (x_1, y_1) and (x_2, y_2), average the x-coordinates to get the x-coordinate of the midpoint, and average the y-coordinates to get the y-coordinate of the midpoint. The formula is midpoint $= \left(\frac{x_1+x_2}{2}, \frac{y_1+y_2}{2}\right)$.

The *Distance* between two points is the same as the length of the hypotenuse of a right triangle with the two given points as endpoints, and the two sides of the right triangle parallel to the x-axis and y-axis, respectively. The length of the segment parallel to the x-axis is the difference between the x-coordinates of the two points. The length of the segment parallel to the y-axis is the difference between the y-coordinates of the two points. Use the Pythagorean Theorem $a^2 + b^2 = c^2$ or $c = \sqrt{a^2 + b^2}$ to find the distance. The formula is: distance $= \sqrt{(x_2 - x_1)^2 + (y_2 - y_1)^2}$.

When a line is in the format $Ax + By + C = 0$, where A, B, and C are coefficients, you can use a point (x_1, y_1) not on the line and apply the formula $d = \frac{|Ax_1 + By_1 + C|}{\sqrt{A^2 + B^2}}$ to find the distance between the line and the point (x_1, y_1).

> **Review Video: Calculations Using Points on a Graph**
> Visit mometrix.com/academy and enter code: 883228

TRANSFORMATION

- Rotation: An object is rotated, or turned, between 0 and 360 degrees, around a fixed point. The size and shape of the object are unchanged.
- Reflection: An object is reflected, or flipped, across a line, so that the original object and reflected object are the same distance from the line of reflection. The size and shape of the object are unchanged.
- Translation: An object is translated, or shifted, horizontally and/or vertically to a new location. The orientation, size, and shape of the object are unchanged.
- Dilation: An object is dilated, or proportionally stretched or shrunken, by a scale factor. The dilated image is the same shape and orientation as the original image but a different size. A polygon and its dilated image are similar.

ROTATION

A line segment begins at (1, 4) and ends at (5, 4). Draw the line segment and rotate the line segment 90° about the point (3, 4).

The point about which the line segment is being rotated is on the line segment. This point should be on both the original and rotated line. The point (3, 4) is the center of the original line segment, and should still be the center of the rotated line segment. The dashed line is the rotated line segment.

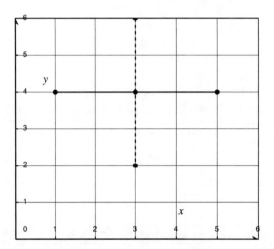

REFLECTION

Example 1: To create a congruent rectangle by reflecting, first draw a line of reflection. The line can be next to or on the figure. Then draw the image reflected across this line.

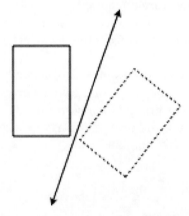

Example 2: A line segment begins at (1, 5) and ends at (5, 4). Draw the line segment, then reflect the line segment across the line *y* = 3.

Mometrix

To reflect a segment, consider folding a piece of paper at the line of reflection. The new image should line up exactly with the old image when the paper is folded. The dashed line is the reflected line segment.

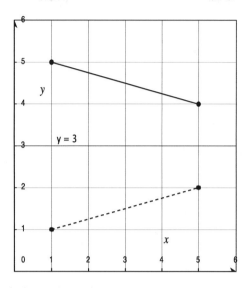

TRANSLATION

Example 1: A line segment on an x-y grid starts at (3, 2) and ends at (4, 1). Draw the line segment, and translate the segment up 2 units and left 2 units.

The solid line segment is the original line segment, and the dashed line is the translated line segment. The *y*-coordinate of each point has increased by 2, because the points moved two units away from 0. The *x*-coordinate of each point has decreased by 2, because the points moved two units closer to 0.

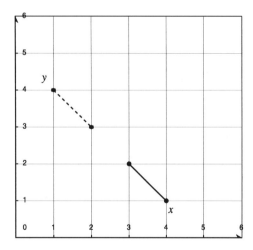

103

Example 2: Identify a transformation that could have been performed on the solid triangle to result in the dashed triangle.

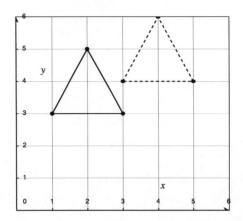

The transformed triangle has the same orientation as the original triangle. It has been shifted up one unit and two units to the right. Because the orientation of the figure has not changed, and its new position can be described using shifts up and to the right, the figure was translated.

DILATION

Example 1: Let $\Delta A'B'C'$ be the image of ΔABC after a dilation with center at the origin and a scale factor of $\frac{1}{3}$. Graph $\Delta A'B'C'$.

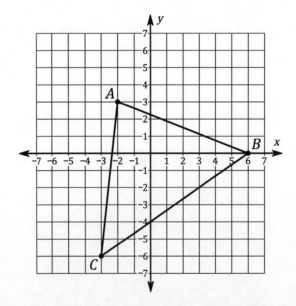

A dilation with center at the origin and a scale factor of k maps a point $P(x, y)$ onto $P'(kx, ky)$. First find the coordinates of the vertices of the given triangle. From the figure, they are: $A(-2, 3)$, $B(6, 0)$, and $C(-3, -6)$. Then use these values to calculate the coordinates of $\Delta A'B'C'$.

$$A(-2, 3) \rightarrow A'\left(-\frac{2}{3}, 1\right)$$

$$B(6, 0) \rightarrow B'(2, 0)$$

$$C(-3,-6) \rightarrow C'(-1,-2)$$

Finally, the triangle can be graphed:

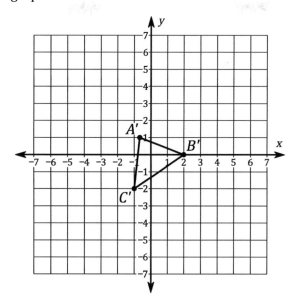

Example 2: In the coordinate plane, ΔDEF is the image of ΔABC after a sequence of transformations. What sequence of transformations can be used to go from ΔABC to ΔDEF?

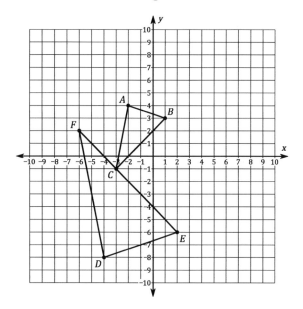

Notice that ΔDEF has the same shape as ΔABC, but it is twice as large. Thus, you need to perform a dilation with a center at the origin and a scale factor of 2. A dilation with center at the origin and a scale factor of k maps a point $P(x, y)$ onto $P'(kx, ky)$. Thus, the coordinates of $\Delta A'B'C'$ are:

$$A(-2,4) \rightarrow A'(-4,8)$$

$$B(1,3) \rightarrow B'(2,6)$$

$$C(-3,-1) \rightarrow C'(-6,-2)$$

105

Graph this triangle.

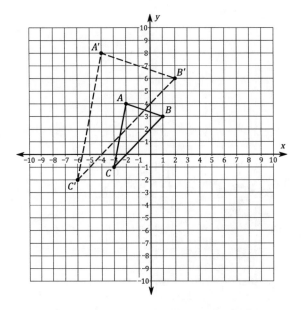

ANGLES

An angle is formed when two lines or line segments meet at a common point. It may be a common starting point for a pair of segments or rays, or it may be the intersection of lines. Angles are represented by the symbol $\angle$.

The vertex is the point at which two segments or rays meet to form an angle. If the angle is formed by intersecting rays, lines, and/or line segments, the vertex is the point at which four angles are formed. The pairs of angles opposite one another are called vertical angles, and their measures are equal.

An acute angle is an angle with a degree measure less than 90°.

A right angle is an angle with a degree measure of exactly 90°.

An obtuse angle is an angle with a degree measure greater than 90° but less than 180°.

A straight angle is an angle with a degree measure of exactly 180°. This is also a semicircle.

A reflex angle is an angle with a degree measure greater than 180° but less than 360°.

A **full angle** is an angle with a degree measure of exactly 360°. This is also a circle.

Review Video: __Angles__
Visit mometrix.com/academy and enter code: 264624

Two angles whose sum is exactly 90° are said to be complementary. The two angles may or may not be adjacent. In a right triangle, the two acute angles are complementary.

Two angles whose sum is exactly 180° are said to be supplementary. The two angles may or may not be adjacent. Two intersecting lines always form two pairs of supplementary angles. Adjacent supplementary angles will always form a straight line.

Two angles that have the same vertex and share a side are said to be adjacent. Vertical angles are not adjacent because they share a vertex but no common side.

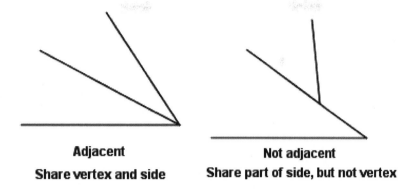

Adjacent

Share vertex and side

Not adjacent

Share part of side, but not vertex

When two parallel lines are cut by a transversal, the angles that are between the two parallel lines are interior angles. In the diagram below, angles 3, 4, 5, and 6 are interior angles.

When two parallel lines are cut by a transversal, the angles that are outside the parallel lines are exterior angles. In the diagram below, angles 1, 2, 7, and 8 are exterior angles.

When two parallel lines are cut by a transversal, the angles that are in the same position relative to the transversal and a parallel line are corresponding angles. The diagram below has four pairs of corresponding angles: angles 1 and 5; angles 2 and 6; angles 3 and 7; and angles 4 and 8. Corresponding angles formed by parallel lines are congruent.

When two parallel lines are cut by a transversal, the two interior angles that are on opposite sides of the transversal are called alternate interior angles. In the diagram below, there are two pairs of alternate interior angles: angles 3 and 6, and angles 4 and 5. Alternate interior angles formed by parallel lines are congruent.

When two parallel lines are cut by a transversal, the two exterior angles that are on opposite sides of the transversal are called alternate exterior angles. In the diagram below, there are two pairs of alternate exterior angles: angles 1 and 8, and angles 2 and 7. Alternate exterior angles formed by parallel lines are congruent.

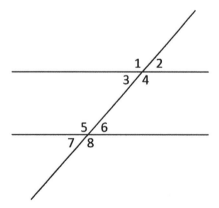

When two lines intersect, four angles are formed. The non-adjacent angles at this vertex are called vertical angles. Vertical angles are congruent. In the diagram, $\angle ABD \cong \angle CBE$ and $\angle ABC \cong \angle DBE$.

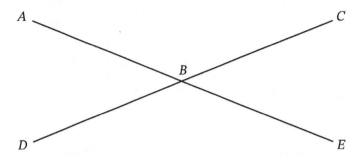

TRIANGLES

An equilateral triangle is a triangle with three congruent sides. An equilateral triangle will also have three congruent angles, each 60°. All equilateral triangles are also acute triangles.

An isosceles triangle is a triangle with two congruent sides. An isosceles triangle will also have two congruent angles opposite the two congruent sides.

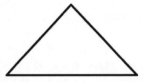

A scalene triangle is a triangle with no congruent sides. A scalene triangle will also have three angles of different measures. The angle with the largest measure is opposite the longest side, and the angle with the smallest measure is opposite the shortest side.

An acute triangle is a triangle whose three angles are all less than 90°. If two of the angles are equal, the acute triangle is also an isosceles triangle. If the three angles are all equal, the acute triangle is also an equilateral triangle.

A right triangle is a triangle with exactly one angle equal to 90°. All right triangles follow the Pythagorean Theorem. A right triangle can never be acute or obtuse.

An obtuse triangle is a triangle with exactly one angle greater than 90°. The other two angles may or may not be equal. If the two remaining angles are equal, the obtuse triangle is also an isosceles triangle.

TRIANGLE TERMINOLOGY

Altitude of a Triangle: A line segment drawn from one vertex perpendicular to the opposite side. In the diagram below, $\overline{BE}$, $\overline{AD}$, and $\overline{CF}$ are altitudes. The three altitudes in a triangle are always concurrent.

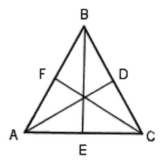

Height of a Triangle: The length of the altitude, although the two terms are often used interchangeably.

Orthocenter of a Triangle: The point of concurrency of the altitudes of a triangle. Note that in an obtuse triangle, the orthocenter will be outside the triangle, and in a right triangle, the orthocenter is the vertex of the right angle.

Median of a Triangle: A line segment drawn from one vertex to the midpoint of the opposite side. This is not the same as the altitude, except the altitude to the base of an isosceles triangle and all three altitudes of an equilateral triangle.

Centroid of a Triangle: The point of concurrency of the medians of a triangle. This is the same point as the orthocenter only in an equilateral triangle. Unlike the orthocenter, the centroid is always inside the triangle. The centroid can also be considered the exact center of the triangle. Any shape triangle can be perfectly balanced on a tip placed at the centroid. The centroid is also the point that is two-thirds the distance from the vertex to the opposite side.

SIMILARITY AND CONGRUENCE RULES

Similar triangles are triangles whose corresponding angles are equal and whose corresponding sides are proportional. Represented by AAA. Similar triangles whose corresponding sides are congruent are also congruent triangles.

Triangles can be shown to be **congruent** in 5 ways:

- **SSS**: Three sides of one triangle are congruent to the three corresponding sides of the second triangle.
- **SAS**: Two sides and the included angle (the angle formed by those two sides) of one triangle are congruent to the corresponding two sides and included angle of the second triangle.
- **ASA**: Two angles and the included side (the side that joins the two angles) of one triangle are congruent to the corresponding two angles and included side of the second triangle.
- **AAS**: Two angles and a non-included side of one triangle are congruent to the corresponding two angles and non-included side of the second triangle.
- **HL**: The hypotenuse and leg of one right triangle are congruent to the corresponding hypotenuse and leg of the second right triangle.

> **Review Video: <u>Similar Triangles</u>**
> Visit mometrix.com/academy and enter code: 398538

GENERAL RULES FOR TRIANGLES

The Triangle Inequality Theorem states that the sum of the measures of any two sides of a triangle is always greater than the measure of the third side. If the sum of the measures of two sides were equal to the third side, a triangle would be impossible because the two sides would lie flat across the third side and there would be no vertex. If the sum of the measures of two of the sides was less than the third side, a closed figure would be impossible because the two shortest sides would never meet.

The sum of the measures of the interior angles of a triangle is always 180°. Therefore, a triangle can never have more than one angle greater than or equal to 90°.

In any triangle, the angles opposite congruent sides are congruent, and the sides opposite congruent angles are congruent. The largest angle is always opposite the longest side, and the smallest angle is always opposite the shortest side.

The line segment that joins the midpoints of any two sides of a triangle is always parallel to the third side and exactly half the length of the third side.

> **Review Video: <u>Proof that a Triangle is 180 Degrees</u>**
> Visit mometrix.com/academy and enter code: 687591

PYTHAGOREAN THEOREM

The side of a triangle opposite the right angle is called the hypotenuse. The other two sides are called the legs. The Pythagorean Theorem states a relationship among the legs and hypotenuse of a right triangle: $a^2 + b^2 = c^2$, where a and b are the lengths of the legs of a right triangle, and c is the length of the hypotenuse. Note that this formula will only work with right triangles.

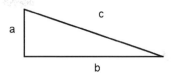

TRIGONOMETRIC FORMULAS

In the diagram below, angle C is the right angle, and side c is the hypotenuse. Side a is the side adjacent to angle B and side b is the side adjacent to angle A. These formulas will work for any acute angle in a right triangle. They will NOT work for any triangle that is not a right triangle. Also, they will not work for the right angle in a right triangle, since there are not distinct adjacent and opposite sides to differentiate from the hypotenuse.

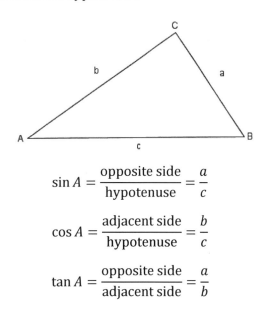

$$\sin A = \frac{\text{opposite side}}{\text{hypotenuse}} = \frac{a}{c}$$

$$\cos A = \frac{\text{adjacent side}}{\text{hypotenuse}} = \frac{b}{c}$$

$$\tan A = \frac{\text{opposite side}}{\text{adjacent side}} = \frac{a}{b}$$

POLYGONS

Each straight line segment of a polygon is called a side.

The point at which two sides of a polygon intersect is called the vertex. In a polygon, the number of sides is always equal to the number of vertices.

A polygon with all sides congruent and all angles equal is called a regular polygon.

A line segment from the center of a polygon perpendicular to a side of the polygon is called the apothem. In a regular polygon, the apothem can be used to find the area of the polygon using the formula $A = \frac{1}{2}ap$, where a is the apothem and p is the perimeter.

A line segment from the center of a polygon to a vertex of the polygon is called a radius. The radius of a regular polygon is also the radius of a circle that can be circumscribed about the polygon.

- Triangle – 3 sides
- Quadrilateral – 4 sides
- Pentagon – 5 sides
- Hexagon – 6 sides
- Heptagon – 7 sides
- Octagon – 8 sides
- Nonagon – 9 sides
- Decagon – 10 sides
- Dodecagon – 12 sides

More generally, an *n*-gon is a polygon that has *n* angles and *n* sides.

> **Review Video: Intro to Polygons**
> Visit mometrix.com/academy and enter code: 271869

The sum of the interior angles of an *n*-sided polygon is $(n - 2) \times 180°$. For example, in a triangle $n = 3$. So the sum of the interior angles is $(3 - 2) \times 180° = 180°$. In a quadrilateral, $n = 4$, and the sum of the angles is $(4 - 2) \times 180° = 360°$.

A diagonal is a line segment that joins two non-adjacent vertices of a polygon.

A convex polygon is a polygon whose diagonals all lie within the interior of the polygon.

A concave polygon is a polygon with a least one diagonal that lies outside the polygon. In the diagram below, quadrilateral *ABCD* is concave because diagonal $\overline{AC}$ lies outside the polygon.

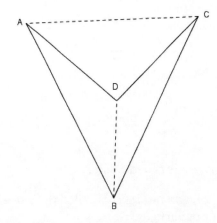

The number of diagonals a polygon has can be found by using the formula: number of diagonals = $\frac{n(n-3)}{2}$, where n is the number of sides in the polygon. This formula works for all polygons, not just regular polygons.

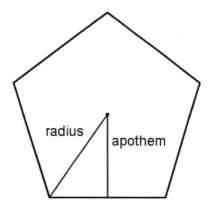

Congruent figures are geometric figures that have the same size and shape. All corresponding angles are equal, and all corresponding sides are equal. It is indicated by the symbol ≅.

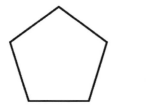 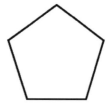

Congruent polygons

Similar figures are geometric figures that have the same shape, but do not necessarily have the same size. All corresponding angles are equal, and all corresponding sides are proportional, but they do not have to be equal. It is indicated by the symbol ~.

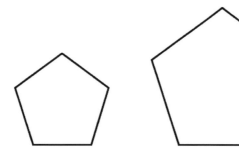

Similar polygons

Note that all congruent figures are also similar, but not all similar figures are congruent.

Line of Symmetry: The line that divides a figure or object into two symmetric parts. Each symmetric half is congruent to the other. An object may have no lines of symmetry, one line of symmetry, or more than one line of symmetry.

Lines of symmetry:

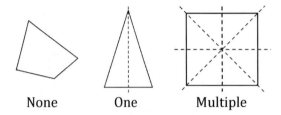

| None | One | Multiple |

Quadrilateral: A closed two-dimensional geometric figure composed of exactly four straight sides. The sum of the interior angles of any quadrilateral is 360°.

Parallelogram: A quadrilateral that has exactly two pairs of opposite parallel sides. The sides that are parallel are also congruent. The opposite interior angles are always congruent, and the consecutive interior angles are supplementary. The diagonals of a parallelogram bisect each other. Each diagonal divides the parallelogram into two congruent triangles.

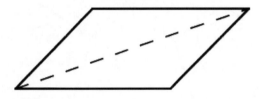

Trapezoid: Traditionally, a quadrilateral that has exactly one pair of parallel sides. Some math texts define trapezoid as a quadrilateral that has at least one pair of parallel sides. Because there are no rules governing the second pair of sides, there are no rules that apply to the properties of the diagonals of a trapezoid.

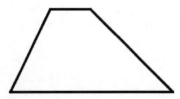

Rectangles, rhombuses, and squares are all special forms of parallelograms.

Rectangle: A parallelogram with four right angles. All rectangles are parallelograms, but not all parallelograms are rectangles. The diagonals of a rectangle are congruent.

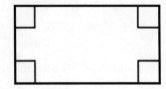

Rhombus: A parallelogram with four congruent sides. All rhombuses are parallelograms, but not all parallelograms are rhombuses. The diagonals of a rhombus are perpendicular to each other.

Square: A parallelogram with four right angles and four congruent sides. All squares are also parallelograms, rhombuses, and rectangles. The diagonals of a square are congruent and perpendicular to each other.

A quadrilateral whose diagonals bisect each other is a parallelogram. A quadrilateral whose opposite sides are parallel (2 pairs of parallel sides) is a parallelogram.

A quadrilateral whose diagonals are perpendicular bisectors of each other is a rhombus. A quadrilateral whose opposite sides (both pairs) are parallel and congruent is a rhombus.

A parallelogram that has a right angle is a rectangle. (Consecutive angles of a parallelogram are supplementary. Therefore if there is one right angle in a parallelogram, there are four right angles in that parallelogram.)

A rhombus with one right angle is a square. Because the rhombus is a special form of a parallelogram, the rules about the angles of a parallelogram also apply to the rhombus.

CIRCLES

The center is the single point inside the circle that is equidistant from every point on the circle. (Point O in the diagram below.)

The radius is a line segment that joins the center of the circle and any one point on the circle. All radii of a circle are equal. (Segments OX, OY, and OZ in the diagram below.)

The diameter is a line segment that passes through the center of the circle and has both endpoints on the circle. The length of the diameter is exactly twice the length of the radius. (Segment XZ in the diagram below.)

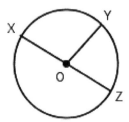

AREA AND CIRCUMFERENCE OF A CIRCLE

The area of a circle is found by the formula $A = \pi r^2$, where r is the length of the radius. If the diameter of the circle is given, remember to divide it in half to get the length of the radius before proceeding.

FIND THE RADIUS OF A CIRCLE

You may have problems that give you the area of a circle. So, you are asked to find the radius.

Example: The area of a circle is 30cm². Find the radius.

First: Set up the equation to set apart the radius.

The equation is $30 = \pi r^2$. Now, divide both sides by π: $\dfrac{30}{\pi} = \dfrac{\pi r^2}{\pi}$

Second: Take the square root of both sides: $\sqrt{9.55} = \sqrt{r^2}$.

So, you are left with: $3.09 = r$.

Note: You may have the area, and you are asked to find the diameter of the circle. So, follow the steps above to find the radius. Then, multiply the radius by 2 for the diameter.

The circumference of a circle is found by the formula $C = 2\pi r$, where r is the radius. Again, remember to convert the diameter if you are given that measure rather than the radius.

FIND THE RADIUS OF A CIRCLE

You may have problems that give you the circumference of a circle. So, you are asked to find the radius. Example: The circumference is 20cm. Find the radius.

First: Set up the equation to set apart the radius.

The equation is $20 = 2\pi r$. Now divide both sides by 2: $\dfrac{20}{2} = \dfrac{2\pi r}{2}$.

Second: Divide both sides by π: $\dfrac{10}{\pi} = \dfrac{\pi r}{\pi}$. So, you are left with $3.18 = r$

Note: You may have the circumference, and you are asked to find the diameter of the circle. So, follow the steps above to find the radius. Then, multiply the radius by 2 for the diameter.

An arc is a portion of a circle. Specifically, an arc is the set of points between and including two points on a circle. An arc does not contain any points inside the circle. When a segment is drawn from the endpoints of an arc to the center of the circle, a sector is formed.

A central angle is an angle whose vertex is the center of a circle and whose legs intercept an arc of the circle. Angle *XOY* in the diagram above is a central angle. A minor arc is an arc that has a measure less than 180°. The measure of a central angle is equal to the measure of the minor arc it intercepts. A major arc is an arc having a measure of at least 180°. The measure of the major arc can be found by subtracting the measure of the central angle from 360°. A semicircle is an arc whose endpoints are the endpoints of the diameter of a circle. A semicircle is exactly half of a circle.

An inscribed angle is an angle whose vertex lies on a circle and whose legs contain chords of that circle. The portion of the circle intercepted by the legs of the angle is called the intercepted arc.

The measure of the intercepted arc is exactly twice the measure of the inscribed angle. In the diagram below, angle *ABC* is an inscribed angle. $\overset{\frown}{AC} = 2(m\angle ABC)$

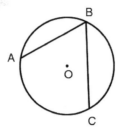

Any angle inscribed in a semicircle is a right angle. The intercepted arc is 180°, making the inscribed angle half that, or 90°. In the diagram below, angle *ABC* is inscribed in semicircle *ABC*, making angle *ABC* equal to 90°.

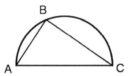

A chord is a line segment that has both endpoints on a circle. In the diagram below, $\overline{EB}$ is a chord.

Secant: A line that passes through a circle and contains a chord of that circle. In the diagram below, $\overleftrightarrow{EB}$ is a secant and contains chord $\overline{EB}$.

A tangent is a line in the same plane as a circle that touches the circle in exactly one point. While a line segment can be tangent to a circle as part of a line that is tangent, it is improper to say a tangent can be simply a line segment that touches the circle in exactly one point. In the diagram below, $\overleftrightarrow{CD}$ is tangent to circle *A*. Notice that $\overline{FB}$ is not tangent to the circle. $\overline{FB}$ is a line segment that touches the circle in exactly one point, but if the segment were extended, it would touch the circle in a second point. The point at which a tangent touches a circle is called the point of tangency. In the diagram below, point *B* is the point of tangency.

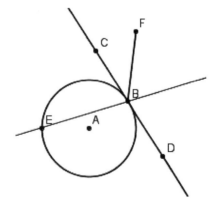

A secant is a line that intersects a circle in two points. Two secants may intersect inside the circle, on the circle, or outside the circle. When the two secants intersect on the circle, an inscribed angle is formed.

When two secants intersect inside a circle, the measure of each of two vertical angles is equal to half the sum of the two intercepted arcs. In the diagram below, m∠AEB = $\frac{1}{2}(\widehat{AB} + \widehat{CD})$ and m∠BEC = $\frac{1}{2}(\widehat{BC} + \widehat{AD})$.

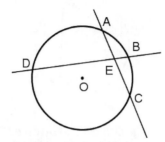

When two secants intersect outside a circle, the measure of the angle formed is equal to half the difference of the two arcs that lie between the two secants. In the diagram below, m∠AEB = $\frac{1}{2}(\widehat{AB} - \widehat{CD})$.

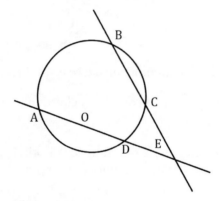

The **arc length** is the length of that portion of the circumference between two points on the circle. The formula for arc length is $s = \frac{\pi r \theta}{180°}$ where s is the arc length, r is the length of the radius, and θ is the angular measure of the arc in degrees, or $s = r\theta$, where θ is the angular measure of the arc in radians (2π radians = 360 degrees).

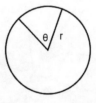

A sector is the portion of a circle formed by two radii and their intercepted arc. While the arc length is exclusively the points that are also on the circumference of the circle, the sector is the entire area bounded by the arc and the two radii.

The area of a sector of a circle is found by the formula, $A = \frac{\theta r^2}{2}$, where A is the area, θ is the measure of the central angle in radians, and r is the radius. To find the area when the central angle is in degrees, use the formula, $A = \frac{\theta \pi r^2}{360}$, where θ is the measure of the central angle in degrees and r is the radius.

OTHER CONIC SECTIONS

An ellipse is the set of all points in a plane, whose total distance from two fixed points called the foci (singular: focus) is constant, and whose center is the midpoint between the foci.

The standard equation of an ellipse that is taller than it is wide is $\frac{(y-k)^2}{a^2} + \frac{(x-h)^2}{b^2} = 1$, where a and b are coefficients. The center is the point (h, k) and the foci are the points $(h, k+c)$ and $(h, k-c)$, where $c^2 = a^2 - b^2$ and $a^2 > b^2$.

The major axis has length $2a$, and the minor axis has length $2b$. Eccentricity (e) is a measure of how elongated an ellipse is, and is the ratio of the distance between the foci to the length of the major axis. Eccentricity will have a value between 0 and 1. The closer to 1 the eccentricity is, the closer the ellipse is to being a circle. The formula for eccentricity is $= \frac{c}{a}$.

Parabola: The set of all points in a plane that are equidistant from a fixed line, called the directrix, and a fixed point not on the line, called the focus. Axis: The line perpendicular to the directrix that passes through the focus.

For parabolas that open up or down, the standard equation is $(x - h)^2 = 4c(y - k)$, where h, c, and k are coefficients. If c is positive, the parabola opens up. If c is negative, the parabola opens down. The vertex is the point (h, k). The directrix is the line having the equation $y = -c + k$, and the focus is the point $(h, c + k)$. For parabolas that open left or right, the standard equation is $(y - k)^2 = 4c(x - h)$, where k, c, and h are coefficients. If c is positive, the parabola opens to the right. If c is negative, the parabola opens to the left. The vertex is the point (h, k). The directrix is the line having the equation $x = -c + h$, and the focus is the point $(c + h, k)$.

A hyperbola is the set of all points in a plane, whose distance from two fixed points, called foci, has a constant difference.

The standard equation of a horizontal hyperbola is $\frac{(x-h)^2}{a^2} - \frac{(y-k)^2}{b^2} = 1$, where a, b, h, and k are real numbers. The center is the point (h, k), the vertices are the points $(h + a, k)$ and $(h - a, k)$, and the foci are the points that every point on one of the parabolic curves is equidistant from and are found using the formulas $(h + c, k)$ and $(h - c, k)$, where $c^2 = a^2 + b^2$. The asymptotes are two lines the graph of the hyperbola approaches but never reaches, and are given by the equations $y = \left(\frac{b}{a}\right)(x - h) + k$ and $y = -\left(\frac{b}{a}\right)(x - h) + k$.

A vertical hyperbola is formed when a plane makes a vertical cut through two cones that are stacked vertex-to-vertex.

The standard equation of a vertical hyperbola is $\frac{(y-k)^2}{a^2} - \frac{(x-h)^2}{b^2} = 1$, where a, b, k, and h are real numbers. The center is the point (h, k), the vertices are the points $(h, k + a)$ and $(h, k - a)$, and the foci are the points that every point on one of the parabolic curves is equidistant from and are found using the formulas $(h, k + c)$ and $(h, k - c)$, where $c^2 = a^2 + b^2$. The asymptotes are two lines the

119

graph of the hyperbola approaches but never reach, and are given by the equations $y = \left(\frac{a}{b}\right)(x - h) + k$ and $y = -\left(\frac{a}{b}\right)(x - h) + k$.

AREA AND PERIMETER FORMULAS: POLYGONS

TRIANGLE

The perimeter of any triangle is found by summing the three side lengths; $P = a + b + c$. For an equilateral triangle, this is the same as $P = 3s$, where s is any side length, since all three sides are the same length.

FIND THE SIDE OF A TRIANGLE

You may have problems that give you the perimeter of a triangle. So, you are asked to find one of the sides.

Example: The perimeter of a triangle is 35 cm. One side length is 10 cm. Another side length is 20cm. Find the length of the missing side.

> First: Set up the equation to set apart a side length.
>
>> Now, the equation is $35 = 10 + 20 + c$. So, you are left with $35 = 30 + c$.
>
> Second: Subtract 30 from both sides: $35 - 30 = 30 - 30 + c$
>
>> Then, you are left with $5 = c$

The area of any triangle can be found by taking half the product of one side length (base or b) and the perpendicular distance from that side to the opposite vertex (height or h). In equation form, $A = \frac{1}{2}bh$. For many triangles, it may be difficult to calculate h, so using one of the other formulas given here may be easier.

FIND THE HEIGHT OR THE AREA OF THE BASE

You may have problems that give you the area of a triangle. So, you are asked to find the height or the base.

Example: The area of a triangle is 70 cm², and the height is 10. Find the base.

> First: Set up the equation to set apart the base.
>
>> The equation is $70 = \frac{1}{2}10b$.
>
>> Now, multiply both sides by 2: $70 \times 2 = \frac{1}{2}10b \times 2$.
>
>> So, you are left with: $140 = 10b$.
>
> Second: Divide both sides by 10 to get the base: $\frac{140}{10} = \frac{10b}{10}$

Then, you have $14 = b$.

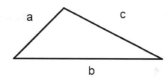

Another formula that works for any triangle is $A = \sqrt{s(s-a)(s-b)(s-c)}$, where A is the area, s is the semiperimeter $s = \frac{a+b+c}{2}$, and a, b, and c are the lengths of the three sides.

The area of an equilateral triangle can be found by the formula $A = \frac{\sqrt{3}}{4}s^2$, where A is the area and s is the length of a side. You could use the $30° - 60° - 90°$ ratios to find the height of the triangle and then use the standard triangle area formula, but this is faster.

The area of an isosceles triangle can be found by the formula, $A = \frac{1}{2}b\sqrt{a^2 - \frac{b^2}{4}}$, where A is the area, b is the base (the unique side), and a is the length of one of the two congruent sides. If you do not remember this formula, you can use the Pythagorean Theorem to find the height so you can use the standard formula for the area of a triangle.

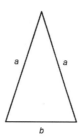

SQUARE

The area of a square is found by using the formula $A = s^2$, where and s is the length of one side.

FIND THE SIDE OF A SQUARE

You may have problems that give you the area of a square. So, you are asked to find the side.

Example: The area of a square is 9 cm². Find the side.

First: Set up the equation to set apart s.

The equation is $9 = s^2$.

Second: Now, you can take the square root of both sides: $\sqrt{9} = \sqrt{s^2}$.

So, you are left with: $3 = s$

The perimeter of a square is found by using the formula $P = 4s$, where s is the length of one side. Because all four sides are equal in a square, it is faster to multiply the length of one side by 4 than to add the same number four times. You could use the formulas for rectangles and get the same answer.

FIND THE SIDE OF A SQUARE

You may have problems that give you the perimeter of a square. So, you are asked to find the side.

Example: The perimeter of a square is 60 cm. Find the side.

First: Set up the equation to set apart s.

The equation is $60 = 4s$.

Second: Now, you can divide both sides by 4: $\frac{60}{4} = \frac{4s}{4}$. You are left with $15 = s$

RECTANGLE

The area of a rectangle is found by the formula $A = lw$, where A is the area of the rectangle, l is the length (usually considered to be the longer side) and w is the width (usually considered to be the shorter side). The numbers for l and w are interchangeable.

FIND THE WIDTH OR LENGTH OF A RECTANGLE

You may have problems that give you the area of a rectangle. So, you are asked to find the width.

Example: The area of a rectangle is 150cm², and the length is 10cm. Find the width.

First: Set up the equation to set apart width. The equation is $150 = 10w$.

Second: Divide both sides by 10: $\frac{150}{10} = \frac{10w}{10}$. You are left with $15 = w$

Note: When you need to find the length, you can follow the steps above to find it.

The perimeter of a rectangle is found by the formula $P = 2l + 2w$ or $P = 2(l + w)$, where l is the length, and w is the width. It may be easier to add the length and width first and then double the result, as in the second formula.

FIND THE WIDTH OR LENGTH OF A RECTANGLE

You may have problems that give you the perimeter of a rectangle. So, you are asked to find the width.

Example: The perimeter of a rectangle is 100cm, and the length is 20cm. Find the width.

First: Set up the equation to set apart the width. The equation is $100 = 2(20 + w)$

Second: Distribute the 2 across $(20 + w)$: $100 = 40 + 2w$

Then, subtract 40 from both sides: $100 - 40 = 40 + 2w - 40$

So, you are left with: $60 = 2w$. Then, divide both sides by 2: $\frac{60}{2} = \frac{2w}{2}$.

Now, you have $30 = w$.

Note: When you need to find the length, you can follow the steps above to find it.

PARALLELOGRAM

The area of a parallelogram is found by the formula $A = bh$, where b is the length of the base, and h is the height. Note that the base and height correspond to the length and width in a rectangle, so this formula would apply to rectangles as well. Do not confuse the height of a parallelogram with the length of the second side. The two are only the same measure in the case of a rectangle.

FIND THE LENGTH OF THE BASE OR THE HEIGHT OF A PARALLELOGRAM

You may have problems that give you the area of a parallelogram. So, you are asked to find the area of the base or the height.

Example: The area of the parallelogram is 84 cm². The base is 7cm. Find the height.

Set up the equation to set apart the height.

So, you have $84 = 7h$. Now, divide both sides by 7: $\frac{84}{7} = \frac{7h}{7}$.

Then, you are left with $12 = h$

The perimeter of a parallelogram is found by the formula $P = 2a + 2b$ or $P = 2(a + b)$, where a and b are the lengths of the two sides.

FIND THE MISSING SIDE OF A PARALLELOGRAM

You may have problems that give you the perimeter of a parallelogram. So, you are asked to find one of the sides. Example: The perimeter of a parallelogram is 100cm, and one side is 20cm. Find the other side.

First: Set up the equation to set apart one of the side lengths.

The equation is $100 = 2(20 + b)$

Second: Distribute the 2 across $(20 + b)$: $100 = 40 + 2b$

Then, subtract 40 from both sides: $100 - 40 = 40 + 2b - 40$

So, you are left with: $60 = 2b$. Then, divide both sides by 2: $\frac{60}{2} = \frac{2b}{2}$

Now, you have $30 = b$.

> **Review Video: <u>Area and Perimeter of a Parallelogram</u>**
> Visit mometrix.com/academy and enter code: 718313

TRAPEZOID

The area of a trapezoid is found by the formula $A = \frac{1}{2}h(b_1 + b_2)$, where h is the height (segment joining and perpendicular to the parallel bases), and b_1 and b_2 are the two parallel sides (bases). Do not use one of the other two sides as the height unless that side is also perpendicular to the parallel bases.

FIND THE HEIGHT OF A TRAPEZOID

You may have problems that give you the area of a trapezoid. So, you are asked to find the height.

Example: The area of a trapezoid is 30cm². B_1 is 3cm, and B_2 is 9cm. Find the height.

First: Set up the equation to set apart the height. The equation is $30 = \frac{1}{2}h(3 + 9)$.

Second: Now, multiply both sides by 2: $30 \times 2 = \frac{1}{2}(12)h \times 2$.

So, you are left with: $60 = (12)h$.

Third: Divide both sides by 12: $\frac{60}{12} = \frac{(12)h}{12}$. Now, you have $5 = h$

FIND A BASE OF A TRAPEZOID

You may have problems that give you the area of a trapezoid and the height. So, you are asked to find one of the bases.

Example: The area of a trapezoid is 90cm². b_1 is 5cm, and the height is 12cm. Find b_2.

First: Set up the equation to set apart b_2.

The equation is $90 = \frac{1}{2}12(5 + b_2)$.

Second: Now, multiply the height by $\frac{1}{2}$: $90 = 6(5 + b_2)$.

So, you can distribute the 6 across $(5 + b_2)$: $90 = 30 + 6b_2$

Third: Subtract 30 from both sides $90 - 30 = 30 + 6b_2 - 30$.

Now, you have $60 = 6b_2$.

Then, divide both sides by 6: $\frac{60}{6} = \frac{6b_2}{6}$. So, $b_2 = 10$.

The perimeter of a trapezoid is found by the formula $P = a + b_1 + c + b_2$, where a, b_1, c, and b_2 are the four sides of the trapezoid.

FIND THE MISSING SIDE OF A TRAPEZOID

Example: The perimeter of a trapezoid is 50cm. B_1 is 20cm, B_2 is 10cm, and a is 5cm. Find the length of side c.

First: Set up the equation to set apart the missing side.

The equation is $50 = 5 + 20 + c + 10$. So, you have $50 = 35 + c$

Second: Subtract 35 from both sides: $50 - 35 = 35 + c - 35$.

So, you are left with $15 = c$

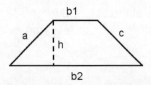

| **Review Video: <u>Area and Perimeter of a Trapezoid</u>** |
| Visit mometrix.com/academy and enter code: 587523 |

VOLUME AND SURFACE AREA

The surface area of a solid object is the area of all sides or exterior surfaces. For objects such as prisms and pyramids, a further distinction is made between base surface area (B) and lateral surface area (LA). For a prism, the total surface area (SA) is $SA = LA + 2B$. For a pyramid or cone, the total surface area is $SA = LA + B$.

SPHERE

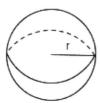

The **surface area of a sphere** can be found with the formula $SA = 4\pi r^2$, where r is the radius.

FIND THE RADIUS OF A SPHERE

You may have problems that give you the surface area of a sphere. So, you are asked to find the radius.

Example: The surface area of a sphere is 100 cm². Find the radius.

First: Set up the equation to set apart the radius.

You begin with: $SA = 4\pi r^2$. Then, you move 4π to the other side of the equal sign and cancel out the 4π on the right side of the formula: $\frac{SA}{4\pi} = r^2$.

Next, you square both sides to set apart the radius:

$\sqrt{\frac{SA}{4\pi}} = \sqrt{r^2}$. So, you are left with $r = \sqrt{\frac{SA}{4\pi}}$

Second: Solve the equation.

$\sqrt{\frac{100}{4\pi}} = \sqrt{\frac{100}{12.57}} = 2.82$. So, the radius equals 2.82 cm.

The **volume of a sphere** can be found with the formula $V = \frac{4}{3}\pi r^3$, where r is the radius. Sometimes, you may be asked to give the volume of a sphere in terms of π. For example, the volume of the sphere is 30π.

FIND THE RADIUS OF A SPHERE

You may have problems that give you the volume of a sphere. So, you are asked to find the radius.
Example: The volume of a sphere is 100 cm³. Find the radius.

First: Set up the equation and cancel out the fraction.

$\frac{3}{4} \times \frac{4}{3}\pi r^3 = 100 \times \frac{3}{4}$. So, you are left with: $\pi r^3 = 75$

Second: Cancel out π.

125

$\frac{\pi r^3}{\pi} = \frac{75}{\pi}$. So, you are left with: $r^3 = \frac{75}{\pi} = 23.87$

Third: Take the cubed root of r³ and 23.87 to solve for the radius.

$\sqrt[3]{r^3} = \sqrt[3]{23.87}$. So, you have the result of r= 2.88

RECTANGULAR PRISM

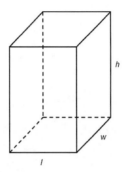

For a rectangular prism, the volume can be found by the formula $V = lwh$, where V is the volume, l is the length, w is the width, and h is the height.

> **Review Video: Volume and Surface Area of a Rectangular Prism**
> Visit momctrix.com/academy and enter code: 282814

FIND THE LENGTH, WIDTH, OR HEIGHT OF A RECTANGULAR PRISM

You may have problems that give you the volume of a rectangular prism. So, you are asked to find the length, width, or height.

Example: The volume of the rectangular prism is 200 cm³. The width is 10cm, and the height is 10cm. Find the length.

First: Set up the equation to set apart the length.

So, you have $200 = l(10)(10)$ that becomes $200 = (100)l$.

Second: Divide both sides by 100.

Now, you have $\frac{200}{100} = \frac{(100)l}{100}$. So, you are left with $2 = l$.

Note: When you need to find the width or height, you can follow the steps above to solve for either.

The surface area can be calculated as $SA = 2lw + 2hl + 2wh$ or $SA = 2(lw + hl + wh)$.

FIND THE LENGTH, WIDTH, OR HEIGHT OF A RECTANGULAR PRISM

You may have problems that give you the surface area of a rectangular prism. So, you are asked to find the length, width, or height.

Example: The surface area of the rectangular prism is 200 cm². The width is 15cm, and the height is 5cm. Find the length.

First: Set up the equation to set apart the length.

So, you have $200 = 2(15)l + 2(5)l + 2(15)(5)$ that becomes: $200 = (40)l + 150$.

Second: Subtract 150 from both sides.

So, $200 - 150 = (40)l + 150 - 150$ becomes $50 = (40)l$.

Then, divide both sides by 40 to set apart l: $\frac{50}{40} = \frac{(40)l}{40}$.

You are left with $1.25 = l$.

Note: When you need to find the width or height, you can follow the steps above to solve for either.

CUBE

The volume of a cube can be found by the formula $V = s^3$, where s is the length of a side.

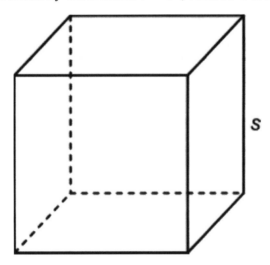

FIND THE SIDE OF A CUBE

You may have problems that give you the volume of a cube. So, you are asked to find the side.

Example: The volume of a cube is 20 cm³. Find the side.

First: Set up the equation to set apart the side length. Then, take the cube root of both sides. So, $20 = s^3$ becomes $\sqrt[3]{20} = \sqrt[3]{s^3}$ Then, you are left with $\sqrt[3]{20} = s$

Second: Solve for the side length.

$\sqrt[3]{20} = 2.71$. So, s equals 2.71.

The surface area of a cube is calculated as $SA = 6s^2$, where SA is the total surface area and s is the length of a side. These formulas are the same as the ones used for the volume and surface area of a rectangular prism, but simplified since all three quantities (length, width, and height) are the same.

FIND THE SIDE OF A CUBE

You may have problems that give you the surface area of a cube. So, you are asked to find the side.

Example: The surface area of a cube is 60 cm². Find the side.

First: Set up the equation to set apart the side length.

So, $60 = 6s^2$ becomes $\frac{60}{6} = \frac{6s^2}{6}$. Then, you are left with $10 = s^2$

Second: Take the square root of both sides to set apart the s.

So, $10 = s^2$ becomes $\sqrt{10} = \sqrt{s^2}$.

Then, you are left with $3.16 = s$

CYLINDER

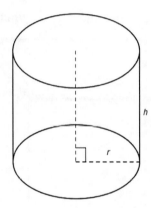

The volume of a cylinder can be calculated by the formula $V = \pi r^2 h$, where r is the radius, and h is the height.

> **Review Video: <u>Finding the Volume and Surface Area of a Right Circular Cylinder</u>**
> Visit mometrix.com/academy and enter code: 226463

FIND THE HEIGHT OF A CYLINDER

You may have problems that give you the volume of a cylinder. So, you are asked to find the height.

Example: The volume of a cylinder is 300 cm³ and the radius is 5 cm. Find the height.

First: Set up the equation and put in the known numbers.

You begin with $300 = \pi 5^2 h$. Now, $\pi 5^2 h = 78.5h$.

So, you have $300 = 78.5h$

Second: Set apart h to solve for the height.

$\frac{300}{78.5} = \frac{78.5h}{78.5}$. So, you are left with: $\frac{300}{78.5} = h$

Solve: $\frac{300}{78.5} = 3.82$cm is the height.

FIND THE RADIUS OF A CYLINDER

You may have problems that give you the volume of a cylinder. So, you are asked to find the radius.

Example: The volume of a cylinder is 200 cm³ and the radius is 15cm. Find the radius.

First: Set up the equation to set apart the radius.

You begin with $200 = \pi(15)r^2$. Now, you move π and (15) to both sides of the equation: $\frac{200}{\pi(15)} = \frac{\pi(15)r^2}{\pi(15)}$. Then, you are left with: $\frac{200}{\pi(15)} = r^2$.

Second: Take the square root of both sides to solve for the radius: $\sqrt{\frac{200}{\pi(15)}} = \sqrt{r^2}$.

Then, you have $\sqrt{4.25} = r$. So, the radius is equal to 2.06.

The surface area of a cylinder can be found by the formula $SA = 2\pi r^2 + 2\pi rh$. The first term is the base area multiplied by two, and the second term is the perimeter of the base multiplied by the height.

FIND THE HEIGHT OF A CYLINDER

You may have problems that give you the surface area of a cylinder. So, you are asked to find the height. Example: The surface area of a cylinder is 150 cm² and the radius is 2 cm. Find the height.

First: Set up the equation and put in the known numbers.

You begin with $150 = 2\pi 2^2 + 2\pi(2)h$.

So, you have $150 = 25.12 + 12.56h$.

Second: Subtract 25.12 from both sides of the equation.

So, $150 - 25.12 = 25.12 + 12.56h - 25.12$ becomes $124.85 = 12.56h$.

Then, divide both sides by 12.56.

Now, you are left with $9.94 = h$.

FIND THE RADIUS OF A CYLINDER

You may have problems that give you the surface area of a cylinder. So, you are asked to find the radius. Example: The surface area of a cylinder is 327 cm², and the height is 12cm. Find the radius.

First: Set up the equation and put in the known numbers.

You begin with $327 = 2\pi r^2 + 2\pi 12(r)$. So, you have $327 = 2\pi r^2 + 75.36r$.

Second: Set up the quadratic formula.

So, you now have $6.28r^2 + 75.36r - 327 = 0$.

Third: Solve the equation using the quadratic formula steps.

$$\text{Now, radius} = \frac{-75.36 \pm \sqrt{(75.36)^2 - 4(6.28)(-327)}}{2(6.28)}$$

So, the radius equals a positive 3.39.

PYRAMID

The **volume of a pyramid** is found with the formula $V = \frac{1}{3}Bh$, where B is the area of the base, and h is the height. The perpendicular distance from the vertex to the base is the height. This formula is the same as $\frac{1}{3}$ times the volume of a prism. Like a prism, the base of a pyramid can be any shape.

FIND THE AREA OF THE BASE OR THE HEIGHT OF A PYRAMID

You may have problems that give you the volume of a pyramid. So, you are asked to find the area of the base or the height.

Example: The volume of the pyramid is 100 cm³. The area of the base is 5cm². Find the height.

First: Set up the equation to set apart the height.

The equation is $100 = \frac{1}{3}5h$.

Now, you start by multiplying both sides by 3: $100 \times 3 = \frac{1}{3}5h \times 3$.

Second: You have $300 = 5h$. Now, divide both sides by 5: $\frac{300}{5} = \frac{5h}{5}$.

So, you have found that the height is 60.

Note: When you need to find the area of the base, you can follow the steps above to find it.

A right pyramid means that the base is a regular polygon. Also, the vertex is directly over the center of that polygon. If the pyramid is a right pyramid, the **surface area** can be calculated as $SA = B + \frac{1}{2}Ph_s$, where P is the perimeter of the base, and h_s is the slant height. The distance from the vertex to the midpoint of one side of the base is the slant height.

If the pyramid is irregular, the area of each triangle side must be calculated one at a time. Then, take the sum of the areas and the base to have the surface area.

FIND THE AREA OF THE BASE, THE PERIMETER OF THE BASE, OR THE HEIGHT

You may have problems that give you the surface area of a pyramid. So, you are asked to find the area of the base, the perimeter of the base, or the height.

Example: The surface area of the pyramid is 100 cm². The area of the base is 40cm², and the height is 12cm.

First: Set up the equation to set apart the perimeter of the base.

The equation is $100 = 40 + \frac{1}{2}12P$

Now, you can multiply the height by $\frac{1}{2}$.

So, you have: $100 = 40 + 6P$

Second: Subtract both sides of the equation by 40: $100 - 40 = 40 + 6P - 40$.

So, you have: $60 = 6P$

Now, divide both sides by 6: $\frac{60}{6} = \frac{6P}{6}$. So, you are left with: P=10cm.

Note: When you need to find the area of the base or the height, you can follow the steps above.

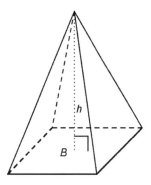

CONE

The **volume of a cone** is found with the formula $V = \frac{1}{3}\pi r^2 h$, where r is the radius, and h is the height. This formula is the same as $\frac{1}{3}$ times the volume of a cylinder.

FIND THE RADIUS OR HEIGHT OF A CONE

You may have problems that give you the volume of a cone. So, you are asked to find the radius or the height.

Example: The volume of the cone is 47.12 cm³. The height is 5cm. Find the radius.

First: Set up the equation to set apart the radius.

The equation is $47.12 = \frac{1}{3}\pi 5 r^2$

Now, you can multiply both sides by 3: $47.12 \times 3 = \frac{1}{3}\pi 5 r^2 \times 3$

So, you have $141.36 = \pi 5 r^2$.

Second: Divide both sides by 5: $\frac{141.36}{5} = \frac{\pi 5 r^2}{5}$.

Now, you have: $28.27 = \pi r^2$

You can divide both sides by π: $\frac{28.27}{\pi} = \frac{\pi r^2}{\pi}$.

So, you have $9 = \pi r^2$.

Third: Take the square root of both sides: $\sqrt{9} = \sqrt{r^2}$.

Now, you have $3 = r$

Note: When you need to find the height, you can follow the steps above to find it.

The **surface area of a cone** can be found with the formula $SA = \pi r^2 + \pi rs$, where s is the slant height. The slant height can be found with the Pythagorean Theorem to be $\sqrt{r^2 + h^2}$. So, the surface area formula for a cone can also be written as $SA = \pi r^2 + \pi r\sqrt{r^2 + h^2}$.

FIND THE RADIUS OF A CONE

You may have problems that give you the surface area of a cone. So, you are asked to find the radius.

Example: The surface area of the cone is 43.96 cm². The slant height is 5cm. Find the radius.

First: Set up the equation to set apart the radius.

The equation is $43.96 = \pi r^2 + 5\pi r$

Then, you can factor out the π: $43.96 = \pi(r^2 + 5r)$

Second: Now, you can divide both sides by π: $\frac{43.96}{\pi} = \frac{\pi(r^2+5r)}{\pi}$

So, you have: $14 = r^2 + 5r$. Then, subtract 14 from both sides, and you have: $x = r^2 + 5r - 14$

Third: Use the quadratic formula

$$x = \frac{-5 \pm \sqrt{5^2 - 4(1)(-14)}}{2(1)}$$

So, the radius equals a positive 2.

FIND THE SLANT HEIGHT OF A CONE

You may have problems that give you the surface area of a cone. So, you are asked to find the slant height.

Example: The surface area of the cone is 37.68 cm². The radius is 2cm. Find the slant height.

First: Set up the equation to set apart the slant height.

The equation is $37.68 = \pi 2^2 + \pi 2s$

Now, calculate both sides: $37.68 = 12.56 + 6.28s$

Second: Divide 6.28 across all three terms: $\frac{37.68}{6.28} = \frac{12.56}{6.28} + \frac{6.28s}{6.28}$

Then, you have $6 = 2 + s$. Now, subtract 2 from both sides: $6 - 2 = 2 + s - 2$

So, you are left with $4 = s$

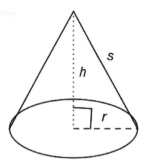

GEOMETRY MODELING

Example 1

The following table lists the four states with the largest populations in 2010 and the area (in square miles) of each state. Find the population density of each and list the states from highest to lowest population density.

State	2010 Population	Area (square miles)
California	37,253,956	158,648
Texas	25,145,561	266,874
New York	19,378,102	49,112
Florida	18,801,310	58,681

California:
$$\frac{37,253,956}{158,648} \approx 235 \text{ people/sq. mi}$$

Texas:
$$\frac{25,145,561}{266,874} \approx 94 \text{ people/sq. mi}$$

New York:
$$\frac{19,378,102}{49,112} \approx 395 \text{ people/sq. mi}$$

Florida:
$$\frac{18,801,310}{58,681} \approx 320 \text{ people/sq. mi}$$

Highest population density: New York, Florida, California.

Lowest population density: Texas.

Example 2

A factory cuts large sheets of cardstock (100 in by 102 in) into cards (3 in by 5 in). Determine the maximum number of cards the factory can cut and which side of the cards should be cut from the 100 in side of the sheets.

Area of the large sheet: $A_{sheet} = l \cdot w = 100 \cdot 102 =$ 10200 square inches	Area of one card: $A_{card} = l \cdot w = 3 \cdot 5 =$ 15 square inches	Number of cards made: $\dfrac{10200}{15} = 680$

Option 1: 3 *in* side cut from 100 *in* side $\dfrac{100}{3} = 33.3333 \;\to\; 99$ *in* used and 33 cards per side $\dfrac{102}{5} = 20.4 \;\to\; 100$ *in* used and 20 cards per side $33 \cdot 20 = 660$ cards total	Option 2: 5 *in* side cut from the 100 *in* side $\dfrac{100}{5} = 20 \;\to\; 100$ *in* used and 20 cards per side $\dfrac{102}{3} = 34 \;\to\; 102$ *in* used and 34 cards per side $34 \cdot 20 = 680$ cards total

Option 2 should be used to achieve the maximum number of cards made and avoid any wasted material.

Example 3

A display box is designed to hold a single baseball so the ball touches all six faces of the box. If the diameter of a baseball is 2.9 in, how much empty space is in the box around the ball?

$V_{box} = s^3 = 2.9^3 = 24.389$ $V_{ball} = \dfrac{4}{3} \cdot \pi r^3 = \dfrac{4}{3} \cdot \pi \cdot (1.45)^3 = 12.77$	$V_{space} = V_{box} - V_{ball} = 24.389 - 12.77$ $= 11.619$

The box has 11.619 cubic inches of space around the baseball.

Data Analysis, Probability, and Statistics

STATISTICS

Statistics is the branch of mathematics that deals with collecting, recording, interpreting, illustrating, and analyzing large amounts of data. The following terms are often used in the discussion of data and statistics:

Data – the collective name for pieces of information (singular is datum).

Quantitative data – measurements (such as length, mass, and speed) that provide information about quantities in numbers

Qualitative data – information (such as colors, scents, tastes, and shapes) that cannot be measured using numbers

Discrete data – information that can be expressed only by a specific value, such as whole or half numbers; For example, since people can be counted only in whole numbers, a population count would be discrete data.

Continuous data – information (such as time and temperature) that can be expressed by any value within a given range

Primary data – information that has been collected directly from a survey, investigation, or experiment, such as a questionnaire or the recording of daily temperatures; Primary data that has not yet been organized or analyzed is called raw data.

Secondary data – information that has been collected, sorted, and processed by the researcher

Ordinal data – information that can be placed in numerical order, such as age or weight

Nominal data – information that cannot be placed in numerical order, such as names or places

MEASURES OF CENTRAL TENDENCY

The quantities of mean, median, and mode are all referred to as measures of central tendency. They can each give a picture of what the whole set of data looks like with just a single number. Knowing what each of these values represents is vital to making use of the information they provide.

The mean, also known as the arithmetic mean or average, of a data set is calculated by summing all of the values in the set and dividing that sum by the number of values. For example, if a data set has 6 numbers and the sum of those 6 numbers is 30, the mean is calculated as $30/6 = 5$.

The median is the middle value of a data set. The median can be found by putting the data set in numerical order, and locating the middle value. In the data set (1, 2, 3, 4, 5), the median is 3. If there is an even number of values in the set, the median is calculated by taking the average of the two middle values. In the data set, (1, 2, 3, 4, 5, 6), the median would be $(3 + 4)/2 = 3.5$.

The mode is the value that appears most frequently in the data set. In the data set (1, 2, 3, 4, 5, 5, 5), the mode would be 5 since the value 5 appears three times. If multiple values appear the same number of times, there are multiple values for the mode. If the data set were (1, 2, 2, 3, 4, 4, 5, 5), the modes would be 2, 4, and 5. If no value appears more than any other value in the data set, then there is no mode.

MEASURES OF DISPERSION

The standard deviation expresses how spread out the values of a distribution are from the mean. Standard deviation is given in the same units as the original data and is represented by a lower-case sigma (σ). A high standard deviation means that the values are very spread out. A low standard deviation means that the values are close together.

If every value in a distribution is increased or decreased by the same amount, the mean, median, and mode are increased or decreased by that amount, but the standard deviation stays the same. If every value in a distribution is multiplied or divided by the same number, the mean, median, mode, and standard deviation will all be multiplied or divided by that number.

The range of a distribution is the difference between the highest and lowest values in the distribution. For example, in the data set (1, 3, 5, 7, 9, 11), the highest and lowest values are 11 and 1, respectively. The range then would be calculated as 11 – 1 = 10.

The three quartiles are the three values that divide a data set into four equal parts. Quartiles are generally only calculated for data sets with a large number of values. As a simple example, for the data set consisting of the numbers 1 through 99, the first quartile (Q1) would be 25, the second quartile (Q2), always equal to the median, would be 50, and the third quartile (Q3) would be 75. The difference between Q1 and Q3 is known as the interquartile range.

PROBABILITY

Probability is a branch of statistics that deals with the likelihood of something taking place. One classic example is a coin toss. There are only two possible results: heads or tails. The likelihood, or probability, that the coin will land as heads is 1 out of 2 (1/2, 0.5, 50%). Tails has the same probability. Another common example is a 6-sided die roll. There are six possible results from rolling a single die, each with an equal chance of happening, so the probability of any given number coming up is 1 out of 6.

> **Review Video: Intro to Probability**
> Visit mometrix.com/academy and enter code: 212374

Terms frequently used in probability:

Event – a situation that produces results of some sort (a coin toss)

Compound event – event that involves two or more items (rolling a pair of dice; taking the sum)

Outcome – a possible result in an experiment or event (heads, tails)

Desired outcome (or success)—an outcome that meets a particular set of criteria (a roll of 1 or 2 if we are looking for numbers less than 3)

Independent events—two or more events whose outcomes do not affect one another (two coins tossed at the same time)

Dependent events—two or more events whose outcomes affect one another (two cards drawn consecutively from the same deck)

Certain outcome—probability of outcome is 100% or 1

Impossible outcome—probability of outcome is 0% or 0

Mutually exclusive outcomes – two or more outcomes whose criteria cannot all be satisfied in a single outcome (a coin coming up heads and tails on the same toss)

Theoretical probability is the likelihood of a certain outcome occurring for a given event. It can be determined without actually performing the event. It is calculated as P (probability of success) = (desired outcomes)/(total outcomes).

Example:

There are 20 marbles in a bag and 5 are red. The theoretical probability of randomly selecting a red marble is 5 out of 20, (5/20 = 1/4, 0.25, or 25%).

Most of the time, when we talk about probability, we mean theoretical probability. Experimental probability, or relative frequency, is the number of times an outcome occurs in a particular experiment or a certain number of observed events.

While theoretical probability is based on what *should* happen, experimental probability is based on what *has* happened. Experimental probability is calculated in the same way as theoretical probability, except that actual outcomes are used instead of possible outcomes.

CONDITIONAL PROBABILITY

Given two events A and B, the **conditional probability** $P(A|B)$ is the probability that event A will occur, given that event B has occurred. For instance, suppose you have a jar containing two red marbles and two blue marbles, and you draw two marbles at random. Note. The first drawn marble is not replaced. Consider event A being the event that the first marble drawn is red, and event B being the event that the second marble drawn is blue. With no conditions set, both P(A) and P(B) are equal to $\frac{1}{2}$. However, if we know that the first marble drawn was red—that is, that event A occurred—then that leaves one red marble and two blue marbles in the jar. In that case, the probability that the second marble is blue given that the first marble was red—that is, P(A|B)—is equal to $\frac{2}{3}$.

Size Color	Small	Medium	Large	Total
Blue	25	40	35	100
White	27	25	22	74
Black	8	23	15	26
Total	60	88	72	220

COMMON CHARTS AND GRAPHS

Charts and *Tables* are ways of organizing information into separate rows and columns. These rows and columns are labeled to find and to explain the information in them. Some charts and tables are organized horizontally with rows giving the details about the labeled information. Other charts and tables are organized vertically with columns giving the details about the labeled information.

Frequency Tables show how many times each value comes up within the set. A *Relative Frequency Table* shows the proportions of each value compared to the entire set. Relative frequencies are given as percents. However, the total percent for a relative frequency table may not equal 100 percent because of rounding.

This is an example of a frequency table with relative frequencies:

Favorite Color	Frequency	Relative Frequency
Blue	4	13%
Red	7	22%
Purple	3	9%
Green	6	19%
Cyan	12	38%

A *Bar Graph* is one of the few graphs that can be drawn correctly in two ways: horizontally and vertically. A bar graph is similar to a line plot because of how the data is organized on the graph. Both axes must have their categories defined for the graph to be useful. A thick line is drawn from zero to the exact value of the data. This line can be used for a number, a percentage, or other numerical value. Longer bar lengths point to greater data values. To understand a bar graph, read the labels for the axes to know the units being reported. Then look where the bars end and match this to the scale on the other axis. This will show you the connection between the axes. This bar graph shows the responses from a survey about the favorite colors of a group.

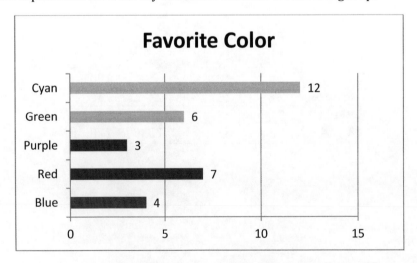

Line Graphs have one or more lines of different styles (e.g., solid or broken). These lines show the different values for a data set. Each point on the graph is shown as an ordered pair. This is similar to a Cartesian plane. In this case, the *x*- and *y*- axes are given certain units (e.g., dollars or time).

Each point that is for one measurement is joined by line segments. Then, these lines show what the values are doing.

The lines may be increasing (i.e., line sloping upward), decreasing (i.e., line sloping downward), or staying the same (i.e., horizontal line). More than one set of data can be put on the same line graph. This is done to compare more than one piece of data. An example of this would be graphing test scores for different groups of students over the same stretch of time. This allows you to see which group had the greatest increase or decrease in performance over a certain amount of years. This example is shown in the graph below.

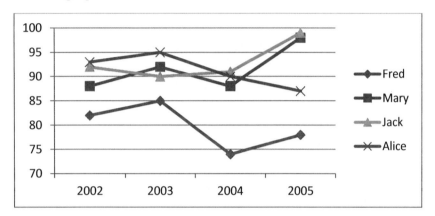

A *Line Plot*, or a *Dot Plot*, has plotted points that are NOT connected by line segments. In this graph, the horizontal axis lists the different possible values for the data. The vertical axis lists how many times one value happens. A single dot is graphed for each value. The dots in a line plot are connected. If the dots are connected, then this will not correctly represent the data.

The *5-Number Summary* of a set of data gives a very informative picture of the set. The five numbers in the summary are the minimum value, maximum value, and the three quartiles. This information gives you the range and the median of the set. Also, this information hints at how the data is spread across the median.

A *Box-and-Whiskers Plot* shows the 5-number summary on a graph. To draw a box-and-whiskers plot, place the points of the 5-number summary on a number line. Draw a box whose ends come through the points for the first and third quartiles. This is called the interquartile range. Draw a vertical line in the box that comes through the median and divides the box in half. Then, draw a line segment from the first quartile point to the minimum value. Also, draw a point from the third quartile point to the maximum value.

A *Pictograph* is a graph that is given in the horizontal format. This graph uses pictures or symbols to show the data. Each pictograph must have a key that defines the picture or symbol. Also, this key should give the number that stands for each picture or symbol. The pictures or symbols on a pictograph are not always shown as whole elements.

In this case, the fraction of the picture or symbol stands for the same fraction of the quantity that a whole picture or symbol represents. For example, there is a row in the pictograph with $3\frac{1}{2}$ ears of corn. Each ear of corn represents 100 stalks of corn in a field. So, this would equal $3\frac{1}{2} \times 100 = 350$ stalks of corn in the field.

Circle Graphs, or *Pie Charts*, show the relationship of each type of data compared to the whole set of data. The circle graph is divided into sections by drawing radii (i.e., plural for radius) to make central angles. These angles stand for a percentage of the circle. Each 1% of data is equal to 3.6° in the graph. So, data that stands for a 90° section of the circle graph makes up 25% of the whole. The pie chart below shows the data from the frequency table where people were asked about their favorite color.

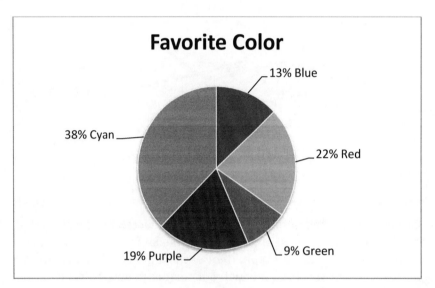

At first glance, a *Histogram* looks like a vertical bar graph. The difference is that a bar graph has a separate bar for each piece of data. A histogram has one bar for each stretch of data. For example, a histogram may have one bar for the stretch of 0–9 and one bar for the stretch of 10–19. A bar graph has numerical values on one axis.

A histogram has numbers on both axes. Each range is of equal size, and they are ordered left to right from lowest to highest. The height of each column on a histogram stands for the number of data values within that range. Like a stem and leaf plot, a histogram makes it easy to look at the graph and find which range has the greatest number of values. Below is an example of a histogram.

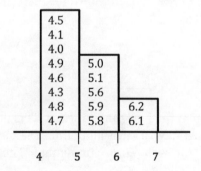

A *Stem and Leaf Plot* can outline groups of data that fall into a range of values. Each piece of data is split into two parts: the first, or left, part is called the stem. The second, or right, part is called the leaf. Each stem is listed in a column from smallest to largest. Each leaf that has the common stem is listed in that stem's row from smallest to largest.

For example, in a set of two-digit numbers, the digit in the tens place is the stem. So, the digit in the ones place is the leaf. With a stem and leaf plot, you can see which subset of numbers (10s, 20s, 30s, etc.) is the largest. This information can be found by looking at a histogram. However, a stem and leaf plot also lets you look closer and see which values fall in that range. Using all of the test scores from the line graph, we can put together a stem and leaf plot:

Test Scores								
7	4	8						
8	2	5	7	8	8			
9	0	0	1	2	2	3	5	8	9

Again, a stem-and-leaf plot is similar to histograms and frequency plots. However, a stem-and-leaf plot keeps all of the original data. In this example, you can see that almost half of the students scored in the 80s. Also, all of the data has been maintained. These plots can be used for larger numbers as well. However, they work better for small sets of data.

Bivariate Data is data from two different variables. The prefix *bi-* means *two*. In a *Scatter Plot*, each value in the set of data is put on a grid. This is similar to the Cartesian plane where each axis represents one of the two variables. When you look at the pattern made by the points on the grid, you may know if there is a relationship between the two variables. Also, you may know what that relationship is and if it exists.

The variables may be directly proportionate, inversely proportionate, or show no proportion. Also, you may be able to see if the data is linear. If the data is linear, you can find an equation to show the two variables. The following scatter plot shows the relationship between preference for brand "A" and the age of the consumers surveyed.

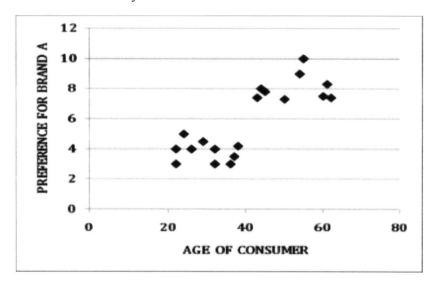

Scatter Plots are useful for knowing the types of functions that are given with the data. Also, they are helpful for finding the simple regression. A regression is a chart that is used to predict future

141

events. Linear scatter plots may be positive or negative. Many nonlinear scatter plots are exponential or quadratic. Below are some common types of scatter plots:

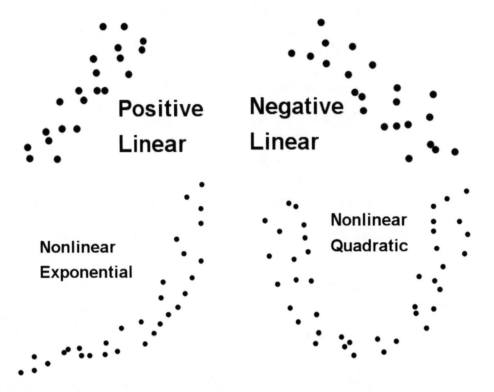

In statistics, *Simple Regression* is using an equation to represent a relation between an independent and dependent variables. The independent variable is also referred to as the explanatory variable or the predictor, and is generally represented by the variable x in the equation. The dependent variable, usually represented by the variable y, is also referred to as the response variable. The equation may be any type of function – linear, quadratic, exponential, etc. The best way to handle this task is to use the regression feature of your graphing calculator. This will easily give you the curve of best fit and provide you with the coefficients and other information you need to derive an equation.

In a scatter plot, the *Line of Best Fit* is the line that best shows the trends of the data. The line of best fit is given by the equation $\hat{y} = ax + b$, where a and b are the regression coefficients. The regression coefficient a is also the slope of the line of best fit, and b is also the y-coordinate of the point at which the line of best fit crosses the x-axis. Not every point on the scatter plot will be on the line of best fit. The differences between the y-values of the points in the scatter plot and the corresponding y-values according to the equation of the line of best fit are the residuals. The line of best fit is also called the least-squares regression line because it is also the line that has the lowest sum of the squares of the residuals.

SHAPE OF DATA DISTRIBUTION
SYMMETRY AND SKEWNESS

Symmetry is a characteristic of the shape of the plotted data. Specifically, it refers to how well the data on one side of the median mirrors the data on the other side.

A skewed data set is one that has a distinctly longer or fatter tail on one side of the peak or the other. A data set that is skewed left has more of its values to the left of the peak, while a set that is skewed right has more of its values to the right of the peak. When actually looking at the graph, these names may seem counterintuitive since, in a left-skewed data set, the bulk of the values seem to be on the right side of the graph, and vice versa. However, if the graph is viewed strictly in relation to the peak, the direction of skewness makes more sense.

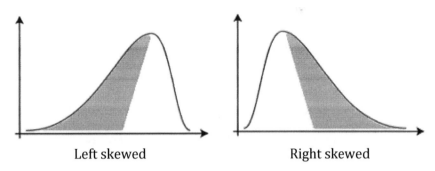

Left skewed   Right skewed

UNIMODAL VS. BIMODAL

If a distribution has a single peak, it would be considered unimodal. If it has two discernible peaks it would be considered bimodal. Bimodal distributions may be an indication that the set of data being considered is actually the combination of two sets of data with significant differences.

UNIFORMITY

A uniform distribution is a distribution in which there is no distinct peak or variation in the data. No values or ranges are particularly more common than any other values or ranges.

OUTLIER

An outlier is an extremely high or extremely low value in the data set. It may be the result of measurement error, in which case, the outlier is not a valid member of the data set. However, it may also be a valid member of the distribution. Unless a measurement error is identified, the experimenter cannot know for certain if an outlier is or is not a member of the distribution. There are arbitrary methods that can be employed to designate an extreme value as an outlier. One method designates an outlier (or possible outlier) to be any value less than $Q_1 - 1.5(IQR)$ or any value greater than $Q_3 + 1.5(IQR)$, where Q_1 and Q_3 are the first and third quartiles and IQR is the interquartile range. For instance, in the data set {42, 71, 22, 500, 33, 38, 62, 44, 58, 37, 61, 25}, the point 500 may be considered an outlier, since 500 is greater than 101.25 (61.5 + 1.5(26.5) = 101.25).

The Reading Test

The 35-minute PreACT Reading Test consists of four reading selections, each followed by 10 questions. One of the four selections is drawn from the humanities, one from social studies, one from the natural sciences, and one from prose fiction.

Key Ideas and Details

SUMMARIZING A COMPLEX TEXT

SUMMARIZE

A helpful tool is the ability to summarize the information that you have read in a paragraph or passage format. This process is similar to creating an effective outline. First, a summary should accurately define the main idea of the passage though the summary does not need to explain this main idea in exhaustive detail. The summary should continue by laying out the most important supporting details or arguments from the passage. All of the significant supporting details should be included, and none of the details included should be irrelevant or insignificant. Also, the summary should accurately report all of these details. Too often, the desire for brevity in a summary leads to the sacrifice of clarity or accuracy. Summaries are often difficult to read because they omit all of the graceful language, digressions, and asides that distinguish great writing. However, an effective summary should contain much the same message as the original text.

> **Review Video: Summarizing Text**
> Visit mometrix.com/academy and enter code: 172903

PARAPHRASE

Paraphrasing is another method that the reader can use to aid in comprehension. When paraphrasing, one puts what they have read into their words by rephrasing what the author has written, or one "translates" all of what the author shared into their words by including as many details as they can.

IDENTIFYING THE LOGICAL CONCLUSION

Identifying a logical conclusion can help you determine whether you agree with the writer or not. Coming to this conclusion is much like making an inference: the approach requires you to combine the information given by the text with what you already know in order to make a logical conclusion. If the author intended the reader to draw a certain conclusion, then you can expect the author's argumentation and detail to be leading in that direction. One way to approach the task of drawing conclusions is to make brief notes of all the points made by the author. When the notes are arranged on paper, they may clarify the logical conclusion. Another way to approach conclusions is to consider whether the reasoning of the author raises any pertinent questions. Sometimes you will be able to draw several conclusions from a passage. On occasion these will be conclusions that were never imagined by the author. Therefore, be aware that these conclusions must be supported directly by the text.

> **Review Video: How to Support a Conclusion**
> Visit mometrix.com/academy and enter code: 281653

DIRECTLY STATED INFORMATION

A reader should always be drawing conclusions from the text. Sometimes conclusions are implied from written information, and other times the information is **stated directly** within the passage. One should always aim to draw conclusions from information stated within a passage, rather than to draw them from mere implications. At times an author may provide some information and then describe a counterargument. Readers should be alert for direct statements that are subsequently rejected or weakened by the author. Furthermore, you should always read through the entire passage before drawing conclusions. Many readers are trained to expect the author's conclusions at either the beginning or the end of the passage, but many texts do not adhere to this format.

INFERENCES

Readers are often required to understand a text that claims and suggests ideas without stating them directly. An **inference** is a piece of information that is implied but not written outright by the author. For instance, consider the following sentence: *After the final out of the inning, the fans were filled with joy and rushed the field.* From this sentence, a reader can infer that the fans were watching a baseball game and their team won the game. Readers should take great care to avoid using information beyond the provided passage before making inferences. As you practice drawing inferences, you will find that they require concentration and attention.

> **Review Video: Inference**
> Visit mometrix.com/academy and enter code: 379203

Test-taking tip: While being tested on your ability to make correct inferences, you must look for contextual clues. An answer can be *true* but not *correct*. The contextual clues will help you find the answer that is the best answer out of the given choices. Be careful in your reading to understand the context in which a phrase is stated. When asked for the implied meaning of a statement made in the passage, you should immediately locate the statement and read the context in which the statement was made. Also, look for an answer choice that has a similar phrase to the statement in question.

IMPLICATIONS

Drawing conclusions from information implied within a passage requires confidence on the part of the reader. **Implications** are things that the author does not state directly, but readers can assume based on what the author does say. Consider the following passage: *I stepped outside and opened my umbrella. By the time I got to work, the cuffs of my pants were soaked.* The author never states that it is raining, but this fact is clearly implied. Conclusions based on implication must be well supported by the text. In order to draw a solid conclusion, readers should have multiple pieces of evidence. If readers have only one piece, they must be assured that there is no other possible explanation than their conclusion. A good reader will be able to draw many conclusions from information implied by the text which will be a great help in the exam.

TOPICS, MAIN IDEAS, AND SUPPORTING DETAILS
TOPICS AND MAIN IDEAS

One of the most important skills in reading comprehension is the identification of **topics** and **main ideas.** There is a subtle difference between these two features. The topic is the **subject** of a text (i.e., what the text is all about). The main idea, on the other hand, is the **most important point** being made by the author. The topic is usually expressed in a few words at the most while the main idea often needs a full sentence to be completely defined. As an example, a short passage might have the topic of penguins and the main idea could be written as *Penguins are different from other birds in many ways.* In most nonfiction writing, the topic and the main idea will be stated directly and often appear in a sentence at the very beginning or end of the text. When being tested on an understanding of the author's topic, you may be able to skim the passage for the general idea, by reading only the first sentence of each paragraph. A body paragraph's first sentence is often—but not always—the main topic sentence which gives you a summary of the content in the paragraph.

However, there are cases in which the reader must figure out an unstated topic or main idea. In these instances, you must read every sentence of the text and try to come up with an overarching idea that is supported by each of those sentences.

> **Review Video: Topics and Main Ideas**
> Visit mometrix.com/academy and enter code: 407801

SUPPORTING DETAILS

Supporting details provide evidence and backing for the main point. In order to show that a main idea is correct, or valid, authors add details that prove their point. All texts contain details, but they are only classified as supporting details when they serve to reinforce some larger point. Supporting details are most commonly found in informative and persuasive texts. In some cases, they will be clearly indicated with terms like *for example* or *for instance*, or they will be enumerated with terms like *first*, *second*, and *last*. However, you need to be prepared for texts that do not contain those indicators. As a reader, you should consider whether the author's supporting details really back up his or her main point. Supporting details can be factual and correct, yet they may not be relevant to the author's point. Conversely, supporting details can seem pertinent, but they can be ineffective because they are based on opinion or assertions that cannot be proven.

> **Review Video: Supporting Details**
> Visit mometrix.com/academy and enter code: 396297

TOPIC AND SUMMARY SENTENCES

Topic and summary sentences are a convenient way to encapsulate the main idea of a text. In some textbooks and academic articles, the author will place a topic or summary sentence at the beginning of each section as a means of preparing the reader for what is to come. Research suggests that the brain is more receptive to new information when it has been prepared by the presentation of the main idea or some key words. The phenomenon is somewhat akin to the primer coat of paint that allows subsequent coats of paint to absorb more easily. A good topic sentence will be clear and not contain any jargon. When topic or summary sentences are not provided, good readers can jot down their own so that they can find their place in a text and refresh their memory.

EVENTS IN A SEQUENCE

Readers must be able to identify a text's **sequence**, or the order in which things happen. Often, when the sequence is very important to the author, the text is indicated with signal words like *first*, *then*, *next*, and *last*. However, a sequence can be merely implied and must be noted by the reader. Consider the sentence *He walked through the garden and gave water and fertilizer to the plants.* Clearly, the man did not walk through the garden before he collected water and fertilizer for the plants. So, the implied sequence is that he first collected water, then he collected fertilizer, next he walked through the garden, and last he gave water or fertilizer as necessary to the plants. Texts do not always proceed in an orderly sequence from first to last. Sometimes they begin at the end and start over at the beginning. As a reader, you can enhance your understanding of the passage by taking brief notes to clarify the sequence.

Review Video: Sequence
Visit mometrix.com/academy and enter code: 489027

CAUSE AND EFFECT

In **cause and effect**, an author presents one thing that makes something else happen. For example, if one were to go to bed very late and awake very early, then they would be tired in the morning. The cause is lack of sleep, with the effect of being tired the next day.

Identifying the cause-and-effect relationships in a text can be tricky, but there are a few ways to approach this task. Often, these relationships are signaled with certain terms. When an author uses words like *because*, *since*, *in order*, and *so*, he or she is likely describing a cause-and-effect relationship. Consider the sentence: *He called her because he needed the homework*. This is a simple causal relationship in which the cause was his need for the homework, and the effect was his phone call. Yet, not all cause-and-effect relationships are marked in this way. Consider the sentences: *He called her. He needed the homework*. When the cause-and-effect relationship is not indicated with a keyword, the relationship can be discovered by asking why something happened. He called her: why? The answer is in the next sentence: He needed the homework.

Persuasive essays, in which an author tries to make a convincing argument and change the minds of readers, usually include cause-and-effect relationships. However, these relationships should not always be taken at face value. Frequently, an author will assume a cause or take an effect for granted. To read a persuasive essay effectively, readers need to judge the cause-and-effect relationships that the author is presenting. For instance, imagine an author wrote the following: *The parking deck has been unprofitable because people would prefer to ride their bikes*. The relationship is clear: the cause is that people prefer to ride their bikes, and the effect is that the parking deck has been unprofitable. However, readers should consider whether this argument is conclusive. Perhaps there are other reasons for the failure of the parking deck: a down economy, excessive fees, etc. Too often, authors present causal relationships as if they are fact rather than opinion. Readers should be on the alert for these dubious claims.

COMPARING IDEAS

Many texts follow the **compare-and-contrast** model in which the similarities and differences between two ideas or things are explored. Analysis of the similarities between ideas is called comparison. In an ideal comparison, the author places ideas or things in an equivalent structure (i.e., the author presents the ideas in the same way). If an author wants to show the similarities between cricket and baseball, then he or she may do so by summarizing the equipment and rules for each game. Be mindful of the similarities as they appear in the passage and take note of any differences that are mentioned. Often, these small differences will only reinforce the more general similarity.

CONTRASTING IDEAS

Thinking critically about ideas and conclusions can seem like a daunting task. One way to ease this task is to understand the basic elements of ideas and writing techniques. Looking at the way different ideas relate to each other can be a good way for readers to begin their analysis. For instance, sometimes authors will write about two ideas that are in opposition to each other. Or one author will provide his or her ideas on a topic, and another author may respond in opposition. The analysis of these opposing ideas is known as **contrast**. Contrast is often marred by the author's obvious partiality to one of the ideas. A discerning reader will be put off by an author who does not engage in a fair fight. In an analysis of opposing ideas, both ideas should be presented in clear and reasonable terms. If the author does prefer a side, you need to read carefully to determine the areas where the author shows or avoids this preference. In an analysis of opposing ideas, you should proceed through the passage by marking the major differences point by point with an eye that is looking for an explanation of each side's view. For instance, in an analysis of capitalism and communism, there is an importance in outlining each side's view on labor, markets, prices, personal responsibility, etc. Additionally, as you read through the passages, you should note whether the opposing views present each side in a similar manner.

> **Review Video: Compare and Contrast**
> Visit mometrix.com/academy and enter code: 798319

THEMES IN PRINT AND OTHER SOURCES

Themes are seldom expressed directly in a text and can be difficult to identify. A theme is an issue, an idea, or a question raised by the text. For instance, a theme of *Cinderella* (the Charles Perrault version) is perseverance as the title character serves her step-sisters and step-mother, and the prince seeks to find the girl with the missing slipper. A passage may have many themes, and you, as a dedicated reader, must take care to identify only themes that you are asked to find. One common characteristic of themes is that they raise more questions than they answer. In a good piece of fiction, authors are trying to elevate the reader's perspective and encourage him or her to consider the themes in a deeper way. In the process of reading, one can identify themes by constantly asking about the general issues that the text is addressing. A good way to evaluate an author's approach to a theme is to begin reading with a question in mind (e.g., How does this text approach the theme of love?) and to look for evidence in the text that addresses that question.

> **Review Video: Themes in Literature**
> Visit mometrix.com/academy and enter code: 732074

SIMILAR THEMES ACROSS CULTURES

A brief study of world literature suggests that writers from vastly different cultures address similar themes. For instance, works like the *Odyssey* and *Hamlet* both consider the individual's battle for self-control and independence. In most cultures, authors address themes of personal growth and the struggle for maturity. Another universal theme is the conflict between the individual and society. Works that are as culturally disparate as *Native Son*, the *Aeneid*, and *1984* dramatize how people struggle to maintain their personalities and dignity in large (sometimes) oppressive groups. Finally, many cultures have versions of the hero's or heroine's journey in which an adventurous person must overcome many obstacles in order to gain greater knowledge, power, and perspective. Some famous works that treat this theme are the *Epic of Gilgamesh*, Dante's *Divine Comedy*, and Cervantes' *Don Quixote*.

DIFFERENCES IN ADDRESSING THEMES IN VARIOUS CULTURES AND GENRES

Authors from different genres (for instance poetry, drama, novel, short story) and cultures may address similar themes, but they often do so quite differently. For instance, poets are likely to address subject matter obliquely, through the use of images and allusions. In a play, on the other hand, the author is more likely to dramatize themes by using characters to express opposing viewpoints. This disparity is known as a dialectical approach. In a novel, the author does not need to express themes directly; rather, they can be illustrated through events and actions. Different movements and styles become popular in different regions. For example, in Greece and England, authors tend to use more irony. In the 1950s Latin American authors popularized the use of unusual and surreal events to show themes about real life in the genre of magical realism. Japanese authors use the well-established poetic form of the haiku to organize their treatment of common themes.

Craft and Structure

WORD MEANING FROM CONTEXT

One of the benefits of reading is the expansion of one's vocabulary. In order to obtain this benefit, however, one needs to know how to identify the definition of a word from its context. This means defining a word based on the words around it and the way it is used in a sentence. Consider the following sentence: *The elderly scholar spent his evenings hunched over arcane texts that few other people even knew existed.* The adjective *arcane* is uncommon, but you can obtain significant information about it based on its use in the sentence. The fact that few other people know of their existence allows you to assume that "arcane texts" must be rare and be of interest to a few people. Also, the texts are being read by an elderly scholar. So, you can assume that they focus on difficult academic subjects. Sometimes, words can be defined by what they are not. Consider the following sentence: *Ron's fealty to his parents was not shared by Karen, who disobeyed their every command.* Someone who disobeys is not demonstrating *fealty*. So, you can infer that the word means something like *obedience* or *respect*.

FIGURATIVE LANGUAGE

There are many types of language devices that authors use to convey their meaning in a descriptive way. Understanding these concepts will help you understand what you read. These types of devices are called *figurative language* – language that goes beyond the literal meaning of a word or phrase. **Descriptive language** that evokes imagery in the reader's mind is one type of figurative language. **Exaggeration** is another type of figurative language. Also, when you compare two things, you are using figurative language. **Similes** and **metaphors** are ways of comparing things, and both are types of figurative language commonly found in poetry. An example of figurative language (a simile in this case): *The child howled like a coyote when her mother told her to pick up the toys.* In this example, the child's howling is compared to that of a coyote and helps the reader understand the sound being made by the child.

METAPHOR

A **metaphor** is a type of figurative language in which the writer equates one thing with a different thing. For instance: *The bird was an arrow arcing through the sky.* In this sentence, the arrow is serving as a metaphor for the bird. The point of a metaphor is to encourage the reader to consider the item being described in a different way. Let's continue with this metaphor for a bird: you are asked to envision the bird's flight as being similar to the arc of an arrow. So, you imagine the flight to be swift and bending. Metaphors are a way for the author to describe an item without being direct and obvious. This literary device is a lyrical and suggestive way of providing information. Note that the reference for a metaphor will not always be mentioned explicitly by the author. Consider the following description of a forest in winter: *Swaying skeletons reached for the sky and groaned as the wind blew through them.* In this example, the author is using *skeletons* as a metaphor for leafless trees. This metaphor creates a spooky tone while inspiring the reader's imagination.

> **Review Video: Metaphors in Writing**
> Visit mometrix.com/academy and enter code: 133295

SIMILE

A **simile** is a figurative expression that is similar to a metaphor, yet the expression requires the use of the distancing words *like* or *as*. Some examples: *The sun was like an orange, eager as a beaver,* and *nimble as a mountain goat.* Because a simile includes *like* or *as*, the device creates a space between the description and the thing being described. If an author says that *a house was like a shoebox*, then the tone is different than the author saying that the house *was* a shoebox. In a simile, authors

explicitly indicate that the description is not the same thing as the thing being described. In a metaphor, there is no such distinction. The decision of which device to use will be made based on the authors' intended tone.

Review Video: **Similes**
Visit mometrix.com/academy and enter code: 642949

PERSONIFICATION

Another type of figurative language is **personification.** This is the description of a nonhuman thing as if the item were human. Literally, the word means the process of making something into a person. The general intent of personification is to describe things in a manner that will be comprehensible to readers. When an author states that a tree *groans* in the wind, he or she does not mean that the tree is emitting a low, pained sound from a mouth. Instead, the author means that the tree is making a noise similar to a human groan. Of course, this personification establishes a tone of sadness or suffering. A different tone would be established if the author said that the tree was *swaying* or *dancing.*

Review Video: **Personification**
Visit mometrix.com/academy and enter code: 260066

DENOTATIVE MEANING OF WORDS

The **denotative** meaning of a word is the literal meaning of the word. The **connotative** meaning goes beyond the denotative meaning to include the emotional reaction that a word may invoke. The connotative meaning often takes the denotative meaning a step further due to associations which the reader makes with the denotative meaning. Readers can differentiate between the denotative and connotative meanings by first recognizing how authors use each meaning. Most non-fiction, for example, is fact-based and authors do not use flowery, figurative language. The reader can assume that the writer is using the denotative meaning of words. In fiction, the author may use the connotative meaning. Readers can determine whether the author is using the denotative or connotative meaning of a word by implementing context clues.

Review Video: **Connotation and Denotation**
Visit mometrix.com/academy and enter code: 310092

STRUCTURE OF TEXTS
PROBLEM-SOLUTION TEXT STRUCTURE

Some nonfiction texts are organized to present a problem followed by a solution. For this type of text, the problem is often explained before the solution is offered. In some cases, as when the problem is well known, the solution may be introduced briefly at the beginning. Other passages may focus on the solution, and the problem will be referenced only occasionally. Some texts will outline multiple solutions to a problem, leaving readers to choose among them. If the author has an interest or an allegiance to one solution, he or she may fail to mention or describe accurately some of the other solutions. Readers should be careful of the author's agenda when reading a problem-solution text. Only by understanding the author's perspective and interests can one develop a proper judgment of the proposed solution.

DESCRIPTIVE TEXT

In a sense, almost all writing is descriptive, insofar as an author seeks to describe events, ideas, or people to the reader. Some texts, however, are primarily concerned with **description.** A descriptive text focuses on a particular subject and attempts to depict the subject in a way that will be clear to readers. Descriptive texts contain many adjectives and adverbs (i.e., words that give shades of meaning and create a more detailed mental picture for the reader). A descriptive text fails when it is unclear to the reader. A descriptive text will certainly be informative and may be persuasive and entertaining as well.

> **Review Video: Descriptive Texts**
> Visit mometrix.com/academy and enter code: 174903

COMPARISON AND CONTRAST

Authors will use different stylistic and writing devices to make their meaning clear for readers. One of those devices is comparison and contrast. As mentioned previously, when an author describes the ways in which two things are alike, he or she is comparing them. When the author describes the ways in which two things are different, he or she is contrasting them. The "compare and contrast" essay is one of the most common forms in nonfiction. These passages are often signaled with certain words: a comparison may have indicating terms such as *both, same, like, too,* and *as well*; while a contrast may have terms like *but, however, on the other hand, instead,* and *yet.* Of course, comparisons and contrasts may be implicit without using any such signaling language. A single sentence may both compare and contrast. Consider the sentence *Brian and Sheila love ice cream, but Brian prefers vanilla and Sheila prefers strawberry.* In one sentence, the author has described both a similarity (love of ice cream) and a difference (favorite flavor).

CAUSE AND EFFECT

One of the most common text structures is cause and effect. A cause is an act or event that makes something happen, and an effect is the thing that happens as a result of the cause. A cause-and-effect relationship is not always explicit, but there are some terms in English that signal causes, such as *since, because,* and *due to.* Furthermore, terms that signal effects include *consequently, therefore, this lead(s) to.* As an example, consider this sentence: *Because the sky was clear, Ron did not bring an umbrella.* The cause is the clear sky, and the effect is that Ron did not bring an umbrella. However, readers may find that sometimes the cause-and-effect relationship will not be clearly noted. For instance, the sentence *He was late and missed the meeting* does not contain any signaling words, but the sentence still contains a cause (he was late) and an effect (he missed the meeting).

> **Review Video: Rhetorical Strategy of Cause-and-Effect Analysis**
> Visit mometrix.com/academy and enter code: 725944

TYPES OF PASSAGES
NARRATIVE PASSAGE

A **narrative** passage is a story that can be fiction or nonfiction. However, there are a few elements that a text must have in order to be classified as a narrative. First, the text must have a plot (i.e., a series of events). Narratives often proceed in a clear sequence, but this is not a requirement. If the narrative is good, then these events will be interesting to readers. Second, a narrative has characters. These characters could be people, animals, or even inanimate objects—so long as they participate in the plot. Third, a narrative passage often contains figurative language which is meant to stimulate the imagination of readers by making comparisons and observations. For instance, a metaphor, a common piece of figurative language, is a description of one thing in terms of another.

The moon was a frosty snowball is an example of a metaphor. In the literal sense this is obviously untrue, but the comparison suggests a certain mood for the reader.

> **Review Video: Style, Tone, and Mood**
> Visit mometrix.com/academy and enter code: 416961

EXPOSITORY PASSAGE

An **expository** passage aims to inform and enlighten readers. The passage is nonfiction and usually centers around a simple, easily defined topic. Since the goal of exposition is to teach, such a passage should be as clear as possible. Often, an expository passage contains helpful organizing words, like *first, next, for example*, and *therefore*. These words keep the reader oriented in the text. Although expository passages do not need to feature colorful language and artful writing, they are often more effective with these features. For a reader, the challenge of expository passages is to maintain steady attention. Expository passages are not always about subjects that will naturally interest a reader, so the writer is often more concerned with clarity and comprehensibility than with engaging the reader. By reading actively, you will ensure a good habit of focus when reading an expository passage.

TECHNICAL PASSAGE

A **technical** passage is written to describe a complex object or process. Technical writing is common in medical and technological fields, in which complex ideas of mathematics, science, and engineering need to be explained simply and clearly. To ease comprehension, a technical passage usually proceeds in a very logical order. Technical passages often have clear headings and subheadings, which are used to keep the reader oriented in the text. Additionally, you will find that these passages divide sections up with numbers or letters. Many technical passages look more like an outline than a piece of prose. The amount of jargon or difficult vocabulary will vary in a technical passage depending on the intended audience. As much as possible, technical passages try to avoid language that the reader will have to research in order to understand the message, yet readers will find that jargon cannot always be avoided.

PERSUASIVE PASSAGE

A **persuasive** passage is meant to change the mind of readers and lead them into agreement with the author. The persuasive intent may be very obvious or quite difficult to discern. In some cases, a persuasive passage will be indistinguishable from one that is informative. Both passages make an assertion and offer supporting details. However, a persuasive passage is more likely to appeal to the reader's emotions and to make claims based on opinion. Persuasive passages may not describe alternate positions, but when they do, they often display significant bias. Readers may find that a persuasive passage is giving the author's viewpoint, or the passage may adopt a seemingly objective tone. A persuasive passage is successful if it can make a convincing argument and win the trust of the reader.

> **Review Video: Persuasive Essay**
> Visit mometrix.com/academy and enter code: 621428

IDENTIFYING AN AUTHOR'S POSITION

In order to be an effective reader, one must pay attention to the author's **position** and purpose. Even those texts that seem objective and impartial, like textbooks, have a position and bias. Readers need to take these positions into account when considering the author's message. When an author uses emotional language or clearly favors one side of an argument, his or her position is clear. However, the author's position may be evident not only in what he or she writes, but also in what he or she doesn't write. In a normal setting, a reader would want to review some other texts on the same topic in order to develop a view of the author's position. If this was not possible, then you would want to acquire some background about the author. However, since you are in the middle of an exam and the only source of information is the text, you should look for language and argumentation that seems to indicate a particular stance on the subject.

> **Review Video: Author's Position**
> Visit mometrix.com/academy and enter code: 827954

PURPOSE

Usually, identifying the **purpose** of an author is easier than identifying his or her position. In most cases, the author has no interest in hiding his or her purpose. A text that is meant to entertain, for instance, should be written to please the reader. Most narratives, or stories, are written to entertain, though they may also inform or persuade. Informative texts are easy to identify, while the most difficult purpose of a text to identify is persuasion because the author has an interest in making this purpose hard to detect. When a reader discovers that the author is trying to persuade, he or she should be skeptical of the argument. For this reason, persuasive texts often try to establish an entertaining tone and hope to amuse the reader into agreement. On the other hand, an informative tone may be implemented to create an appearance of authority and objectivity.

An author's purpose is evident often in the organization of the text (e.g., section headings in bold font points to an informative text). However, you may not have such organization available to you in your exam. Instead, if the author makes his or her main idea clear from the beginning, then the likely purpose of the text is to inform. If the author begins by making a claim and provides various arguments to support that claim, then the purpose is probably to persuade. If the author tells a story or seems to want the attention of the reader more than to push a particular point or deliver information, then his or her purpose is most likely to entertain. As a reader, you must judge authors on how well they accomplish their purpose. In other words, you need to consider the type of passage (e.g., technical, persuasive, etc.) that the author has written and whether the author has followed the requirements of the passage type.

> **Review Video: Understanding the Author's Intent**
> Visit mometrix.com/academy and enter code: 511819

PERSUASIVE WRITING

In a persuasive essay, the author is attempting to change the reader's mind or convince him or her of something that he or she did not believe previously. There are several identifying characteristics of persuasive writing. One is opinion presented as fact. When authors attempt to persuade readers, they often present their opinions as if they were fact. Readers must be on guard for statements that sound factual but which cannot be subjected to research, observation, or experiment. Another characteristic of persuasive writing is emotional language. An author will often try to play on the emotions of readers by appealing to their sympathy or sense of morality. When an author uses colorful or evocative language with the intent of arousing the reader's passions, then the author may be attempting to persuade. Finally, in many cases, a persuasive text will give an unfair explanation of opposing positions, if these positions are mentioned at all.

> **Review Video: Using Rhetorical Strategies for Persuasion**
> Visit mometrix.com/academy and enter code: 302658

INFORMATIVE TEXTS

An **informative text** is written to educate and enlighten readers. Informative texts are almost always nonfiction and are rarely structured as a story. The intention of an informative text is to deliver information in the most comprehensible way. So, look for the structure of the text to be very clear. In an informative text, the thesis statement is one or two sentences that normally appears at the end of the first paragraph. The author may use some colorful language, but he or she is likely to put more emphasis on clarity and precision. Informative essays do not typically appeal to the emotions. They often contain facts and figures and rarely include the opinion of the author; however, readers should remain aware of the possibility for a bias as those facts are presented. Sometimes a persuasive essay can resemble an informative essay, especially if the author maintains an even tone and presents his or her views as if they were established fact.

> **Review Video: Informational Text**
> Visit mometrix.com/academy and enter code: 924964

ENTERTAINING TEXTS

The success or failure of an author's intent to **entertain** is determined by those who read the author's work. Entertaining texts may be either fiction or nonfiction, and they may describe real or imagined people, places, and events. Entertaining texts are often narratives or poems. A text that is written to entertain is likely to contain colorful language that engages the imagination and the emotions. Such writing often features a great deal of figurative language, which typically enlivens the subject matter with images and analogies.

Though an entertaining text is not usually written to persuade or inform, authors may accomplish both of these tasks in their work. An entertaining text may appeal to the reader's emotions and cause him or her to think differently about a particular subject. In any case, entertaining texts tend to showcase the personality of the author more than other types of writing.

> **Review Video: Figurative Language**
> Visit mometrix.com/academy and enter code: 584902

EXPRESSION OF FEELINGS

When an author intends to **express feelings,** he or she may use expressive and bold language. An author may write with emotion for any number of reasons. Sometimes, authors will express feelings because they are describing a personal situation of great pain or happiness. In other situations, authors will attempt to persuade the reader and will use emotion to stir up the passions. This kind of expression is easy to identify when the writer uses phrases like *I felt* and *I sense*. However, readers may find that the author will simply describe feelings without introducing them. As a reader, you must know the importance of recognizing when an author is expressing emotion and not to become overwhelmed by sympathy or passion. Readers should maintain some detachment so that they can still evaluate the strength of the author's argument or the quality of the writing.

POINT OF VIEW

Another element that impacts a text is the author's point-of-view. The **point of view** of a text is the perspective from which a passage is told. An author will always have a point of view about a story before he or she draws up a plot line. The author will know what events they want to take place, how they want the characters to interact, and how they want the story to resolve. An author will also have an opinion on the topic or series of events which is presented in the story that is based on their prior experience and beliefs.

The two main points of view that authors use--especially in a work of fiction--are first person and third person. If the narrator of the story is also the main character, or *protagonist*, the text is written in first-person point of view. In first person, the author writes from the perspective of *I*. Third-person point of view is probably the most common that authors use in their passages. Using third person, authors refer to each character by using *he* or *she*. In third-person omniscient, the narrator is not a character in the story and tells the story of all of the characters at the same time.

Integration of Knowledge and Ideas

FACT AND OPINION

Readers must always be conscious of the distinction between fact and opinion. A fact can be subjected to analysis and can be either proved or disproved. An opinion, on the other hand, is the author's personal thoughts or feelings which may not be alterable by research or evidence. If the author writes that the distance from New York to Boston is about two hundred miles, then he or she is stating a fact. If an author writes that New York is too crowded, then he or she is giving an opinion because there is no objective standard for overpopulation.

An opinion may be indicated by words like *believe*, *think*, or *feel*. Readers must be aware that an opinion may be supported by facts. For instance, the author might give the population density of New York as a reason for an overcrowded population. An opinion supported by fact tends to be more convincing. On the other hand, when authors support their opinions with other opinions, readers should not be persuaded by the argument to any degree.

> **Review Video: Distinguishing Fact and Opinion**
> Visit mometrix.com/academy and enter code: 870899

BIASES AND STEREOTYPES

Every author has a point-of-view, but authors demonstrate a bias when they ignore reasonable counterarguments or distort opposing viewpoints. A bias is evident whenever the author is unfair or inaccurate in his or her presentation. Bias may be intentional or unintentional, and readers should be skeptical of the author's argument. Remember that a biased author may still be correct; however, the author will be correct in spite of his or her bias, not because of the bias. A stereotype is like a bias, yet a stereotype is applied specifically to a group or place. Stereotyping is considered to be particularly abhorrent because the practice promotes negative generalizations about people. Readers should be very cautious of authors who stereotype in their writing. These faulty assumptions typically reveal the author's ignorance and lack of curiosity.

> **Review Video: Bias and Stereotype**
> Visit mometrix.com/academy and enter code: 644829

EVALUATING AN ARGUMENT

Argumentative and persuasive passages take a stand on a debatable issue, seek to explore all sides of the issue, and find the best possible solution. Argumentative and persuasive passages should not be combative or abusive. The word *argument* may remind you of two or more people shouting at each other and walking away in anger. However, an argumentative or persuasive passage should be a calm and reasonable presentation of an author's ideas for others to consider. When an author writes reasonable arguments, his or her goal is not to win or have the last word. Instead, authors want to reveal current understanding of the question at hand and suggest a solution to a problem. The purpose of argument and persuasion in a free society is to reach the best solution.

EVIDENCE

The term **text evidence** refers to information that supports a main point or minor points and can help lead the reader to a conclusion. Information used as text evidence is precise, descriptive, and factual. A main point is often followed by supporting details that provide evidence to back up a claim. For example, a passage may include the claim that winter occurs during opposite months in the Northern and Southern hemispheres. Text evidence based on this claim may include countries where winter occurs in opposite months along with reasons that winter occurs at different times of the year in separate hemispheres (due to the tilt of the Earth as it rotates around the sun).

> **Review Video: Textual Evidence**
> Visit mometrix.com/academy and enter code: 486236

Evidence needs to be provided that supports the thesis and additional arguments. Most arguments must be supported by facts or statistics. Facts are something that is known with certainty and have been verified by several independent individuals. Examples and illustrations add an emotional component to arguments. With this component, you persuade readers in ways that facts and statistics cannot. The emotional component is effective when used with objective information that can be confirmed.

CREDIBILITY

The text used to support an argument can be the argument's downfall if the text is not credible. A text is **credible**, or believable, when the author is knowledgeable and objective, or unbiased. The author's motivations for writing the text play a critical role in determining the credibility of the text and must be evaluated when assessing that credibility. Reports written about the ozone layer by an environmental scientist and a hairdresser will have a different level of credibility.

APPEAL TO EMOTION

Sometimes, authors will appeal to the reader's emotion in an attempt to persuade or to distract the reader from the weakness of the argument. For instance, the author may try to inspire the pity of the reader by delivering a heart-rending story. An author also might use the bandwagon approach, in which he suggests that his opinion is correct because it is held by the majority. Some authors resort to name-calling, in which insults and harsh words are delivered to the opponent in an attempt to distract. In advertising, a common appeal is the celebrity testimonial, in which a famous person endorses a product. Of course, the fact that a famous person likes something should not really mean anything to the reader. These and other emotional appeals are usually evidence of poor reasoning and a weak argument.

COUNTER ARGUMENTS

When authors give both sides to the argument, they build trust with their readers. As a reader, you should start with an undecided or neutral position. If an author presents only his or her side to the argument, then you will need to be concerned at best.

Building common ground with neutral or opposed readers can be appealing to skeptical readers. Sharing values with undecided readers can allow people to switch positions without giving up what they feel is important. For people who may oppose a position, they need to feel that they can change their minds without betraying who they are as a person. This appeal to having an open mind can be a powerful tool in arguing a position without antagonizing other views. Objections can be countered on a point-by-point basis or in a summary paragraph. Be mindful of how an author points out flaws in counter arguments. If they are unfair to the other side of the argument, then you should lose trust with the author.

PRIMARY SOURCES AND INTERNET SOURCES

PRIMARY SOURCES

When conducting research, it is important to depend on reputable primary sources. A primary source is the documentary evidence closest to the subject being studied. For instance, the primary sources for an essay about penguins would be photographs and recordings of the birds, as well as accounts of people who have studied penguins in person. A secondary source would be a review of a movie about penguins or a book outlining the observations made by others. A primary source should be credible and, if it is on a subject that is still being explored, recent. One way to assess the credibility of a work is to see how often it is mentioned in other books and articles on the same subject. Just by reading the works cited and bibliographies of other books, one can get a sense of what the reliable sources authorities in the field are.

INTERNET SOURCES

The Internet was once considered a poor place to find sources for an essay or article, but its credibility has improved greatly over the years. Still, students need to exercise caution when performing research online. The best sources are those affiliated with established institutions, such as universities, public libraries, and think tanks. Most newspapers are available online, and many of them allow the public to browse their archives. Magazines frequently offer similar services. When obtaining information from an unknown website, however, one must exercise considerably more caution. A website can be considered trustworthy if it is referenced by other sites that are known to be reputable. Also, credible sites tend to be properly maintained and frequently updated. A site is easier to trust when the author provides some information about himself, including some credentials that indicate expertise in the subject matter.

MAKING PREDICTIONS AND DRAWING CONCLUSIONS
PREDICTIONS

A prediction is a guess about what will happen next. Readers constantly make predictions based on what they have read and what they already know. Consider the following sentence: *Staring at the computer screen in shock, Kim blindly reached over for the brimming glass of water on the shelf to her side.* The sentence suggests that Kim is agitated, and that she is not looking at the glass that she is going to pick up. So, a reader might predict that Kim is going to knock over the glass. Of course, not every prediction will be accurate: perhaps Kim will pick the glass up cleanly. Nevertheless, the author has certainly created the expectation that the water might be spilled. Predictions are always subject to revision as the reader acquires more information.

> **Review Video: Predictive Reading**
> Visit mometrix.com/academy and enter code: 437248

FORESHADOWING

Foreshadowing uses hints in a narrative to let the audience anticipate future events in the plot. Foreshadowing can be indicated by a number of literary devices and figures of speech, as well as through dialogue between characters.

DRAWING CONCLUSIONS

In addition to inference and prediction, readers must often **draw conclusions** about the information they have read. When asked for a *conclusion* that may be drawn, look for critical "hedge" phrases, such as *likely, may, can, will often*, among many others. When you are being tested on this knowledge, remember the question that writers insert into these hedge phrases to cover every possibility. Often an answer will be wrong simply because there is no room for exception. Extreme positive or negative answers (such as always or never) are usually not correct. The reader should not use any outside knowledge that is not gathered from the passage to answer the related questions. Correct answers can be derived straight from the passage.

The Science Test

The Science test may scare you. For even the most accomplished student, many of the terms will be unfamiliar. General test-taking skill will help the most. Make sure you don't run out of time: move quickly and use the easy pacing methods we outline in the test-taking tactics section.

The most important thing you can do is to ignore your fears and jump into the test immediately. Don't be overwhelmed by all of the strange-sounding terms. You have to jump into the test like jumping into a pool; all at once is the easiest way. Once you get past the jargon, you'll find that the Science Reasoning test is in some ways easier than even the Reading Test. Unfortunately, most students don't finish this test. This is why managing your time on this test is at least as important as on the Math test.

The test lasts 35-minutes, 5 minutes per section.

The first thing to do is to read the passage. Use 2 minutes to do this. Really try to understand what's going on, treating all of the scientific terms as you would characters in a novel; just accept their names as they are, and follow the story. Use another 3 minutes to answer as many questions as you can. It's important to answer all of the easy questions.

Overall, the Science Reasoning is the test that is the hardest to study for and has the lowest test average for all test-takers, even lower than the Math. If science is a subject you take because you have to, and not because you want to, your primary goal on Science Reasoning is damage control; you want to prevent it from dragging down your higher scores when the PreACT averages your test scores to get the composite.

In addition, the Science Reasoning test is probably unlike any other science test you've ever taken in high school. It's vital that you work a few practice Science Reasoning tests before the test day. Familiarity alone will boost your score by 1-2 points.

Life Science

FUNCTIONS FOR LIFE AND ENERGY

CELLULAR RESPIRATION

Cellular respiration is a set of metabolic reactions. These reactions change chemical bonds into energy that is stored in the form of ATP. Respiration has many oxidation and reduction reactions. This happens with the electron transport system inside the cell.

Oxidation is a loss of electrons. Reduction is a gain of electrons. Electrons in C-H (carbon/hydrogen) and C-C (carbon/carbon) bonds are given to oxygen atoms. Some systems in cellular respiration are glycolysis, the Krebs cycle, and the electron transport chain.

The two forms of respiration are aerobic and anaerobic. Aerobic respiration is very common. With aerobic respiration, oxygen is the final electron acceptor. In anaerobic respiration, the final electron acceptor is not oxygen. Aerobic respiration causes more ATP than anaerobic respiration.

PHOTOSYNTHESIS

Photosynthesis changes sunlight into energy in plant cells. This can also happen in some types of bacteria and protists. Carbon dioxide and water are changed into glucose during photosynthesis. Light is needed in this process. Cyanobacteria are thought to come from the first organisms to use photosynthesis about 3.5 billion years ago.

Photosynthesis is a form of cellular respiration. It happens in chloroplasts that use thylakoids. These thylakoids are structures in the membrane that have light reaction chemicals. Chlorophyll is a pigment that takes in light. During the process, water is used, and oxygen is released.

The equation for the chemical reaction that happens during photosynthesis:

$6H_2O + 6CO_2 \rightarrow C_6H_{12}O_6 + 6O_2$.

During photosynthesis, six molecules of water and six molecules of carbon dioxide react. So, one molecule of sugar and six molecules of oxygen are the products.

> **Review Video: Photosynthesis**
> Visit mometrix.com/academy and enter code: 227035

HOMEOSTASIS

Homeostasis is when an organism, cell, or body makes changes to stay balanced. A human body can maintain homeostasis with the release of hormones. Some hormones work in pairs. When a condition reaches an upper limit, a hormone is released to correct the condition. When a condition reaches the lower limit, another hormone is released. Hormones that work in this way are known as antagonistic. Insulin and glucagon are a pair of antagonistic hormones that help to manage the level of glucagon in the blood. Positive feedback loops can unbalance systems by increasing changes. A negative feedback loop acts to make a system more stable by handling changes.

CELL STRUCTURE

NUCLEAR PARTS OF A CELL

All eukaryotic cells have a nucleus. The nucleus is a small structure that holds the chromosomes. Also, the nucleus manages the DNA of a cell. The nucleus is the defining structure of eukaryotic cells. The nucleus is responsible for passing on genetic traits between generations. The nucleus has a nuclear envelope, nucleoplasm, a nucleolus, nuclear pores, chromatin, and ribosomes.

Chromosomes: These are tight, threadlike rods of DNA (deoxyribonucleic acid). DNA is the genetic material that stores information about the plant or animal.

Review Video: Cell Structure
Visit mometrix.com/academy and enter code: 591293

Review Video: Chromosomes
Visit mometrix.com/academy and enter code: 132083

Chromatin: This is a combination of DNA and protein that makes up chromosomes.

Nucleolus: This structure inside the nucleus is made of protein. The nucleolus is small and round. It does not have a membrane. This piece works in protein synthesis. Also, it combines and stores RNA (ribonucleic acid).

Nuclear envelope: This surrounds the structures of the nucleus. It has inner and outer membranes that are made of lipids.

Nuclear pores: These help in the trade of material between the nucleus and the cytoplasm.

Nucleoplasm: This is the liquid inside the nucleus. It is similar to cytoplasm.

OTHER PARTS OF A CELL

Ribosomes: Ribosomes help to put together proteins from amino acids. There are many in one cell. They make up about one fourth of the cell. Some cells have thousands of ribosomes. Some are free to move. Others are tied down in the rough endoplasmic reticulum.

Golgi complex (i.e., Golgi apparatus): This helps to put together materials. An example is proteins that are moved out of the cell. It is near the nucleus and has layers of membranes.

Vacuoles: These are sacs used for storage, digestion, and waste removal. There is one large vacuole in plant cells. Animal cells have small vacuoles. Sometimes animal cells have many vacuoles.

Vesicle: This is a small organelle inside a cell. It has a membrane and has many roles. One role is moving materials inside a cell.

Cytoskeleton: This has microtubules that help to shape and to support the cell.

Microtubules: These are part of the cytoskeleton and help support the cell. They are made of protein.

Cytosol: This is the liquid material in the cell. The liquid is mostly water. However, it also has some floating molecules.

Cytoplasm: This is a general term for the cytosol and the substructures (i.e., organelles) inside the plasma membrane. This is not for the parts in the nucleus.

Cell membrane (or plasma membrane): This is a barrier for the cell. It keeps cytoplasm in and keeps substances not inside the cell out of the cell. It decides what can enter and exit the cell.

Endoplasmic reticulum: There are two types of endoplasmic reticulum. One is rough that has ribosomes on the surface. The other is smooth and does not have ribosomes on the surface. It is a network of tubes that is the transport system of a cell. It is tied to the nuclear membrane. Also, it goes through the cytoplasm to the cell membrane.

Mitochondrion (plural: mitochondria): These cell structures can be different in their size and how many are in a cell. Some cells may have one mitochondrion. Other cells may have thousands. The mitochondrion has many roles. One important role is to make ATP. The mitochondrion also helps with cell growth and death. Mitochondria have their own DNA. This DNA is separate from what is in the nucleus.

CELL CYCLE

A cell cycle is when a cell reproduces. This includes cell growth, the copy of genetic material, and cell division. Complex organisms with many cells use the cell cycle. The cell cycle replaces cells as they wear out. The entire cell cycle in animal cells can take 24 hours. The time needed is different for different cell types. An example is human skin cells. They are always reproducing. Other cells rarely divide.

When neurons are mature, they do not grow or divide. The two ways that cells can make more cells are through meiosis and mitosis. When cells make copies through mitosis, the "daughter cell" is an exact copy of the parent cell. When cells divide through meiosis, the daughter cells have different genetic coding than the parent cell. Meiosis only happens in special reproductive cells called gametes.

CELL DIVISION

Cell division happens in organisms so they can grow and replace cells that are old, worn out, or damaged.

Chromatids: During cell division, the DNA is copied. So, the chromatids are the two exact copies of chromosomes that are joined at the centromere to make an "X."

Gametes: These are cells used by organisms to reproduce sexually. Gametes in humans are haploid. This means that they have 23 chromosomes. This is half of the organism's genetic information. Other human cells have all 46 chromosomes.

Haploid/diploid: Haploid means there is one set of chromosomes. Diploid means there are two sets of chromosomes. There is one set from each parent.

MITOSIS

The following are the stages of **mitosis**:

Interphase: The cell gets ready for division by making copies of its genetic and cytoplasmic material. This step can be further divided into G_1, S, and G_2.

Prophase: The chromatin thickens into chromosomes. Then, the nuclear membrane begins to break down. Pairs of centrioles move to opposite sides of the cell. Then, spindle fibers are made. The mitotic spindle is made from cytoskeleton parts. This spindle moves chromosomes inside the cell.

Metaphase: The spindle moves to the center of the cell. Then, chromosome pairs line up along the center of the spindle structure.

Anaphase: The pairs of chromosomes are called sisters. In this stage, these pairs begin to pull apart and can bend. When they are pulled apart, they are called daughter chromosomes. In the cell membrane, grooves can be seen.

Telophase: In this stage, the spindle breaks down, the nuclear membranes are made again, and the chromosomes return to chromatin. In animal cells, the membrane is divided. In plant cells, a new cell wall is made.

Cytokinesis: This is the physical splitting of the cell into two cells. Some think that this happens after telophase. Others say that it happens from anaphase through telophase.

> **Review Video: Mitosis**
> Visit mometrix.com/academy and enter code: 849894

MEIOSIS

Meiosis has the same phases as mitosis. However, these stages happen twice. Also, different events happen during some phases of meiosis than mitosis. The events that happen in the first phase of meiosis are interphase (I), prophase (I), metaphase (I), anaphase (I), telophase (I), and cytokinesis (I).

In this first phase of meiosis, chromosomes cross over and genetic material is traded. Also, tetrads (i.e., four) of four chromatids are made. The nuclear membrane dissolves. Homologous pairs of chromatids are separated. Then, they move to different poles. At this point, one cell has been divided to make two cells.

Next, each cell goes through a second cell division. The stages are prophase (II), metaphase (II), anaphase (II), telophase (II), and cytokinesis (II). This makes four daughter cells with different sets of chromosomes. The daughter cells are haploid. This means that they have half the genetic material of the parent cell.

> **Review Video: Meiosis**
> Visit mometrix.com/academy and enter code: 247334

IMPORTANT VOCABULARY

Meiosis: This is when the cell divides and the number of chromosomes in the parent cell is halved to make four gamete cells.

Mitosis: This is when the cell nucleus separates and the parent cell divides into two daughter cells.

Organelle: A general term for an organ or smaller structure inside a cell. Membrane-bound organelles are in eukaryotic cells.

RNA: Ribonucleic acid is a type of molecule that has a long chain (i.e., polymer) of nucleotide units.

Polymer: This is a compound of large molecules made by repeating monomers.

Monomer: A monomer is a small molecule. It is a single compound that makes chemical bonds with other monomers to make a polymer.

Nucleotides: These are molecules that combine to make DNA and RNA.

Nucleoid: This is the nucleus-like mass of DNA that has the chromatin in a prokaryotic cell.

Gene expression: This is the use of information in a gene. Usually, this is done in the processes of transcription and translation and ends in a protein product.

Transcription: This is the putting together of RNA. The information for this event comes from DNA.

Translation: This is the decoding of mRNA (i.e., messenger RNA) that is used in the building of protein. It happens after transcription.

Cellular differentiation: This is the event where a less specialized cell becomes a more specialized cell.

GENETICS
DNA

Chromosomes are made of genes. A gene is a single unit of genetic information. Genes are made of deoxyribonucleic acid. DNA is a nucleic acid in the cell nucleus. DNA is also in the mitochondria. DNA makes copies of itself to pass on genetic information. The DNA in almost all cells is the same. It is also part of the biosynthesis of proteins.

The model of DNA is known as a double helix. A helix is a curve. So, a double helix is two congruent curves that are connected by horizontal pieces. The model can be compared to a spiral staircase.

The British scientist Rosalind Elsie Franklin is the one who took the x-ray diffraction image in 1952. This image was used by Francis Crick and James Watson to put together the double-helix model of DNA. With this information, they were able to think about its important role in carrying and moving genetic information.

> **Review Video: DNA**
> Visit mometrix.com/academy and enter code: 639552

DNA STRUCTURE

DNA has the shape of a double helix. This shape looks like a twisted ladder. It is made of nucleotides. Nucleotides have a five-carbon sugar (i.e., pentose), a phosphate group, and a nitrogenous base. Two bases pair up to make the bars of the ladder. The "side rails" or backbone is made of the covalently bonded sugar and phosphate. The bases are connected to each other with hydrogen bonds. These bonds can be easily separated for replication to happen.

There are four types of nitrogenous bases: adenine (A), guanine (G), cytosine (C), and thymine (T). Adenine (A) pairs with thymine (T). Cytosine (C) pairs with guanine (G). There are about 3 billion bases in human DNA. The bases are almost the same in everybody. However, their order is different. The order of these bases makes diversity in people.

MENDELIAN GENETICS
MENDEL'S LAWS

Mendel's laws are the law of segregation (the first law), the law of independent assortment (the second law), and the law of dominance (the third law). The law of segregation states that there are two alleles and that half of the total number of alleles are contributed by each parent organism. The law of independent assortment states that traits are passed on randomly and are not influenced by other traits. The exception to this is linked traits. A Punnett square can illustrate how alleles combine from the contributing genes to form various phenotypes. One set of a parent's genes are put in columns, while the genes from the other parent are placed in rows. The allele combinations are shown in each cell. The law of dominance states that when two different alleles are present in a pair, the dominant one is expressed. A Punnett square can be used to predict the outcome of crosses.

> **Review Video: What is a Punnett Square?**
> Visit mometrix.com/academy and enter code: 853855

NON-MENDELIAN TERMS

Polygenic inheritance: This goes past Mendel's idea that one gene affects one trait. This idea says that traits are affected by more than one gene. Also, environmental influences on development are important with this idea. An example is an individual who inherits genes that help decide height. However, if the person does not have the needed nutrients, then they may not reach their full height.

Genetic disposition: This is an increased chance of a certain disease that is genetically inherited. However, it may not carry out in a person. For example, people with certain skin types are more likely to have skin cancer. If they limit their time in the Sun, then they may not experience skin cancer.

Multiple alleles: Only two alleles make up a gene. When there are three or more possible alleles, it is known as a multiple allele. A gene where only two alleles are possible is called polymorphic.

Complete dominance: This is when a homozygous pair of dominant alleles (AA) and a heterozygous pair of alleles (Aa) carries out the same phenotype. Dominant genes have the following characteristics:

- they are expressed in each generation
- they are passed on to about half the offspring
- a parent that does not express the trait cannot pass it on to offspring.

Mendel's idea for complete dominance says that one gene that has two alleles is the only piece in the creation of a phenotype. However, most traits are more complex.

> **Review Video: Mendelian and Non-Mendelian Genetics**
> Visit mometrix.com/academy and enter code: 113159

EVOLUTION

THREE TYPES OF EVOLUTION

Three types of evolution are divergent, convergent, and parallel.

Divergent evolution is when two species become different over time. This can be caused by one of the species changing to a different environment.

Convergent evolution is when two species start out fairly different. However, they evolve to share many similar traits.

Parallel evolution is when species do not become more or less similar over time. Also, this is for species that are not similar.

Mechanisms of evolution are descent (i.e., the passing on of genetic information), mutation, migration, natural selection, and genetic variation and drift. The biological definition of **species** is a group of individuals that can mate and reproduce. **Speciation** is the evolution of a new biological species. The biological species concept (BSC) says that a species is a community of individuals that can reproduce and have a clear role in nature.

THEORIES OF EVOLUTION

NATURAL SELECTION

Natural selection: This theory says that the traits that give a species a better chance of survival are passed on to future generations. Members of a species that do not have the trait die before they reproduce. Charles Darwin's four principles are:

- From generation to generation, there are different members in a species
- Genes decide differences
- More members are born than will survive to a mature stage
- Certain genes help an organism to survive

GRADUALISM

Gradualism: This is the idea that evolution goes at a steady pace. Also, it does not have sudden additions of new species or features from one generation to the next. This can be contrasted with punctuated equilibrium.

PUNCTUATED EQUILIBRIUM

Punctuated equilibrium: This idea says that evolution has very long stretches of time with no change (i.e., stasis). Then, this stasis is followed by smaller amounts of time (e.g., hundreds of thousands of years) of fast change. This can be contrasted with gradualism.

Chemistry

Matter is a substance that has mass and takes up space (i.e., volume). Solid, liquid, and gas are the three states of matter. These states come from the differences in the distances and angles between molecules or atoms. This causes differences in the energy that keeps them together.

STATES OF MATTER

In the past, there were three states of matter. **Solid** states are rigid or nearly rigid and have strong bonds. The molecules or atoms in **liquids** move around and have weak bonds. However, these bonds are not weak enough to break. Molecules or atoms of **gases** move almost independently of each other. They are far apart and do not make bonds.

Today, matter has four states. The fourth is **plasma**. This is an ionized gas that has some electrons. These electrons are described as free because they are not tied to an atom or molecule.

THE ATOM

All matter is made of **atoms**. These atoms are made of a nucleus and electrons. The **nucleus** has **protons** and **neutrons**. They have mass and an electrical charge. The nucleus has a positive charge because of protons. Neutrons are the uncharged atomic particles that are in the nucleus. **Electrons** have a negative charge, and they orbit the nucleus. The nucleus has much more mass than the surrounding electrons.

The number of protons in the nucleus is the atomic number of an element. Carbon atoms have six protons. So, the atomic number of carbon is 6. The nucleon is the combination of neutrons and protons.

Atoms can bond together to make molecules. Atoms that have an equal number of protons and electrons are electrically neutral. The number of protons and electrons in an atom may not be equal. In this case, the atom has a positive or negative charge and is an ion. The number of protons minus the number of electrons gives the charge of an atom.

ATOMIC NUMBER AND ATOMIC MASS

The atomic number of an element is the number of protons in the nucleus of an atom. Atoms with a neutral charge have an atomic number that is equal to the number of electrons.

Atomic mass is also known as the mass number. The atomic mass (A) is equal to the number of protons (Z) plus the number of neutrons (N). This can be seen in the equation $A = Z + N$. The mass of electrons in an atom is not counted because it is so small.

Atomic mass unit (amu) is the smallest unit of mass. This is equal to 1/12 of the mass of the carbon isotope carbon-12. A mole (mol) is a measurement of molecular weight. This measurement is equal to the molecule's amu in grams. As an example, carbon has an amu of 12. So, a mole of carbon weighs 12 grams. One mole is equal to about 6.02×10^{23} atoms or molecules. This amount is also known as the Avogadro constant or Avogadro's number (NA). Another way to say this is that one mole of a substance is the same as one Avogadro's number of that substance. As an example, one mole of chlorine is 6.02×10^{23} chlorine atoms.

> **Review Video: What is the Mole Concept?**
> Visit mometrix.com/academy and enter code: 593205

ELECTRONS

Electrons orbit the nucleus at different levels. These levels are known as layers, shells, or clouds. An electron will move to the lowest energy level that it can. An atom has a stable layout of electrons when an atom has all its electrons in the lowest available positions.

The outermost electron shell of an atom in its uncombined state is known as the **valence shell**. The electrons there are called valence electrons. Their number decides their bonding behavior. Atoms will act to fill or to empty their valence shells. Electrons can absorb or release energy. This can change the location of their orbit. Also, this can allow them to break free from the atom. The valence layer can have or share eight electrons.

Chemical bonds have a negative-positive attraction between an electron or electrons and the nucleus of an atom or nuclei of more than one atom. The attraction keeps the atom connected. Also, it helps to make bonds with other atoms and molecules.

PHYSICAL AND CHEMICAL PROPERTIES

Chemical properties cannot be seen or measured without chemical reactions. Physical properties can be seen or measured without chemical reactions. These properties are color, elasticity, mass, volume, and temperature.

Mass measures how much of a substance is in an object.

Weight measures the gravitational pull of the Earth on an object.

Density is a measure of the amount of mass per unit volume.

The formula to find density is mass divided by volume (D=m/V). It is expressed in terms of mass per cubic unit (e.g., grams per cubic centimeter (g/cm^3)).

Volume measures the amount of space taken up.

The volume of an irregular shape can be known by finding out how much water it displaces.

Specific gravity measures the ratio of a substance's density to the density of water.

> **Review Video: Mass, Weight, Volume, Density, and Specific Gravity**
> Visit mometrix.com/academy and enter code: 920570

Physical changes and chemical reactions are everyday events. Physical changes do not bring about different substances. An example is when water becomes ice. It has gone through a physical change, not a chemical change. It has changed its state, not what it is made of. In other words, it is still H_2O.

Chemical properties deal with the particles that make up the structure of a substance. Chemical properties can be seen when chemical changes happen. The chemical properties of a substance are influenced by its electron configuration. This is decided somewhat by the number of protons in the nucleus (i.e., the atomic number). An example is carbon that has 6 protons and 6 electrons. The outermost valence electrons of an element mainly decides its chemical properties. Chemical reactions may give or take energy.

PROPERTIES OF WATER

The important properties of water (H_2O) are high polarity, hydrogen bonding, cohesiveness, adhesiveness, high specific heat, high latent heat, and high heat of vaporization. Water is vital to life as we know it. The reason is that water is one of the main parts of many living things.

Water is a liquid at room temperature. The high specific heat of water means that it does not easily break its hydrogen bonds. Also, it resists heat and motion. This is why it has a high boiling point and high vaporization point.

Most substances are denser in their solid forms. However, water is different because its solid-state floats in its liquid state. Water is cohesive. This means that it is drawn to itself. It is also adhesive. This means that it draws in other molecules. If water will attach to another substance, the substance is said to be hydrophilic. Because of its cohesive and adhesive properties, water makes a good solvent. Substances with polar ions and molecules easily dissolve in water.

VOCABULARY

Elements: These are substances that are made of only one type of atom.

Compounds: These are substances that have two or more elements. Compounds are made from chemical reactions. Often, they have different properties than the original elements. Compounds are broken down by a chemical reaction. They are not separated by a physical reaction.

Solutions: These are homogeneous mixtures. They are made of two or more substances that have become one.

Mixtures: Two or more substances that are combined. However, they have not reacted chemically with each other. Mixtures can be separated with physical methods and compounds cannot.

Heat: This is the transfer of energy from a body or system from thermal contact. Heat is made of random motion and the vibration of atoms, molecules, and ions. Higher temperatures cause more motion with atoms or molecules.

Energy: The capacity to do work.

Work: the amount of energy that must be transferred to overcome a force. An example of work is lifting an object in the air. The opposing force that must be overcome is gravity. Work is measured in joules (J). The rate that work is done is known as power.

Earth and Space Science

ASTRONOMY

Astronomy studies the positions, movements, and structures of celestial objects. Celestial is something that is in the sky or outer space. Objects are the Sun, the Moon, planets, asteroids, meteors, comets, stars, galaxies, the universe, and other space objects. The term astronomy has its roots in the Greek words "astro" and "nomos," which means "laws of the stars."

> **Review Video: Astronomy**
> Visit mometrix.com/academy and enter code: 640556

GALAXIES

Galaxies are made of stars and dark matter. Dwarf galaxies can have as few as 10 million stars. Giant galaxies can have as many as 1 trillion stars. Galaxies are gravitationally bound. This means that the stars, star systems, gases, and dust spin around the galaxy's center. The Earth is in the Milky Way galaxy. The nearest galaxy to the Milky Way is the Andromeda galaxy.

Galaxies can be labeled by their visual shape. Examples are the elliptical, spiral, irregular, and starburst galaxies. It is estimated that there are more than 100 billion galaxies in the universe. The space between two galaxies is a gas that has an average density of less than one atom per cubic meter. Galaxies are organized into clusters which make superclusters. Up to 90% of the mass of galaxies may be dark mark. Today, dark matter is not understood very well.

> **Review Video: Dark Matter**
> Visit mometrix.com/academy and enter code: 251909

STARS

There are different life cycles for stars after they begin and enter into the main sequence stage. Small, somewhat cold red dwarfs with low masses burn hydrogen slowly. They will remain in the main sequence for hundreds of billions of years. Large, hot supergiants will leave the main sequence after just a few million years. Hydrogen--in its plasma state--is the most common chemical element in stars' main sequences.

A nuclear fusion reaction is when multiple atomic nuclei collide to make a new nucleus. If nuclear fusion of hydrogen into helium begins, a star is born. The "main sequence" of a star's life has nuclear fusion reactions. During this time, the star shrinks over billions of years to make up for the lost heat and light energy. As the star shrinks, the temperature, density, and pressure rise at the star's core. So, the cycle continues.

The Sun is a mid-sized star that may be in the main sequence for 10 billion years. After the main sequence, the star will grow to become a red giant. Depending on the original mass of the star, it can become a black dwarf. Then, it will become a small, cooling white dwarf. Massive stars become red supergiants and sometimes blue supergiants. Then, they explode in a supernova and become neutron stars. The largest stars can become black holes.

SOLAR SYSTEM

A solar system has a star and other objects that move in or around it. The start to the solar system began with the collapse of a cloud of interstellar gas and dust. This collapse made the solar nebula. The reason for the collapse is that the cloud was disturbed. As it collapsed, it heated up and compressed at the center. This made a flat protoplanetary disk with a protostar at the center. A

171

protoplanetary disk is spinning disk of gas that is around a new star. Planets were made from the growth of the disk.

Then, gas cooled and condensed into small pieces of rock, metal, and ice. These pieces collided and made larger pieces. Then, the pieces became the size of small asteroids. Eventually, some became large enough to have enough gravity to affect objects around it.

Objects move around and are tied by gravity to a star called the Sun. These objects include: planets, dwarf planets, moons, asteroids, meteoroids, cosmic dust, and comets. The definition of planets has changed. At one time, there were nine planets in the solar system. There are now eight. Planetary objects in the solar system include four inner planets: Mercury, Venus, Earth, and Mars. These planets are small, dense, and rocky. They do not have rings, and they have few or no moons.

The four outer planets are Jupiter, Saturn, Uranus, and Neptune. These planets are large and have low densities, and they have rings and moons. They are also known as gas giants. The asteroid belt comes between the inner and outer planets. Beyond Neptune is the Kuiper belt. Inside this belt are five dwarf planets: Ceres, Pluto, Haumea, Makemake, and Eris.

> **Review Video: <u>The Solar System</u>**
> Visit mometrix.com/academy and enter code: 273231
>
> **Review Video: <u>Terrestrial Planets</u>**
> Visit mometrix.com/academy and enter code: 100346

EARTH'S ATMOSPHERE

The atmosphere is made of 78% nitrogen, 21% oxygen, and 1% argon. Other pieces are water vapor, carbon dioxide, dust particles, and chemicals from Earth. The air in the atmosphere becomes thinner at higher levels above the Earth's surface. At about 3 km above sea level, you will have difficulty breathing. As you go higher, the atmosphere begins to fade into space.

> **Review Video: <u>Earth's Atmosphere</u>**
> Visit mometrix.com/academy and enter code: 417614

ATMOSPHERIC LAYERS

Earth's atmosphere has five main layers. From lowest to highest, these are the troposphere, the stratosphere, the mesosphere, the thermosphere, and the exosphere. A transition layer is between each pair of layers. This layer is known as a pause.

The lowest layer of the atmosphere is called the *troposphere*. Its thickness is different at the poles and the equator. The thickness at the poles is about 7 km. The thickness at the equator is about 17 km. Most weather events happen at this layer. As you go higher in this layer, the temperature decreases. The troposphere has the tropopause which is the transitional layer of the stratosphere.

The *stratosphere* is the next level. This layer goes to a height of about 51 km. In the stratosphere, the temperature is reversed. In other words, the temperature increases as you go higher in this layer. The stratosphere includes the ozone layer. The ozone layer helps to block ultraviolet light from the Sun. The stratopause is the transitional layer to the mesosphere.

The *mesosphere* goes from the stratosphere to a height of about 81 km. In this layer, meteors are likely to burn. This is the coldest layer. So, as you go higher in this layer, the temperature drops.

This layer is thought of as the coldest place on Earth. The average temperature is -85 degrees Celsius.

The next layer is the *thermosphere*. This is where the International Space Station orbits. Temperature increases as you go higher in the thermosphere. The transitional layer to the exosphere is known as the thermopause.

Just past the thermosphere is the exobase. This is the base layer of the *exosphere*. The exosphere is the outermost layer that goes to 10,000 km. This layer is mostly made of hydrogen and helium.

Beyond the five main layers are the ionosphere, homosphere, heterosphere, and magnetosphere.

LAYERS OF EARTH

The Earth has many layers. Each has its own traits:

- Crust is the outermost layer of the Earth. It has the continents and the ocean basins. There are different thicknesses in different areas. For example, it is 35-70 km in the continents. Ocean basins can be about 5-10 km in thickness. Also, it is made of aluminosilicates.
- Mantle is about 2900 km thick. It is made of ferro-magnesium silicates. The mantle is divided into an upper and lower mantle. Most of the internal heat of the Earth is in the mantle. Large convective cells circulate heat. So, this may cause plate tectonic movement.
- Core is separated into the liquid outer core and the solid inner core. The outer core is 2300 km thick. This is made of nickel-iron alloy. The inner core is almost entirely iron. It is 12 km thick. The Earth's magnetic field is thought to be controlled by the liquid outer core.

> **Review Video: Earth's Structure**
> Visit mometrix.com/academy and enter code: 713016

GEOLOGY

WATER CYCLE

The water cycle is the movement of water on the Earth. Water can be in any of its three states for different parts of the cycle. The three states of water are liquid water, frozen ice, and water vapor.

The parts of the water cycle are precipitation, canopy interception, snow melt, runoff, infiltration, subsurface flow, evaporation, sublimation, advection, condensation, and transpiration.

> **Review Video: Hydrologic Cycle**
> Visit mometrix.com/academy and enter code: 426578

HUMAN AFFAIRS AND THE ENVIRONMENT

With the industrial revolution, science and technology have made a great influence on humans. There have been more discoveries in many fields. Many discoveries have led to better things for many people. These discoveries have led to longer life because of better nutrition, better medical care, and better workplaces. These changes have helped the lives of many humans. However, they have brought changes to the environment. Not every problem has been solved. Many still exist in one way or another. For example, there are ways to recycle, yet not everyone recycles because of the cost.

ECOSYSTEMS

Human influences on ecosystems have many forms and causes. These changes have an influence on plants and animals in many biomes and ecosystems. So, the changes can be seen in widespread areas and small areas. Humans take many natural resources to have food or to make energy. This changes their environment to make food, energy, and shelter. Changes come from:

- use or overuse of pesticides
- the invasion of a habitat
- over hunting and over fishing
- bringing plant and animal species into non-native ecosystems
- people refusing to recycle
- people bringing dangerous wastes into the environment

These actions have many effects. Some are acid rain, decrease of ozone, destruction of forests, and loss of more species. Other effects are genetic flaws and harm to animals.

GREENHOUSE EFFECT

The greenhouse effect is a natural and important event. Greenhouse gases (e.g., ozone, carbon dioxide, water vapor, and methane) trap infrared radiation that is reflected to the atmosphere. So, warm air is trapped as well. Without the greenhouse effect, temperatures on Earth would be 30 degrees less on average. Some human activity puts out more greenhouse gas than necessary. These events put more greenhouse gases into the air:

- burning natural gas and oil
- farming actions that release methane and nitrous oxide
- factory actions that make gases
- destroying forests put more greenhouse gases into the air

So, those events decrease the amount of oxygen available to balance out greenhouse gases. Now, too many greenhouse gases trap infrared radiation. So, this increases the temperature at the Earth's surface.

GLOBAL WARMING

Rising temperatures may lead to:

- higher sea levels as polar ice melts
- lower amounts of fresh water as coastal areas flood
- species extinction from changes in habitat
- increases in certain diseases
- lower standard of living for humans

Less fresh water and loss of habitat can lead to less agricultural production and food supply. Global warming brings drier and warmer weather. When dry areas become very arid, this upsets habitats for humans and other species. Increases in damaging weather (e.g., hurricanes or snowstorms) may be seen at unlikely latitudes. There may be more moisture in the atmosphere from evaporation. Global warming may cause the loss of glaciers and permafrost. Also, there is a greater chance for air pollution and acid rain.

Physics

NEWTON'S LAWS

FIRST LAW

An object at rest or in motion will stay at rest or in motion. This will continue until an outside force acts on the object. When a body stays in its present state of motion, the object is in a state known as inertia.

SECOND LAW

An object's acceleration depends on two things. One is the net force that acts on the object. The other is the mass of the object. This can be seen with the formula: $F = ma$. F is the net force acting on a body, m is the mass of the body, and a is its acceleration. Note that the mass is always a positive quantity. So, the acceleration is always in the same direction as the force.

THIRD LAW

This law says that for every action, there is an equal and opposite reaction. An example is a hammer that strikes a nail. In this event, the nail hits the hammer just as hard. Think about two objects: A and B. Now, you can show the contact between these two bodies with the equation $F_{AB} = -F_{BA}$. In the equation, the order of the subscripts shows which body is applying the force.

At first glance, you may think that this law does not allow any movement. Every force is being countered with an equal and opposite force. However, these equal and opposite forces are acting on different objects with different masses. So, they will not cancel out each other.

GRAVITATIONAL FORCE

Gravitational force is a universal force. This causes every object to apply a force on every other object. The **gravitational force** between two objects can be seen with the formula, $F = \frac{Gm_1m_2}{r^2}$. In this example, m_1 and m_2 are the masses of two objects, r is the distance between them, and G is the gravitational constant, $G = 6.672 \times 10^{-11} \frac{\text{N m}^2}{\text{kg}^2}$.

For this force to have an effect that can be noticed, one or both of the objects must be extremely large. So, the equation is used only in problems that deal with objects in space. Problems that deal with objects on Earth are affected by Earth's gravitational pull. So, the force of gravity is calculated as $F = mg$. In this formula, g is $9.81 \frac{\text{m}}{\text{s}^2}$ toward the ground.

WORK

Work is the amount of energy that comes from finishing a set goal. A basic equation for mechanical work (W) is $W = Fd$. In the equation, F is the force put on the object, and d is the displacement of the object. This equation needs the force to be applied in the same direction as the displacement. If force and displacement have the same direction, then work is positive. If they are in opposite directions, then work is negative. If they are perpendicular, the work done is zero.

An example is a man who pushes a block horizontally across a surface. He uses a constant force of 10 N for a distance of 20 m. So, the work done by the man is 200 N-m or 200 J.

Another example is that the block is sliding, and the man tries to slow it down by pushing against it. So, his work done is -200 J. The reason is that he is pushing in the opposite direction of the block.

Now, let's say that the man pushes down on the block while it slides. In this example, his work done is zero. The reason is that his force vector is perpendicular to the displacement vector of the block.

Review Video: <u>Work</u>
Visit mometrix.com/academy and enter code: 681834

MACHINES

Simple machines are the inclined plane, lever, wheel and axle, and pulley. These simple machines have no source of energy inside them. More complex or compound machines can be made from simple machines. Simple machines give a force that is known as a mechanical advantage. This advantage makes it easier to finish a task.

SIMPLE MACHINES

Inclined plane: helps a force that is less than the object's weight to push an object to a greater height.

Lever: helps to multiply a force.

Wheel and axle: allows for movement with less resistance.

Single or double pulleys allow for easier direction of force.

Wedge: turns a small force that is working over a greater distance into a larger force.

Screw: this is an inclined plane that is wrapped around a shaft.

A certain amount of work is needed to move an object. The amount cannot be reduced. However, you can change the way the work is done. So, a mechanical advantage can be gained. A certain amount of work can be done to raise an object to a given height. By getting to the given height at an angle, the effort needed is reduced. However, the distance that is needed to reach a given height is increased. An example of this is walking up a hill.

A lever has a bar (i.e., plank) and a pivot point (i.e., fulcrum). Work is done with the bar. This bar moves at the pivot point to change the direction of the force. There are three types of levers: first, second, and third class. Examples of a first-class lever are balances, see-saws, and nail removers.

In a second-class lever, the fulcrum is placed at one end of the bar. So, the work is done at the other end. The weight or load to be moved is in between. When the weight is closer to the fulcrum, then the weight is easier to move. Force can be increased, but the distance that it is moved is decreased. Examples are pry bars, bottle openers, nutcrackers, and wheelbarrows.

In a third-class lever, the fulcrum is at one end. So, the positions of the weight and the location where the work is done are reversed. Examples are fishing rods, hammers, and tweezers.

The center of a wheel and axle can be compared to a fulcrum on a rotating lever. As it turns, the wheel moves a greater distance than the axle but with less force. However, this type of simple machine can be used to apply a greater force. An example is a person who can turn the handles of a winch. They can apply a greater force at the turning axle to move an object.

A clear example of the wheel and axle is the wheels of a car. Other examples are steering wheels, wrenches, faucets, waterwheels, windmills, gears, and belts. The four basic types of gears are spur, rack and pinion, bevel, and worm gears. Gears work together to change a force. The larger gear turns slower than the smaller. However, this larger gear applies a greater force. Gears at angles can be used to change the direction of forces.

A single pulley has a rope or line that is placed around a wheel. This allows force to go in a downward motion to lift an object. The force that is needed is not decreased. Instead, the force just changes its direction. The load is moved the same distance as the rope pulling it.

A combination pulley (e.g., a double pulley) moves the weight half the distance of the rope. In this way, the work effort is doubled. Pulleys are never 100% efficient because of friction. Examples of pulleys are cranes, chain hoists, block and tackles, and elevators.

> **Review Video: <u>Simple Machines</u>**
> Visit mometrix.com/academy and enter code: 950789

THERMODYNAMICS

Thermodynamics is a branch of physics that studies the conversion of energy into work and heat. It is especially concerned with variables such as temperature, volume, and pressure. Thermodynamic equilibrium refers to objects that have the same temperature because heat is transferred between them to reach equilibrium. Thermodynamics takes places within three different types of systems; open, isolated, and closed systems. Open systems are capable of interacting with a surrounding environment and can exchange heat, work (energy), and matter outside their system boundaries. A closed system can exchange heat and work, but not matter. An isolated system cannot exchange heat, work, or matter with its surroundings. Its total energy and mass stay the same. In physics, surrounding environment refers to everything outside a thermodynamic system (system). The terms "surroundings" and "environment" are also used. The term "boundary" refers to the division between the system and its surroundings.

The laws of thermodynamics are generalized principles dealing with energy and heat.

- The zeroth law of thermodynamics states that two objects in thermodynamic equilibrium with a third object are also in equilibrium with each other. Being in thermodynamic equilibrium basically means that different objects are at the same temperature.
- The first law deals with conservation of energy. It states that neither mass nor energy can be destroyed; only converted from one form to another.
- The second law states that the entropy (the amount of energy in a system that is no longer available for work or the amount of disorder in a system) of an isolated system can only increase. The second law also states that heat is not transferred from a lower-temperature system to a higher-temperature one unless additional work is done.
- The third law of thermodynamics states that as temperature approaches absolute zero, entropy approaches a constant minimum. It also states that a system cannot be cooled to absolute zero.

Thermal contact refers to energy transferred to a body by a means other than work. A system in thermal contact with another can exchange energy with it through the process of heat transfer. Thermal contact does not necessarily involve direct physical contact. Heat is energy that can be transferred from one body or system to another without work being done. Everything tends to become less organized and less useful over time (entropy). In all energy transfers, therefore, the overall result is that the heat is spread out so that objects are in thermodynamic equilibrium and the heat can no longer be transferred without additional work.

ELECTRICITY AND MAGNETISM

ELECTRIC CHARGE

Much like gravity, electricity is an everyday observable phenomenon which is very complex, but may be understood as a set of behaviors. As the gravitational force exists between objects with mass, the electric force exists between objects with electrical charge. In all atoms, the protons have a positive charge, while the electrons have a negative charge. An imbalance of electrons and protons in an object results in a net charge. Unlike gravity, which only pulls, electrical forces can push objects apart as well as pull them together.

Similar electric charges repel each other. Opposite charges attract each other.

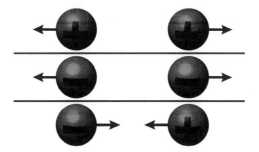

Review Video: Electric Charge
Visit mometrix.com/academy and enter code: 323587

CURRENT

The term for the rate at which the charge flows through a conductive material is *current*. Because each electron carries a specific charge, current can be thought of as the number of electrons passing a point in a length of time. Current is measured in Amperes (A).

VOLTAGE

Voltage is the potential for electric work. It can also be thought of as the push behind electrical work. Voltage is similar to gravitational potential energy.

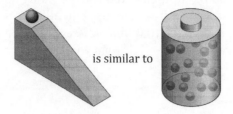

is similar to

Anything used to generate a voltage, such as a battery or a generator, is called a voltage source. Voltage is conveniently measured in Volts (V).

MAGNETISM

Magnetism is an attraction between opposite poles of magnetic materials and a repulsion between similar poles of magnetic materials. Magnetism can be natural or induced with the use of electric currents. Magnets almost always exist with two polar sides: north and south. A magnetic force exists between two poles on objects. Different poles attract each other. Like poles repel each other.

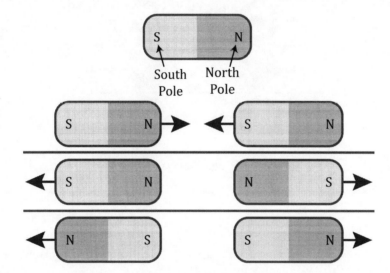

Interpretation of Data

METRIC SYSTEM

Using the metric system is generally accepted as the preferred method for taking measurements. Having a universal standard allows individuals to interpret measurements more easily, regardless of where they are located.

The basic units of measurement are: the meter, which measures length; the liter, which measures volume; and the gram, which measures mass. The metric system starts with a base unit and increases or decreases in units of 10. The prefix and the base unit combined are used to indicate an amount.

For example, deka is 10 times the base unit. A dekameter is 10 meters; a dekaliter is 10 liters; and a dekagram is 10 grams. The prefix hecto refers to 100 times the base amount; kilo is 1,000 times the base amount. The prefixes that indicate a fraction of the base unit are deci, which is 1/10 of the base unit; centi, which is 1/100 of the base unit; and milli, which is 1/1000 of the base unit.

S.I. UNITS OF MEASUREMENT

SI uses second(s) to measure time. Fractions of seconds are usually measured in metric terms using prefixes such as millisecond (1/1,000 of a second) or nanosecond (1/1,000,000,000 of a second). Increments of time larger than a second are measured in minutes and hours, which are multiples of 60 and 24. An example of this is a swimmer's time in the 800-meter freestyle being described as 7:32.67, meaning 7 minutes, 32 seconds, and 67 one-hundredths of a second. One second is equal to 1/60 of a minute, 1/3,600 of an hour, and 1/86,400 of a day.

Other SI base units are the ampere (A) (used to measure electric current), the kelvin (K) (used to measure thermodynamic temperature), the candela (cd) (used to measure luminous intensity), and the mole (mol) (used to measure the amount of a substance at a molecular level). Meter (m) is used to measure length and kilogram (kg) is used to measure mass.

METRIC PREFIXES FOR MULTIPLES AND SUBDIVISIONS

The prefixes for multiples are as follows:

deka (da), 10^1 (deka is the American spelling, but deca is also used)

hecto (h), 10^2

kilo (k), 10^3

mega (M), 10^6

giga (G), 10^9

tera (T), 10^{12}

The prefixes for subdivisions are as follows:

deci (d), 10^{-1}

centi (c), 10^{-2}

milli (m), 10^{-3}

micro (μ), 10^{-6}

nano (n), 10^{-9}

pico (p), 10^{-12}

The rule of thumb is that prefixes greater than 10^3 are capitalized when abbreviating. Abbreviations do not need a period after them. A decimeter (dm) is a tenth of a meter, a deciliter (dL) is a tenth of a liter, and a decigram (dg) is a tenth of a gram. Pluralization is understood. For example, when referring to 5 mL of water, no "s" needs to be added to the abbreviation.

LINE GRAPH

A line graph is a type of graph that is typically used for measuring trends over time. The graph is set up along a vertical and a horizontal axis. The variables being measured are listed along the left side and the bottom side of the axes. Points are then plotted along the graph as they correspond with their values for each variable. For instance, imagine a line graph measuring a person's income for each month of the year. If the person earned $1500 in January, there should be a point directly above January (perpendicular to the horizontal axis) and directly to the right of $1500 (perpendicular to the vertical axis). Once all of the lines are plotted, they are connected with a line from left to right. This line provides a nice visual illustration of the general trends. For instance, using the earlier example, if the line sloped up, then one would see that the person's income had increased over the course of the year.

> **Review Video: How to Create a Line Graph**
> Visit mometrix.com/academy and enter code: 480147

BAR GRAPH

The bar graph is one of the most common visual representations of information. Bar graphs are used to illustrate sets of numerical data. The graph has a vertical axis (along which numbers are listed), and a horizontal axis (along which categories, words, or some other indicators are placed). One example of a bar graph is a depiction of the respective heights of famous basketball players: the vertical axis would contain numbers ranging from five to eight feet, and the horizontal axis would contain the names of the players. The length of the bar above the player's name would illustrate his height, and the top of the bar would stop perpendicular to the height listed along the left side. In this representation, one would see that Yao Ming is taller than Michael Jordan because Yao's bar would be higher.

PIE CHART

A **pie chart**, also known as a circle graph, is useful for depicting how a single unit or category is divided. The standard pie chart is a circle with designated wedges. Each wedge is proportional in size to a part of the whole. For instance, consider a pie chart representing a student's budget. If the student spends half of his or her money on rent, then the pie chart will represent that amount with a line through the center of the pie. If she spends a quarter of her money on food, there will be a line extending from the edge of the circle to the center at a right angle to the line depicting rent. This illustration would make it clear that the student spends twice the amount of money on rent as she does on food.

A pie chart is effective at showing how a single entity is divided into parts. They are not effective at demonstrating the relationships between parts of different wholes. For example, an unhelpful use

of a pie chart would be to compare the respective amounts of state and federal spending devoted to infrastructure since these values are only meaningful in the context of the entire budget.

Scientific Investigation

LAB GLASSWARE

GRADUATED CYLINDERS AND BURETTES

Graduated cylinders are used for an intermediate amount of precision. More precise than beakers and Erlenmeyer flasks but not quite as precise as volumetric flasks or pipettes, they are made of either polypropylene (which is shatter-resistant and resistant to chemicals but cannot be heated) or polymethylpentene (which is known for its clarity). They are lighter to ship and less fragile than glass.

To read a graduated cylinder, it should be placed on a flat surface and read at eye level. The surface of a liquid in a graduated cylinder forms a lens-shaped curve. The measurement should be taken from the bottom of the curve. A ring may be placed at the top of tall, narrow cylinders to help avoid breakage if they are tipped over.

A burette, or buret, is a piece of lab glassware used to accurately dispense liquid. It looks similar to a narrow graduated cylinder, but includes a stopcock and tip. It may be filled with a funnel or pipette.

FLASKS, BEAKERS, AND PIPETTES

Two types of flasks commonly used in lab settings are Erlenmeyer flasks and volumetric flasks, which can also be used to accurately measure liquids. Erlenmeyer flasks and beakers can be used for mixing, transporting, and reacting, but are not appropriate for accurate measurements.

A pipette can be used to accurately measure small amounts of liquid. Liquid is drawn into the pipette through the bulb and a finger is then quickly placed at the top of the container. The liquid measurement is read exactly at the meniscus. Liquid can be released from the pipette by lifting the finger. There are also plastic disposal pipettes. A repipette is a hand-operated pump that dispenses solutions.

BALANCES

Unlike laboratory glassware that measures volume, balances such as triple-beam balances, spring balances, and electronic balances measure mass and force. An electronic balance is the most accurate, followed by a triple-beam balance and then a spring balance.

One part of a triple-beam balance is the plate, which is where the item to be weighed is placed. There are also three beams that have hatch marks indicating amounts and hold the weights that rest in the notches. The front beam measures weights between 0 and 10 grams, the middle beam measures weights in 100-gram increments, and the far beam measures weights in 10-gram increments.

The sum of the weight of each beam is the total weight of the object. A triple beam balance also includes a set screw to calibrate the equipment and a mark indicating the object and counterweights are in balance. Analytical balances are accurate to within 0.0001 g.

SCIENTIFIC INQUIRY

SCIENTIFIC METHOD

The scientific method of inquiry is a general method by which ideas are tested and either confirmed or refuted by experimentation. The first step in the scientific method is formulating the problem that is to be addressed. It is essential to define clearly the limits of what is to be observed, since that allows for a more focused analysis.

Once the problem has been defined, it is necessary to form a hypothesis. This educated guess should be a possible solution to the problem that was formulated in the first step.

The next step is to test that hypothesis by experimentation. This often requires the scientist to design a complete experiment. The key to making the best possible use of an experiment is observation. Observations may be quantitative, that is, when a numeric measurement is taken, or they may be qualitative, that is, when something is evaluated based on feeling or preference. This measurement data will then be examined to find trends or patterns that are present.

From these trends, the scientist will draw conclusions or make generalizations about the results, intended to predict future results. If these conclusions support the original hypothesis, the experiment is complete and the scientist will publish his conclusions to allow others to test them by repeating the experiment. If they do not support the hypothesis, the results should then be used to develop a new hypothesis, which can then be verified by a new or redesigned experiment.

EXPERIMENTAL DESIGN

Designing relevant experiments that allow for meaningful results is not a simple task. Every stage of the experiment must be carefully planned to ensure that the right data can be safely and accurately taken.

Ideally, an experiment should be controlled so that all of the conditions except the ones being manipulated are held constant. This helps to ensure that the results are not skewed by unintended consequences of shifting conditions. A good example of this is a placebo group in a drug trial. All other conditions are the same, but that group is not given the medication.

In addition to proper control, it is important that the experiment be designed with data collection in mind. For instance, if the quantity to be measured is temperature, there must be a temperature device such as a thermocouple integrated into the experimental setup. While the data are being collected, they should periodically be checked for obvious errors. If there are data points that are orders of magnitude from the expected value, then it might be a good idea to make sure that no experimental errors are being made, either in data collection or condition control.

Once all the data have been gathered, they must be analyzed. The way in which this should be done depends on the type of data and the type of trends observed. It may be useful to fit curves to the data to determine if the trends follow a common mathematical form. It may also be necessary to perform a statistical analysis of the results to determine what effects are significant. Data should be clearly presented.

CONTROLS

A valid experiment must be carefully controlled. All variables except the one being tested must be carefully maintained. This means that all conditions must be kept exactly the same except for the independent variable.

Additionally, a set of data is usually needed for a control group. The control group represents the "normal" state or condition of the variable being manipulated. Controls can be negative or positive. Positive controls are the variables that the researcher expects to have an effect on the outcome of the experiment. A positive control group can be used to verify that an experiment is set up properly. Negative control groups are typically thought of as placebos. A negative control group should verify that a variable has no effect on the outcome of the experiment.

The better an experiment is controlled, the more valid the conclusions from that experiment will be. A researcher is more likely to draw a valid conclusion if all variables other than the one being manipulated are being controlled.

VARIABLES

Every experiment has several variables; however, only one variable should be purposely changed and tested. This variable is the manipulated or independent variable. As this variable is manipulated or changed, another variable, called the responding or dependent variable, is observed and recorded.

> **Review Video: Identifying Independent and Dependent Variables**
> Visit mometrix.com/academy and enter code: 627181

All other variables in the experiment must be carefully controlled and are usually referred to as constants. For example, when testing the effect of temperature on solubility of a solute, the independent variable is the temperature, and the dependent variable is the solubility.

All other factors in the experiment such as pressure, amount of stirring, type of solvent, type of solute, and particle size of the solute are the constants.

> **Review Video: Percent Yield**
> Visit mometrix.com/academy and enter code: 565738

EVENTS AND OBJECTS

EVENTS

Another regular writing device is **cause and effect**. A cause is an act or event that makes something happen. An effect is what results from the cause. A cause and effect relationship is not always easy to find. So, there are some words and phrases that show causes: *since, because,* and *due to.* Words and phrases that show effects include *consequently, therefore, this lead(s) to, as a result.* For example, *Because the sky was clear, Ron did not bring an umbrella.* The cause is the clear sky, and the effect is that Ron did not bring an umbrella. Readers may find that the cause and effect relationship is not clear. For example, *He was late and missed the meeting.* This does not have any words that show cause or effect. Yet, the sentence still has a cause (e.g., he was late) and an effect (e.g., he missed the meeting).

Remember the chance for a single cause to have many effects. (e.g., *Single cause*: Because you left your homework on the table, your dog eats the homework. *Many effects*: (1) As a result, you fail

185

your homework. (2) Your parents do not let you see your friends. (3) You miss out on the new movie. (4) You miss holding the hand of an important person.)

Also, there is a chance of a single effect to have many causes. (e.g., *Single effect*: Alan has a fever. *Many causes*: (1) An unexpected cold front came through the area, and (2) Alan forgot to take his multi-vitamin.)

Now, an effect can become the cause of another effect. This is known as a cause and effect chain. (e.g., As a result of her hatred for not doing work, Lynn got ready for her exam. This led to her passing her test with high marks. Hence, her resume was accepted, and her application was accepted.)

SCALE

From the largest objects in outer space to the smallest pieces of the human body, there are objects that can come in many different sizes and shapes. Many of those objects need to be measured in different ways. So, it is important to know which unit of measurement is needed to record the length or width and the weight of an object.

An example is taking the measurements of a patient. When measuring the total height of a patient or finding the length of an extremity, the accepted measure is given in meters. However, when one is asked for the diameter of a vein, the accepted measure is given in millimeters. Another example would be measuring the weight of a patient which would be given in kilograms, while the measurement of a human heart would be given in grams. The same idea for scale holds true with time as well. When measuring the lifespan of a patient, the accepted measure is given in days, months, or years. However, when measuring the number of breaths that a patient takes, the accepted measure is given in terms of minutes (e.g., breaths per minute).

Evaluation of Models

REVIEW A SCIENTIFIC EXPLANATION WITH LOGIC AND EVIDENCE

DATA COLLECTION

A valid experiment must be measurable. Data tables should be formed, and meticulous, detailed data should be collected for every trial. First, the researcher must determine exactly what data are needed and why those data are needed. The researcher should know in advance what will be done with those data at the end of the experimental research. The data should be repeatable, reproducible, and accurate. The researcher should be sure that the procedure for data collection will be reliable and consistent. The researcher should validate the measurement system by performing practice tests and making sure that all of the equipment is correctly calibrated and periodically retesting the procedure and equipment to ensure that all data being collected are still valid.

> **Review Video: Data Interpretation of Graphs**
> Visit mometrix.com/academy and enter code: 200439

SCIENTIFIC PROCESS SKILLS

Perhaps the most important skill in science is that of observation. Scientists must be able to take accurate data from their experimental setup or from nature without allowing bias to alter the results. Another important skill is hypothesizing. Scientists must be able to combine their knowledge of theory and of other experimental results to logically determine what should occur in their own tests.

The data-analysis process requires the twin skills of ordering and categorizing. Gathered data must be arranged in such a way that it is readable and readily shows the key results. A skill that may be integrated with the previous two is comparing. Scientists should be able to compare their own results with other published results. They must also be able to infer, or draw logical conclusions, from their results. They must be able to apply their knowledge of theory and results to create logical experimental designs and determine cases of special behavior.

Lastly, scientists must be able to communicate their results and their conclusions. The greatest scientific progress is made when scientists are able to review and test one another's work and offer advice or suggestions.

SCIENTIFIC STATEMENTS

Hypotheses are educated guesses about what is likely to occur, and are made to provide a starting point from which to begin design of the experiment. They may be based on results of previously observed experiments or knowledge of theory, and follow logically forth from these.

Assumptions are statements that are taken to be fact without proof for the purpose of performing a given experiment. They may be entirely true, or they may be true only for a given set of conditions under which the experiment will be conducted. Assumptions are necessary to simplify experiments; indeed, many experiments would be impossible without them.

Scientific models are mathematical statements that describe a physical behavior. Models are only as good as our knowledge of the actual system. Often models will be discarded when new discoveries are made that show the model to be inaccurate. While a model can never perfectly represent an actual system, they are useful for simplifying a system to allow for better understanding of its behavior.

Scientific laws are statements of natural behavior that have stood the test of time and have been found to produce accurate and repeatable results in all testing. A theory is a statement of behavior that consolidates all current observations. Theories are similar to laws in that they describe natural behavior, but are more recently developed and are more susceptible to being proved wrong. Theories may eventually become laws if they stand up to scrutiny and testing.

> **Review Video: What is the Scientific Method?**
> Visit mometrix.com/academy and enter code: 191386

The Writing Test

Overview of Writing

BRAINSTORM

Spend the first three to five minutes brainstorming for ideas. Write down any ideas that you might have on the topic. The purpose is to pull any helpful information from the depths of your memory. In this stage, anything goes down in a margin for notes regardless of how good or bad the idea may seem at first glance.

STRENGTH THROUGH DIFFERENT VIEWPOINTS

The best papers will contain several examples and mature reasoning. As you brainstorm, you should consider different perspectives. There are more than two sides to every topic. In an argument, there are countless perspectives that can be considered. On any topic, different groups are impacted and many reach the same conclusion or position. Yet, they reach the same conclusion through different paths. Before writing your essay, try to *see* the topic through as many different *eyes* as you can.

In addition, you don't have to use information on how the topic impacts others. You can draw from your own experience as you wish. If you prefer to use a personal narrative, then explain the experience and your emotions from that moment. Anything that you've seen in your community can be expanded upon to round out your position on the topic.

Once you have finished with your creative flow, you need to stop and review what you brainstormed. *Which idea allowed you to come up with the most supporting information?* Be sure to pick an angle that will allow you to have a thorough coverage of the prompt.

Every garden of ideas has weeds. The ideas that you brainstormed are going to be random pieces of information of different values. Go through the pieces carefully and pick out the ones that are the best. The best ideas are strong points that will be easy to write a paragraph in response.

Now, you have your main ideas that you will focus on. So, align them in a sequence that will flow in a smooth, sensible path from point to point. With this approach, readers will go smoothly from one idea to the next in a reasonable order. Readers want an essay that has a sense of continuity (i.e., Point 1 to Point 2 to Point 3 and so on).

START YOUR ENGINES

Now, you have a logical flow of the main ideas for the start of your essay. Begin by expanding on the first point, then move to your second point. Pace yourself. Don't spend too much time on any one of the ideas that you are expanding on. You want to have time for all of them. Make sure that you watch your time. If you have twenty minutes left to write out your ideas and you have four ideas, then you can only use five minutes per idea. Writing so much information in so little time can be an intimidating task. Yet, when you pace yourself, you can get through all of your points. If you find that you are falling behind, then you can remove one of your weaker arguments. This will allow you to give enough support to your remaining paragraphs.

Once you finish expanding on an idea, go back to your brainstorming session where you wrote out your ideas. You can scratch through the ideas as you write about them. This will let you see what you need to write about next and what you have left to cover.

Your introductory paragraph should have several easily identifiable features.

- First, the paragraph should have a quick description or paraphrasing of the topic. Use your own words to briefly explain what the topic is about.
- Second, you should list your writing points. What are the main ideas that you came up with earlier? If someone was to read only your introduction, they should be able to get a good summary of the entire paper.
- Third, you should explain your opinion of the topic and give an explanation for why you feel that way. What is your decision or conclusion on the topic?

Each of your following paragraphs should develop one of the points listed in the main paragraph. Use your personal experience and knowledge to support each of your points. Examples should back up everything.

Once you have finished expanding on each of your main points, you need to conclude your essay. Summarize what you written in a conclusion paragraph. Explain once more your argument on the prompt and review why you feel that way in a few sentences. At this stage, you have already backed up your statements. So, there is no need to do that again. You just need to refresh your readers on the main points that you made in your essay.

DON'T PANIC

Whatever you do during essay, do not panic. When you panic, you will put fewer words on the page and your ideas will be weak. Therefore, panicking is not helpful. If your mind goes blank when you see the prompt, then you need to take a deep breath. Force yourself to go through the steps listed above: brainstorm and put anything on scratch paper that comes to mind.

Also, don't get clock fever. You may be overwhelmed when you're looking at a page that is mostly blank. Your mind is full of random thoughts and feeling confused, and the clock is ticking down faster. You have already brainstormed for ideas. Therefore, you don't have to keep coming up with ideas. If you're running out of time and you have a lot of ideas that you haven't written down, then don't be afraid to make some cuts. Start picking the best ideas that you have left and expand on them. Don't feel like you have to write on all of your ideas.

A short paper that is well written and well organized is better than a long paper that is poorly written and poorly organized. Don't keep writing about a subject just to add sentences and avoid repeating a statement or idea that you have explained already. The goal is 1 to 2 pages of quality writing. That is your target, but you should not mess up your paper by trying to get there. You want to have a natural end to your work without having to cut something short. If your essay is a little long, then that isn't a problem as long as your ideas are clear and flow well from paragraph to paragraph. Remember to expand on the ideas that you identified in the brainstorming session.

Leave time at the end (at least three minutes) to go back and check over your work. Reread and make sure that everything you've written makes sense and flows well. Clean up any spelling or grammar mistakes. Also, go ahead and erase any brainstorming ideas that you weren't able to include. Then, clean up any extra information that you might have written that doesn't fit into your paper.

As you proofread, make sure that there aren't any fragments or run-ons. Check for sentences that are too short or too long. If the sentence is too short, then look to see if you have a specific subject and an active verb. If it is too long, then break up the long sentence into two sentences. Watch out for any "big words" that you may have used. Be sure that you are using difficult words correctly.

Don't misunderstand; you should try to increase your vocabulary and use difficult words in your essay. However, your focus should be on developing and expressing ideas in a clear and precise way.

THE SHORT OVERVIEW

Depending on your preferences and personality, the essay may be your hardest or your easiest section. You are required to go through the entire process of writing a paper in a limited amount of time which is very challenging.

Stay focused on each of the steps for brainstorming. Go through the process of creative flow first. You can start by generating ideas about the prompt. Next, organize those ideas into a smooth flow. Then, pick out the ideas that are the best from your list.

Create a recognizable essay structure in your paper. Start with an introduction that explains what you have decided to argue. Then, choose your main points. Use the body paragraphs to touch on those main points and have a conclusion that wraps up the topic.

Save a few moments to go back and review what you have written. Clean up any minor mistakes that you might have made and make those last few critical touches that can make a huge difference. Finally, be proud and confident of what you have written!

Practice Test

Want to take this practice test in an online interactive format?
Check out the bonus page, which includes interactive practice questions and
much more: **mometrix.com/bonus948/preact**

English

United States Coast Guard

The United States Coast Guard (1) <u>was founded in 1790</u> as the branch of military service responsible for safeguarding the country's sea-related interests. (2)

(3) <u>It was originally created</u> to protect the US (4) <u>from smugglers, and to enforce</u> tariff and trade laws. It may seem like this would be a job for the Navy, but the purpose of the Navy is very different from that of the Coast Guard. The Navy's job is (5) <u>to engage in combat and defend the seas</u> from threats to the US and its interests worldwide.

(6) The United States Coast Guard is actually a part of the Department of Homeland Security and is considered a federal law enforcement agency.

The mission of the department is to protect and to enforce laws on our coastlines and in our ports and to safeguard other interests within American waters.

In addition to enforcing maritime (7) <u>law, we need to recognize that the United States Coast Guard also serves</u> as a guardian of the environment.

(8) This includes stopping waste and other types of pollution from being dumped into the ocean, preventing and helping to clean up oil spills, and even ensuring that species of marine life that could threaten the balance of existing environments are prevented from being introduced.

(9) <u>This is a real important</u> job for the Coast Guard because there would not be much of a coastline to protect if our seas were too polluted to entertain or to sustain us. (10)

On the whole, the United States Coast Guard personnel (11) <u>perform the following in a single day:</u> save 12 lives; respond to 64 search and rescue cases; keep 842 pounds of cocaine off the streets; service 116 buoys and fix 24 discrepancies; screen 720 commercial vessels and 183,000 crew and passengers; issue 173 credentials to merchant mariners; investigate 13 marine accidents; inspect 68 containers and 29 vessels for compliance with air emissions standards; perform 28 safety and environmental examinations of foreign vessels; board 13 fishing boats to ensure compliance with fisheries laws; and (12) <u>explore and investigate 10 pollution incidents</u>.

The United States Coast Guard (1) <u>was founded in 1790</u> as the branch of military service responsible for safeguarding the country's sea-related interests.

1.
- A. NO CHANGE
- B. was founded in 1790,
- C. were founded in 1790
- D. will have been founded in 1790

2. The author wants to add the following statement:

While this branch of military service has seen several changes in its tasks, the mission of the branch has not changed since its founding.

Should the author make the addition here?
- F. Yes, this sentence offers a smooth transition to the following sentence and informs readers of what they can expect for the remainder of the passage.
- G. No, this sentence is vague and distracting for readers.
- H. Yes, the purpose of the passage is to address the many responsibilities of the US Coast Guard.
- J. No, the dependent phrase of this sentence is already addressed in the next sentence, and the independent clause is addressed in the following paragraphs.

(3) <u>It was originally created</u> to protect the US from smugglers, and to enforce tariff and trade laws.

3.
- A. NO CHANGE
- B. It was originally established
- C. The branch was originally created
- D. Originally, it was created

It was originally created to protect the US (4) <u>from smugglers, and to enforce</u> tariff and trade laws.

4.
- F. NO CHANGE
- G. from smugglers, and enforce
- H. from smugglers, and to promote
- J. from smugglers and to enforce

The Navy's job is (5) <u>to engage in combat and defend the seas</u> from threats to the US and its interests worldwide.

5.
- A. NO CHANGE
- B. to engage in combats and defend the seas
- C. to engage in combat, and defend the seas
- D. to engage in combat and to defend the seas

6. How can the following sentence be revised for conciseness?

(6) The United States Coast Guard is actually a part of the Department of Homeland Security and is considered a federal law enforcement agency

    F.   NO CHANGE

    G. As part of the Department of Homeland Security, the United States Coast Guard is considered a federal law enforcement agency.

    H. As part of the Department of Homeland Security, we know the United States Coast Guard to be a federal law enforcement agency.

    J.   The Department of Homeland Security considers the United States Coast Guard to be actually a part a federal law enforcement agency.

In addition to enforcing maritime (7) <u>law, we need to recognize that the United States Coast Guard also serves</u> as a guardian of the environment.

7.

    A. NO CHANGE

    B. law, also serving the United States Coast Guard

    C. law we need to recognize that the United States Coast Guard serves

    D. law, the United States Coast Guard also serves

8. Which of the following sentences, if placed before sentence 10, would create a better transition from the second paragraph to the third paragraph?

    F.   The "Coastie" life is one that just about anyone would want to choose.

    G. The life of a Coast Guard member (or "Coastie") can be routine and boring, depending on what type of job the "Coastie" has.

    H. There are many things that the Coast Guard can do to enforce laws while at sea or patrolling our waterways.

    J.   Enforcement of laws and protection of the environment are just two of the many responsibilities that a member of the Coast Guard (or "Coastie") can expect to have in the line of duty.

(9) <u>This is a real important</u> job for the Coast Guard because there would not be much of a coastline to protect if our seas were too polluted to entertain or to sustain us.

9.

    A. NO CHANGE

    B. This is not a real important

    C. This is a real, important

    D. This is a really important

194

This is a real important job for the Coast Guard because there would not be much of a coastline to protect if our seas were too polluted to entertain or to sustain us. (10)

On the whole, the United States Coast Guard personnel perform the following in a single day...

10. The author wants to add the following statement:

If we do our part to maintain clean coastlines, then this will allow the Coast Guard to focus more on performing routine inspections or search and rescue missions.

Should the author make the addition here?

   F. Yes, this comes as helpful information to readers who are not familiar with the responsibilities of the Coast Guard.

   G. No, this sentence would distract from author's original purpose of the passage which is to inform, not persuade.

   H. Yes, this leads in well to the next paragraph on the responsibilities of Coast Guard members.

   J. No, this sentence suggests that readers are responsible for cleaning coastlines.

On the whole, the United States Coast Guard personnel (11) <u>perform the following in a single day:</u> save 12 lives...

11.

   A. NO CHANGE

   B. complete the following in a single day:

   C. accomplish the following in one day:

   D. perform the following in a day:

... board 13 fishing boats to ensure compliance with fisheries laws; and (12) <u>respond to and investigate 10 pollution incidents.</u>

12.

   F. NO CHANGE

   G. investigate 10 pollution incidents

   H. explore, and investigate 10 pollution incidents

   J. explore to investigate 10 pollution incidents

13. Adding which of the following sentences to paragraph 3 would make it more credible?

   A. This information comes from the official Coast Guard Web site.

   B. The average age of Coast Guard members is 28.

   C. The Coast Guard has a long history of service.

   D. There are 33,200 enlisted Coast Guard members.

14. If the writer's main goal were to explain the requirements for becoming a member of the United States Coast Guard, then would this passage achieve that goal?

   F. Yes, the author lists the daily objectives of Coast Guard members and notes how they are "a guardian of the environment."

   G. No, the author only provides a general listing of the things that Coast Guard members are expected to accomplish a day.

   H. Yes, the author notes the difference between the US Navy and the Coast Guard in the second paragraph

   J. No, the author gives clarity on some of the differences between the US Navy and the Coast Guard and mentions none of the necessary pieces to becoming a member of the US Coast Guard.

15. Which of the following would be the best conclusion for this essay?

A. There is much more that we can learn about the Coast Guard. To list all of the great things about this organization would take all day. The opportunities available to members of the Coast Guard are endless, and we should all consider becoming a "Coastie."

B. Being a "Coastie" would be the fulfillment of anyone's dreams. Who wouldn't want a career that is full of adventure and honor? There is no better job that a person could pursue as their life's work.

C. The Coast Guard is a very diverse and exciting branch of the US military. Though many may not believe it is as important as the Navy, the Army, the Marines, or the Air Force, it's plain to see that the Coast Guard plays a vital role in ensuring our nation's security and prosperity.

D. The Coast Guard provides little support toward defending our nation from threats, as its members are always so close to home. Greater purpose can be found in a different branch of service. The threats that the Coast Guard faces are insignificant when compared to those faced by the Army, the Navy, the Marines, or the Air Force.

New Zealand Inhabitants

[1]

(16) The islands of New Zealand are among the most remote of all the Pacific islands.

(17) New Zealand is an archipelago, with two large (18) islands, and a number of smaller ones. Its climate is far cooler than the rest of Polynesia.

(19) Nevertheless, according to Maori legends, it was colonized in the early fifteenth century by a wave of Polynesian voyagers who traveled southward in their canoes and settled on North Island. (20) At this time, New Zealand has been known already to the Polynesians, who had probably first landed there some 400 years earlier.

At this time the Polynesians knew their surroundings in New Zealand after landing there probably some 400 years earlier.

[2]

The Polynesian (21) southward migration was limited by the availability of food. Traditional Polynesian tropical crops such as taro and yams will grow on North Island, but the climate of the South Island is too cold for them. (22)

(23) The first settlers were forced to rely on hunting and gathering, and, (24) of course, fishing. Especially on the South Island, most settlements remained close to the sea. At the time of the Polynesian incursion, enormous flocks of moa birds had their rookeries on the island shores. These flightless birds were easy prey for the settlers, and within a few centuries had been hunted to extinction. (25) Fish, shellfish and the roots of the fern were other important sources of food, but even these began to diminish in quantity as the human population increased. The Maori had few other choices (26) of meat among: dogs, smaller birds, and rats. Archaeological evidence shows that human flesh was also eaten, and (27) that tribal warfare increased after the moa disappeared markedly.

[3]

By far the most important farmed crop in prehistoric New Zealand was the sweet potato. This tuber is hearty enough to grow throughout the islands and could be stored to provide food during the winter months when other food-gathering activities were difficult. (28) The availability of the (29) <u>sweet potato made possible a significant increase in the human population</u>. (30)

(16) The islands of New Zealand are among the most remote of all the Pacific islands.

16.

    F. NO CHANGE
    G. The island of New Zealand is among the most remote
    H. The islands of New Zealand are between the most remote
    J. The islands of New Zealand are among the more remote

(17) New Zealand is an archipelago, with two large islands, and a number of smaller ones. Its climate is far cooler than the rest of Polynesia.

17. What is the BEST way to revise and combine sentence 2 and sentence 3?

    A. Its climate is far cooler than the rest of Polynesia because New Zealand is an archipelago, with two large islands and a number of smaller ones.
    B. New Zealand is an archipelago, with two large islands and a number of smaller ones, and its climate is far cooler than the rest of Polynesia.
    C. Its climate is far cooler than the rest of Polynesia; however, New Zealand is an archipelago, with two large islands and a number of smaller ones.
    D. New Zealand is an archipelago, with two large islands and a number of smaller ones; thus, its climate is far cooler than the rest of Polynesia.

New Zealand is an archipelago, with two large (18) <u>islands, and a number of smaller</u> ones.

18.

    F. NO CHANGE
    G. islands and the amount of smaller
    H. islands and a number of smaller
    J. islands and an amount of smaller

19. How can the following sentence be revised for precision and conciseness?

Nevertheless, according to Maori legends, it was colonized in the early fifteenth century by a wave of Polynesian voyagers who traveled southward in their canoes and settled on North Island.

    A. NO CHANGE
    B. According to Maori legends, New Zealand was colonized in the early fifteenth century by Polynesian voyagers who traveled in their canoes to settle on North Island.
    C. Nevertheless, it was colonized according to Maori legends, by a wave of Polynesian voyagers who traveled southward in their canoes and settled on North Island.
    D. Those who traveled southward in their canoes settled on North Island because it was colonized in the early fifteenth century by a wave of Polynesian voyagers according to Maori legends.

(20) At this time, New Zealand has been known already to the Polynesians, who had probably first landed there some 400 years earlier.

20.

F.   NO CHANGE
G.   New Zealand will have been known already to the Polynesians who had probably first landed there some 400 years earlier.
H.   The Polynesians, who had probably first landed there some 400 years earlier, at this time have known New Zealand.
J.   At this time, the Polynesians knew their surroundings in New Zealand after landing there probably some 400 years earlier.

The Polynesian (21) <u>southward migration was limited by</u> the availability of food.

21.

A.   NO CHANGE
B.   Southward migration is limited by
C.   southward migration had been limited by
D.   Southward migration has been limited by

Traditional Polynesian tropical crops such as taro and yams will grow on North Island, but the climate of the South Island is too cold for them. (22) The first settlers were forced to rely on hunting and gathering, and, of course, fishing. Especially on the South Island, most settlements remained close to the sea.

22.   The author is thinking about adding this sentence to the passage.

Coconuts will not grow on either island.

Should the author add this sentence at this point in the paragraph?

F.   Yes. This information is evidence that will help readers understand the predicament of Polynesian people.
G.   No. While the statement is true, the sentence does not transition well in the paragraph.
H.   Yes. This statement transitions well from the previous sentence to the next on the struggle to find and maintain food for Polynesians.
J.   No. This statement does include an explanation of the purpose of coconuts to the Polynesian people.

(23) <u>The first settlers were forced</u> to rely on hunting and gathering, and, of course, fishing.

23.

A.   NO CHANGE
B.   The first settlers forced themselves
C.   The first settlers will have been forced
D.   This harsh environment forced the first settlers

The first settlers were forced to rely on hunting and gathering, and, <u>of course, fishing.</u> Especially on the South Island, most settlements remained close to the sea.

24. Which choice most effectively transitions from sentence 9 to sentence 10 (reproduced above) at the underlined portion?

    F. of course, fishing, but especially on South Island

    G. of course, fishing; however, on South Island

    H. of course, fishing: especially on South Island

    J. of course, fishing; therefore, on South Island

(25) <u>Fish, shellfish and the roots of the fern</u> were other important sources of food, but even these began to diminish in quantity as the human population increased.

25.

    A. NO CHANGE

    B. Fish, shellfish, and the roots of the fern

    C. Fish, Shellfish, and the roots of the fern

    D. Fish, shellfish and the root of the fern

The Maori had few other choices (26) of meat among: dogs, smaller birds, and rats.

26.

    F. NO CHANGE

    G. of meat among: dogs, smaller birds and rats

    H. with: dogs, smaller birds, and rats

    J. of meat: dogs, smaller birds, and rats

Archaeological evidence shows that human flesh was also eaten, and that tribal warfare (27) <u>increased after the moa disappeared markedly</u>.

27.

    A. NO CHANGE

    B. increased markedly after the moa disappeared.

    C. increased after the moa disappeared.

    D. increased markedly after their disappearance.

28. Which is the best placement for sentence 18 in this passage?

    F. Before sentence 16

    G. After sentence 16

    H. After sentence 19

    J. In its current place

The availability of the sweet potato made possible a (29) <u>significant increase in the human population</u>.

29.

    A. NO CHANGE

    B. increase in the human population.

    C. significant increase in the Maori population.

    D. significant increase in the population.

30. The author wants to add the following statement at the end of the passage:

Thus, Maori tribes often were located near the best sweet potato farmlands in encampments called pa, which were fortified with earthen embankments.

Should the author make the addition at the end of this passage?

F. Yes, this information is evidence that supports the topic of the third paragraph.
G. No, this sentence is unnecessary and does not support the topic of the third paragraph.
H. Yes, this sentence is further proof that the Maori tribe was the most advanced of New Zealand inhabitants.
J. No. While this information supports the topic, the author should reconsider the placement of the sentence in this passage.

The Wright Brothers

After Orville and (31) <u>Wilbur Wright will have flown their</u> first airplane in 1903, the age of flying slowly began. Many new pilots (32) <u>learned how to fly in World War I, which</u> the United States joined in 1917. During the war, the American public loved hearing stories about the daring pilots and their air fights. But after the war ended, many Americans thought that men and women belonged on the ground and not in the air.

(33) In the years after the war and through the Roaring Twenties, America's pilots found themselves without jobs. Some of them gave up flying altogether. **A**

Pilot Eddie (34) <u>Rickenbacker, who used to be called America's Ace of Aces, became</u> a car salesman. But other (35) <u>pilots found new and creative things</u> to do with their airplanes.

B The (36) <u>airplane was used by pilot Casey Jones</u> to help get news across the country. (37) <u>When a big news story broke, Jones</u> flew news photos to newspapers in different cities. (38) <u>Another pilot, Roscoe Turner, traveled</u> around the country with a lion cub in his plane. The cub was the mascot of an oil company, and Turner convinced the company that flying the cub around would be a good advertisement. The Humane Society wasn't very happy (39) <u>about this idea, and they convinced Turner</u> to make sure the lion cub always wore a parachute. **C**

(40) Other pilots took people for short airplane rides, often charging five dollars for a five-minute ride (by comparison, you could buy a loaf of bread for about ten cents in 1920).

These pilots, called barnstormers, often used dangerous tricks to get customers: two barnstormers once stood on a plane's wings and played tennis while the plane flew at 70 miles per hour! Many barnstormers advertised their shows as a 'flying circus.' **D**

During the 1920s, the US Post Office developed airmail. Before airmail, the post traveled on trains and (42) <u>can take weeks to reach a destination.</u>

(43) Flying for the post office was dangerous work. Early pilots didn't have sophisticated instruments and safety equipment on their planes.

Many of them had to bail out and use their parachutes when their planes iced up in the cold air or had other trouble.

After Orville and (31) <u>Wilbur Wright will have flown their</u> first airplane in 1903, the age of flying slowly began.

31.
- A. NO CHANGE
- B. Wilbur Wright, have flew their
- C. Wilbur Wright flew their
- D. Wilbur Wright will have flied their

Many new pilots (32) <u>learned how to fly in World War I, which</u> the United States joined in 1917.

32.
- F. NO CHANGE
- G. trained for flight in World War I, which
- H. studied flying during World War I, which
- J. learned how to fly in World War I which

In the years after the war and through the Roaring Twenties, America's pilots found themselves without jobs. Some of them gave up flying altogether.

33. What is the best way to combine sentences 5 and 6?
- A. Some of America's pilots in the years after the war and through the Roaring Twenties found themselves without jobs because they gave up flying altogether.
- B. In the years after the war and through the Roaring Twenties, America's pilots found themselves without jobs; thus some of them gave up flying altogether.
- C. Some of America's pilots gave up flying altogether in the years after the war and through the Roaring Twenties, and they found themselves without jobs.
- D. In the years after the war and through the Roaring Twenties, America's pilots found themselves without jobs because some of them gave up flying altogether.

Pilot Eddie (34) <u>Rickenbacker, who used to be called America's Ace of Aces, became</u> a car salesman.

34.
- F. NO CHANGE
- G. Rickenbacker, who will have been known as America's Ace of Aces, became
- H. Rickenbacker who used to be called America's Ace of Aces became
- J. Rickenbacker, who used to be called America's ace of aces, became

But other (35) <u>pilots found new and creative things</u> to do with their airplanes.

35.
- A. NO CHANGE
- B. pilots found creative things
- C. pilots attempted new and creative things
- D. pilots found new, creative tricks

The (36) <u>airplane was used by pilot Casey Jones</u> to help get news across the country.

36.
- F. NO CHANGE
- G. The airplane was used by Casey Jones, a pilot,
- H. Pilot Casey Jones used his airplane
- J. The airplane was flown by pilot Casey Jones

(37) <u>When a big news story broke, Jones</u> flew news photos to newspapers in different cities.

37.

    A. NO CHANGE

    B. When a big, news story broke, Jones

    C. When an important story broke, Jones

    D. When a big news story arrived, Jones

(38) <u>Another pilot, Roscoe Turner, traveled</u> around the country with a lion cub in his plane.

38.

    F. NO CHANGE

    G. Another pilot, Roscoe Turner, flew

    H. A pilot, Roscoe Turner, traveled

    J. Roscoe Turner, another pilot, traveled

The Humane Society wasn't very happy **(39)** <u>about this idea, and they convinced Turner</u> to make sure the lion cub always wore a parachute.

39.

    A. NO CHANGE

    B. about this idea: they convinced Turner

    C. about this idea; Turner was convinced

    D. about this idea and they convinced Turner

40. What is the best revision to the following sentence?

Other pilots took people for short airplane rides, often charging five dollars for a five-minute ride (by comparison, you could buy a loaf of bread for about ten cents in 1920).

    F. NO CHANGE

    G. In the same time period that you could buy a loaf of bread for about ten cents, there were pilots who took people for short airplane rides by charging five dollars for a five-minute ride.

    H. Pilots took people for short airplane rides by charging five dollars for a five-minute ride, or you could buy a loaf of bread for about ten cents in 1920.

    J. Often charging five dollars for a five-minute ride, pilots took people for short airplane rides, however; you could buy a loaf of bread for about ten cents in 1920 by comparison.

These pilots, called barnstormers, often used dangerous tricks <u>to get customers: two barnstormers once stood</u> on a plane's wings and played tennis while the plane flew at 70 miles per hour!

41.

    A. NO CHANGE

    B. customers, two barnstormers once stood

    C. customers: two "barnstormers" once stood

    D. customers: two barnstormers stood

(42) Before airmail, the post traveled on trains and <u>can take weeks to reach a destination.</u>

42.

    F. NO CHANGE

    G. can take weeks to finally reach a destination.

    H. could take weeks to reach a destination.

    J. could take weeks to reach it's destination.

Flying for the post office was dangerous work. Early pilots didn't have sophisticated instruments and safety equipment on their planes.

43. What is the best way to combine sentences 15 and 16?

A. Flying for the post office was dangerous work, but early pilots didn't have sophisticated instruments and safety equipment on their planes.
B. Early pilots didn't have sophisticated instruments and safety equipment on their planes which made flying for the post office dangerous work.
C. Flying for the post office was dangerous work; however, early pilots didn't have sophisticated instruments and safety equipment on their planes.
D. Early pilots didn't have sophisticated instruments and safety equipment on their planes, nor was flying for the post office dangerous work.

44. The author wants to add the following statement:

The most famous pilot of the 1920s, Charles A. Lindbergh, participated in an air race to fly across the Atlantic Ocean in May 1927.

Where is the best place for this sentence to be added in the passage?

F. Point A in Paragraph 1
G. Point B in Paragraph 2
H. Point C in Paragraph 2
J. Point D in Paragraph 3

45. If the author wanted to argue that the purpose of the passage was to explain the reasons for men and women needing to remain on the ground after the war, would the author be able to maintain this claim?

A. Yes, the first paragraph reviews the contribution that pilots made during WWI.
B. No, the passage does not focus enough on the practical aspects of the airplane compared to entertainment.
C. Yes, the author gives context to the privileges of flight and the early achievements of flight.
D. No, the author does not provide reasons for why the American public thought that the pilots should remain on the ground instead of pursuing more opportunities with flight.

Buddhism, Western Society, and the Self

[1]

(46) In Western society, the American individual self is generally prioritized over the collective self. This is evidenced in such things as the privatization of medicine and conceptions of ownership. In recent decades, however, there has been an increased tension (47) beside Western societies with institutions and ideologies that prioritize the individual and those that prioritize the collective. This is evidenced in the struggles that Western Buddhists face.

[2]

Central to Buddhist belief is the idea of "egolessness." While this term may seem to imply the absence of the individual ego or selfhood, this is (49) not the case; consequently, "egolessness" is a prioritization of the relationships between and among people over selfish concerns. "Egolessness" may also be thought of as an antonym of "ego-toxicity," that condition where an individual (50) places his or her concerns before any other person or group's concerns. (51) In Western societies, ego-toxicity is the reigning condition. Buddhists who live in such societies often find themselves caught between their ideology of egolessness and environmental ego-toxicity.

[3]

While a Western perspective might find it difficult to (53) <u>understand how a Buddhist can keep egolessness;</u> in Western society, Buddhists are able to maintain such a perspective as a natural consequent of their beliefs. The Western perspective expects moral actions to be quid pro quo; to put it another way, (54) <u>a Westerner assumes that if he or she does something considered</u> "good," then he or she should and will be rewarded. Buddhists, on the other hand, believe that good should be done out of compassion for all (55) <u>beings, and to do good is to do good for all beings, including</u> the self. Approaching society and social action in an egoless manner has begun to become more prevalent in secular institutions and movements (56) <u>as can be seen in the healthcare field</u>. The struggle between the ego and the collective continues, however.

[4]

Buddhist practitioners show through their actions that it is possible to do good in the world without giving up one's personhood. (57) <u>When ego-toxicity is abandoned, it is possible to care for one's self and the rest of the world through compassionate, egoless behavior.</u>

(46) <u>In Western society, the American individual self</u> is generally prioritized over the collective self.

46.

   F. NO CHANGE
   G. In Western society, the self
   H. In western society, the American self
   J. In Western society, the individual self

In recent decades, however, there has been an increased tension (47) <u>beside Western societies</u> with institutions and ideologies that prioritize the individual and those that prioritize the collective.

47.

   A. NO CHANGE
   B. among Western societies
   C. between Western societies
   D. underneath western societies

48. What is the purpose of the first paragraph?

   F. To criticize Buddhist notions of the self.
   G. To criticize contemporary Western notions of the self.
   H. To introduce the tension between individuality and collectivity in Western society.
   J. To introduce the idea of "egolessness."

While this term may seem to imply the absence of the individual ego or selfhood, this is (49) <u>not the case; consequently, "egolessness" is a prioritization of the relationships</u> between and among people over selfish concerns.

49.

    A. NO CHANGE

    B. not the case; rather, "egolessness" is a prioritization

    C. not the case; therefore", egolessness" is a prioritization

    D. not the case; accordingly ",egolessness" is a priority

"Egolessness" may also be thought of as an antonym of "ego-toxicity," that condition where an individual (50) <u>places his or her concerns before any other person or group's concerns.</u>

50.

    F. NO CHANGE

    G. places their concerns before any other person's concerns.

    H. places his or her concerns before any other person's or group's concerns.

    J. places their concerns before any other person or group's concerns.

51. This sentence appears in the second paragraph: "In Western societies, ego-toxicity is the reigning condition." Which of the following would be the most logical organization?

    A. NO CHANGE

    B. Move it to the end of the paragraph

    C. Move it to the paragraph's beginning

    D. Move it out of the paragraph entirely

52. Which of the following best describes the purpose of the second paragraph?

    F. It introduces the distinction between "egolessness" and "ego-toxicity."

    G. It makes light of the conflicts that Buddhists in Western societies experience.

    H. It praises egolessness as the only moral way of living.

    J. It harshly denounces ego-toxicity.

While a Western perspective might find it difficult to (53) <u>understand how a Buddhist can keep egolessness;</u> in Western society, Buddhists are able to maintain such a perspective as a natural consequent of their beliefs.

53.

    A. NO CHANGE

    B. understand how a Buddhist could maintain egolessness,

    C. understand how a Buddhist could stay egolessness

    D. believe what a Buddhist could maintain egolessness

The Western perspective expects moral actions to be quid pro quo; to put it another way, a Westerner assumes that if he or she does something considered "good," (54) <u>then he or she should and will be rewarded.</u>

54.

    F. NO CHANGE

    G. then he or she will be rewarded.

    H. then they should be rewarded.

    J. then they will be rewarded.

Buddhists, on the other hand, believe that good should be done out of compassion for all (55) **beings, and to do good is to do good for all beings, including** the self.

55.
- A. NO CHANGE
- B. beings, and to do good is good for all beings, including
- C. beings and to do good is to do good for all beings including
- D. beings, and this is done for all beings including

56. Which of the following choices gives the most specific information about how social action in an egoless manner has become more prevalent in secular institutions and movements?

Approaching society and social action in an egoless manner has begun to become more prevalent in secular institutions and movements (56) **as can be seen in the healthcare field.**
- F. NO CHANGE
- G. like the restoration of generosity among those in healthcare.
- H. such as the transition to a more socialized form of medical treatment in some Western countries.
- J. as was seen with the members of the medical field in Europe.

(57) When ego-toxicity is abandoned, it is possible to care for one's self and the rest of the world through compassionate, egoless behavior.

57.
- A. NO CHANGE
- B. When ego-toxicity can be abandoned it is possible for one's self to care for the rest of the world through compassionate, egoless behavior.
- C. When ego-toxicity is abandoned it could be possible to care for one's self and the rest of the world through compassionate, egoless behavior.
- D. When ego-toxicity is abandoned, it is possible to care for one's self and the rest of the world through compassionate, egoless behavior.

58. In this passage, which sentence in the first paragraph states a main idea that is developed in subsequent paragraphs?
- F. The second sentence
- G. The fourth sentence
- H. The third sentence
- J. The first sentence

59. The style, mode, or type of text in this passage is best characterized as which of these?
- A. Description
- B. Persuasion
- C. Exposition
- D. Narration

60. Which of these accurately describes a pattern in the first and/or last sentences of all the paragraphs in this passage?
- F. The last sentence of each paragraph identifies half a main conflict; the final sentence completes it.
- G. The first sentence of each paragraph identifies a main conflict, with the final sentence reiterating.
- H. The first sentence of each paragraph identifies a main conflict, with the final sentence resolving it.
- J. The last sentence of each paragraph identifies a main conflict, with the final sentence resolving it

The Beginnings of Basketball

[1]

(61) <u>Basketball is, arguably, one of the most popular</u> and most exciting sports of our time.

(62) Behind this fast-paced sport, however, is a rich history. **A** There have been many changes made to the game over the years, but the essence remains the same.

From its humble beginnings in 1891, (63) <u>basketball has grown to have worldwide appeal.</u>

[2]

In 1891, Dr. James Naismith, a teacher and (64) <u>Presbyterian minister, needed</u> an indoor game to keep college students busy during long winter days in Springfield, (65) <u>Massachusetts at the Springfield YMCA Training School</u>. This need prompted the creation of basketball, which was originally played by tossing a soccer ball into an empty peach basket nailed to the gym wall. **B**(67) Additionally, <u>there was two teams</u> but only one basket in the original game.

[3]

Because of the simplicity of (68) <u>basketball, the game spread</u> across the nation within 30 years of its invention in Massachusetts. **C** As more teams formed, the need for a league became apparent. The smaller National Basketball League (NBL) formed soon after. On (69) <u>June 6, 1946 the Basketball Association of America (BAA) was formed.</u> In 1948, the BAA absconded the NBL, and the National Basketball Association (NBA) was born. The NBA played its first full season in 1948-49 and is still going strong today.

[4]

Though much has changed in our world since 1891, the (72) <u>popularity of the sport of basketball has remained strong.</u> From (72) <u>it's humble start in a YMCA gym to the multi-million-dollar empire</u> it is (74) <u>today, the simple fun of the sport has endured.</u> Although many changes have been made over the years, the essence of basketball has remained constant. **D** Its rich history and simplicity ensure that basketball will always be a popular sport around the world.

(61) Arguably the sport of highest popularity and greatest excitement <u>of our time, is basketball.</u>
61.
   A. NO CHANGE
   B. of our time is basketball.
   C. among our time, is basketball.
   D. of our day and age, is basketball.

Behind this fast-paced sport, however, is a rich history. There have been many changes made to the game over the years, but the essence remains the same.

62. What is the BEST way to revise and combine sentence 2 and sentence 3?

    F.   Behind this fast-paced sport is a rich history; however, there have been many changes made to the game over the years.

    G.   Over the years the essence remains the same for this fast-paced sport with its rich history.

    H.   Behind this fast-paced sport is a rich history, but the essence remains the same.

    J.   The essence remains the same for this fast-paced sport with its rich history even though there have been many changes made to the game over the years.

From its humble beginnings in 1891, (63) basketball has grown to have worldwide appeal.

63.

    A.   NO CHANGE

    B.   basketball has grown to have world-wide appeal.

    C.   basketball grew to have worldwide appeal.

    D.   basketball has grown due to its worldwide appeal.

In 1891, Dr. James Naismith, a teacher and (64) <u>Presbyterian minister, needed</u> an indoor game to keep college students busy during long winter days in Springfield, Massachusetts at the Springfield YMCA Training School.

64.

    F.   NO CHANGE

    G.   Presbyterian Minister needed

    H.   presbyterian minister, needed

    J.   a Presbyterian Minister, founded

In 1891, Dr. James Naismith, a teacher and Presbyterian Minister, needed an indoor game to keep college students busy during long winter days in Springfield, (65) <u>Massachusetts at the Springfield YMCA Training School</u>.

65.

    A.   NO CHANGE

    B.   Massachusetts, at the Springfield YMCA training school.

    C.   Massachusetts, at the Springfield YMCA Training School.

    D.   Massachusetts at the Springfield YMCA training school.

What is the BEST placement for this sentence in the passage?

One thing that sets the history of basketball apart from other major sports is the fact that it was created with the intent to be played indoors.

66.

    F.   Point A in Paragraph 1

    G.   Point B in Paragraph 2

    H.   Point C in Paragraph 3

    J.   Point D in Paragraph 4

(67) Additionally, <u>there was two teams but only one</u> basket in the original game.

67.

    A. NO CHANGE

    B. there were two teams; but only one

    C. there was two teams, but only one

    D. there were two teams but only one

Because of the simplicity of **(68)** <u>basketball, the game spread</u> across the nation within 30 years of its invention in Massachusetts.

68.

    F. NO CHANGE

    G. basketball, the sport had spread

    H. basketball the game spread

    J. basketball, the game had spread

69. The style, mode, or type of text in this passage is best characterized as which of these?

    A. Description

    B. Persuasion

    C. Exposition

    D. Narration

On **(70)** June 6, 1946 the Basketball Association of America (BAA) was formed.

70.

    F. NO CHANGE

    G. June 6, 1946, the Basketball Association of America (BAA)

    H. June 6, 1946 the basketball association of America (BAA)

    J. June 6, 1946; the Basketball Association of America (BAA)

Though much has changed in our world since 1891, the **(71)** <u>popularity of the sport of basketball has remained strong.</u>

71.

    A. NO CHANGE

    B. popularity of basketball has remained strong.

    C. popularity of the sport of basketball has been constant.

    D. attention of the sport of basketball has been constant.

From **(72)** <u>it's humble start in a YMCA gym to the multi-million-dollar</u> empire it is today, the simple fun of the sport has endured.

72.

    F. NO CHANGE

    G. it's humble start in a YMCA gymnasium to the multi-million-dollar

    H. it's humble start in a YMCA gym to the multi-million dollar

    J. its humble start in a YMCA gym to the multi-million-dollar

From it's humble start in a YMCA gym to the multi-million-dollar empire it is (73) <u>today, the simple fun of the sport has</u> endured.

73.

    A. NO CHANGE
    B. today, the fun of the sport has
    C. today: the simple fun of the sport has
    D. today, the simple fun of the sport had

[3]

(9) Because of the simplicity of basketball, the game had spread across the nation within 30 years of its invention in Massachusetts. (10) As more teams formed, the need for a league became apparent. (11) The smaller National Basketball League (NBL) formed soon after. (12) On June 6, 1946 the Basketball Association of America (BAA) was formed. (13) In 1948, the BAA absconded the NBL, and the National Basketball Association (NBA) was born. (14) The NBA played its first full season in 1948-49 and is still going strong today.

74. Which of the following changes would most improve the organization and clarity of paragraph 3 of this essay?

    F. The paragraph is correct as it is written
    G. Move sentence 10 to the beginning of the paragraph
    H. Switch sentences 11 and 12
    J. Switch sentences 13 and 14

75. If the author wanted to argue that the purpose of the passage was to explain the influence of the YMCA on sports, would the author be able to maintain this claim?

    A. Yes, the author demonstrated that James Naismith invented a sport.
    B. No, the thirty years after its invention was influential than the YMCA.
    C. Yes, some of the most respected athletes in America were members at a YMCA.
    D. No, the author would need to show how the YMCA influenced more than just basketball.

Mathematics

1. Determine the number of diagonals of a dodecagon.

    A. 12
    B. 24
    C. 54
    D. 72
    E. 108

2. The expression $-2i \times 7i$ is equal to

    F. -14
    G. 14
    H. $14\sqrt{-1}$
    J. $-14\sqrt{-1}$
    K. None of the above.

3. On a road map, $\frac{1}{4}$ inch represents 8 miles of actual road distance. The towns of Dinuba and Clovis are measured to be $2\frac{1}{8}$ inches apart on the map. What is the actual distance, in miles, between the two towns?

    A. 32
    B. 40
    C. 60
    D. 64
    E. 68

4. Put the following numbers in order from the least to greatest $2^3, 4^2, 6^0, 9, 10^1$.

    F. $2^3, 4^2, 6^0, 9, 10^1$
    G. $6^0, 9, 10^1, 2^3, 4^2$
    H. $10^1, 2^3, 6^0, 9, 4^2$
    J. $6^0, 2^3, 9, 10^1, 4^2$
    K. $2^3, 9, 10^1, 4^2, 6^0$

5. The volume of a rectangular box is found by multiplying its length, width, and height. If the dimensions of a box are $\sqrt{3}, 2\sqrt{5}$, and 4, what is its volume?

    A. $2\sqrt{60}$
    B. $2\sqrt{15}$
    C. $4\sqrt{15}$
    D. $8\sqrt{15}$
    E. $24\sqrt{5}$

6. Abe averages 3 miles per hour running and Beatriz averages 4 miles per hour running. How much further can Beatriz go in $\frac{1}{2}$ hour than Abe can?

    F. 2 miles

    G. 1 mile

    H. $\frac{1}{2}$ mile

    J. $\frac{1}{4}$ mile

    K. $\frac{1}{8}$ mile

7. In the figure below, ΔJKL is dilated to the image $\Delta J'K'L'$.

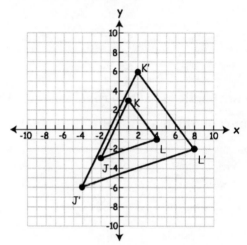

What is the scale factor of the dilation?

    A. $\frac{1}{3}$

    B. $\frac{1}{2}$

    C. 2

    D. 3

    E. $\frac{1}{4}$

8. Which of the following expressions is equivalent to $(x-3)^2$?

    F. $x^2 - 3x + 9$

    G. $x^2 - 6x - 9$

    H. $x^2 - 6x + 9$

    J. $x^2 + 3x - 9$

    K. $x^2 + 3x + 9$

9. Given the double bar graph shown below, which of the following statements is true?

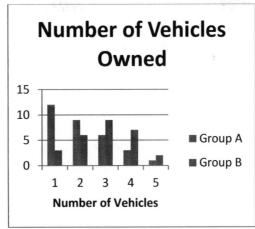

A. Group A is negatively skewed, while Group B is approximately normal.
B. Group A is positively skewed, while Group B is approximately normal.
C. Group A is positively skewed, while Group B is neutral.
D. Group A is approximately normal, while Group B is negatively skewed.
E. Group A is approximately normal, while Group B is positively skewed.

10. Which of the following is true about the relationship between the two triangles shown below?

 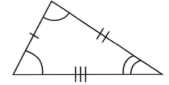

F. The triangles are similar.
G. The triangles are congruent.
H. The triangles are equilateral.
J. The triangles are both congruent and equilateral.
K. The triangles are both similar and congruent.

11. Elijah spends $30 for a state fair ticket and $3.50 per ride. Which of the following expressions could be used to find the total amount spent, if riding x rides?

A. $3.50 + 30x$
B. $33.50x$
C. $30 + 3.50x$
D. $33.50 + 3.50x$
E. $33.50 - 3.50x$

12. The matrix represents the number of students in the class periods of each teacher. Which of the following statements can be made from the information in the matrix?

$$\begin{array}{c} \\ 1st \\ 2nd \\ 3rd \end{array} \begin{array}{cc} \text{Smith} & \text{Tan} \\ \begin{bmatrix} 31 & 25 \\ 29 & 27 \\ 34 & 30 \end{bmatrix} \end{array}$$

F. Smith has 12 more students than Tan.
G. Smith is more popular with students than Tan.
H. Tan has smaller class sizes because she teaches harder classes.
J. Smith wants 3 students from 1st period to transfer into Tan's class.
K. None of the above.

13. If rectangle *ABCD* is dilated by a scale factor of $\frac{1}{2}$ to create its image *A′B′C′D′*, how does the slope of $\overline{AC}$ compare to the slope of $\overline{A'C'}$?

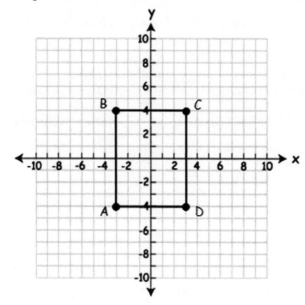

A. The slope of $\overline{A'C'}$ is half the slope of $\overline{AC}$.
B. The slope of $\overline{A'C'}$ is double the slope of $\overline{AC}$.
C. The slope of $\overline{A'C'}$ is the same as the slope of $\overline{AC}$.
D. The slope of $\overline{A'C'}$ is the reciprocal of the slope of $\overline{AC}$.
E. The slope of $\overline{A'C'}$ is not comparable to the slope of $\overline{AC}$.

14. A dress is marked down by 20% and placed on a clearance rack, on which is posted a sign reading, "Take an extra 25% off already reduced merchandise." What fraction of the original price is the final sale price of the dress?

F. $\frac{2}{5}$

G. $\frac{9}{20}$

H. $\frac{11}{20}$

J. $\frac{3}{5}$

K. $\frac{1}{4}$

15. Given the equation, $ax + b = c$, what is the value of x?

A. $\frac{c+b}{a}$

B. $\frac{ca}{b}$

C. $c - ba$

D. $\frac{c-b}{a}$

E. $c + ba$

16. Anna walks from her house to school each day. If she walks 8 blocks east of her house, then turns and walks 6 blocks south to arrive at school, how far is her school in a direct line from her house?

F. 10 blocks

G. 12 blocks

H. 14 blocks

J. 16 blocks

K. 18 blocks

17. In Figure 1 (pictured below), the distance from A to D is 48. The distance from A to B is equal to the distance from B to C. If the distance from C to D is twice the distance of A to B, how far apart are B and D?

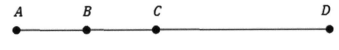

Figure 1

A. 12

B. 16

C. 19

D. 24

E. 36

18. A company is building a track for a local high school. There are two straight sections and two semi-circular turns. Given the dimensions, which of the following most closely measures the perimeter of the entire track?

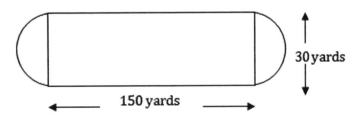

F. 300 yards

G. 180 yards

H. 360 yards

J. 395 yards

K. 120 yards

19. Solve: $\begin{bmatrix} 4 & 2 \\ 7 & 12 \end{bmatrix} + \begin{bmatrix} -1 & 15 \\ 3 & -5 \end{bmatrix}$.

A. $\begin{bmatrix} 3 & 17 \\ 10 & 7 \end{bmatrix}$

B. $\begin{bmatrix} 3 & 1 \\ 10 & 15 \end{bmatrix}$

C. $\begin{bmatrix} 19 & 17 \\ 2 & 7 \end{bmatrix}$

D. $\begin{bmatrix} 19 & 1 \\ 2 & 15 \end{bmatrix}$

E. $\begin{bmatrix} 3 & 17 \\ 2 & 15 \end{bmatrix}$

20. Approximately what percentage of 81 is 36?

F. 34

G. 44

H. 54

J. 64

K. 74

21. Which of the following represents the solution to the system of linear equations
$\begin{cases} 5x + 9y = -7 \\ 2x - 4y = 20 \end{cases}$?

$5x + 9y = -7$
$2x - 4y = 20$?

A. $x = 3, y = 2$

B. $x = 4, y = 3$

C. $x = 4, y = -3$

D. $x = 3, y = -2$

E. $x = 3, y = -3$

22. Raul, Eli, Henry, and Lex all bought the same shirt from different stores for different prices. They spent $18.00, $18.50, $15.39 and $19.99 respectively. What is the average price the four men spent for the shirt?

F. $15.97

G. $16.97

H. $17.97

J. $18.97

K. $19.97

23. Simplify: $(3 - 6i)(5 + 4i)$

A. $39 - 18i$

B. $15 - 24i$

C. $-9 - 18i$

D. $-18i^2$

E. $8 - 2i$

216

24. A farmer installed a new grain silo on his property for the fall harvest. The silo is in the shape of a cylinder with a diameter of 8 m and a height of 24 m. How much grain will the farmer be able to store in the silo, in cubic meters, rounded to the nearest integer multiple of pi?

   F. 192π m³
   G. 384π m³
   H. 512π m³
   J. 768π m³
   K. 1536π m³

25. John puts his money into a bank account that pays monthly interest. His monthly balance (in dollars) after t months is given by the exponential function $b(t) = 315(1.05)^t$. How much money did John initially put into the account?

   A. $5
   B. $105
   C. $300
   D. $315
   E. $350

26. A building is installing a new ramp at their front entrance.

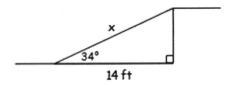

Based on the figure above, what is the length of the ramp, shown by x?

   F. $14 \cos 34°$ ft
   G. $\dfrac{14}{\cos 34°}$ ft
   H. $\dfrac{14}{\tan 34°}$ ft
   J. $\dfrac{14}{\sin 34°}$ ft
   K. None of the above.

27. If Fahrenheit, (°F) and Celsius, (°C) are related by the formula $°F = \left(\dfrac{9}{5}\right)°C + 32$, what is the temperature in Fahrenheit of a location with an average temperature of 20 °C?

   A. 58°
   B. 63°
   C. 68°
   D. 73°
   E. 78°

28. A rectangle with a perimeter of 92 inches has a length of 14 inches longer than its width. What is its width in inches?

   F. 8
   G. 16
   H. 32
   J. 40
   K. 44

29. Given the table below, which of the following best represents the probability that a student is enrolled at TAMU or prefers lattes?

	Latte	Cappuccino	Frappuccino	Total
TAMU	350	225	175	750
NMSU	325	300	275	900
Total	675	525	450	1650

- A. 55%
- B. 60%
- C. 65%
- D. 70%
- E. 75%

30. A librarian makes time-and-a-half for each hour that he works over 40 hours per week. The linear function $s(h) = 27h + 720$ represents his weekly salary (in dollars) if he works h hours more than 40 hours that week. For example, his weekly salary is $s(10) = 990$ dollars if he works 50 hours in one week (because 50 hours means 10 hours of overtime). What is his hourly salary after he has already worked the initial 40 hours in one week?

- F. $7.20 per hour
- G. $18.00 per hour
- H. $27.00 per hour
- J. $48.00 per hour
- K. $72.00 per hour

31. Edward draws a card from a deck of cards, does not replace it, and then draws another card. What is the probability that he draws a heart and then a spade?

- A. $\dfrac{1}{16}$
- B. $\dfrac{1}{2}$
- C. $\dfrac{1}{17}$
- D. $\dfrac{13}{204}$
- E. $\dfrac{1}{3}$

32. There are 100 bacteria in a Petri dish. The number of bacteria doubles every day, so that on the first day, there are 100 bacteria; on the second, there are 200; on the third, there are 400; and so on. Write a formula for the number of bacteria on the nth day.

- F. $b(n) = 100 \times 2^{n-1}$
- G. $b(n) = 100n$
- H. $b(n) = 100n^2$
- J. $b(n) = 200(n-1)$
- K. $b(n) = 200n^2$

Questions 33–34 refer to the following information:

The 180 campers in Group A got to choose which kind of sandwich they wanted on the picnic. The results of the choice are given in the table below.

Sandwich	# of Campers
PB & J	60
Turkey	45
Egg salad	15
Veggie	60

33. Approximately what percentage of the campers chose either turkey or egg salad?

    A. 66

    B. 45

    C. 33

    D. 15

    E. 7

34. Which expression correctly provides the ratio of campers who chose veggie sandwiches to those who chose turkey?

    F. 1:3

    G. 1:4

    H. 2:3

    J. 3:2

    K. 4:3

35. In the figure below, circle O is a unit circle, and the measure of $\angle AOB$ is $\frac{\pi}{3}$ (radians).

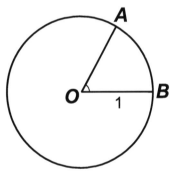

What is the length of $\overarc{AB}$?

    A. $\frac{\pi}{6}$

    B. $\frac{\pi}{3}$

    C. $\frac{2\pi}{3}$

    D. π

    E. 2π

36. Evaluate the quotient and express in standard form: $\frac{15-5i}{4-2i}$.

   F. $\dfrac{25+5i}{6}$

   G. $\dfrac{7+5i}{2}$

   H. $\dfrac{5+i}{2}$

   J. $\dfrac{7+i}{2}$

   K. $\dfrac{7+5i}{6}$

37. Donald rolls a die. If the die lands on a 1 or 2, he wins $5.00. If the die lands on a 3, he loses $1.00. If the die lands on a 4, 5 or 6, he loses $2.50. Which of the following statements is true?

   I. He can expect to win $0.25 after 1 roll.

   II. He can expect to lose $0.50 after 1 roll.

   III. His expected winnings for 50 rolls sum to $12.50.

   IV. His expected losses for 50 rolls sum to $25.00.

   A. I only

   B. I and III only

   C. II only

   D. II and IV only

   E. IV only

38. If $A = \begin{bmatrix} 1 & -3 \\ -4 & 2 \end{bmatrix}$ and $B = \begin{bmatrix} 1 & -3 \\ -4 & -2 \end{bmatrix}$, then what is $A - B$?

   F. $\begin{bmatrix} 2 & -6 \\ -8 & 0 \end{bmatrix}$

   G. $\begin{bmatrix} 0 & 0 \\ 0 & 0 \end{bmatrix}$

   H. $\begin{bmatrix} 0 & 0 \\ 0 & 4 \end{bmatrix}$

   J. $\begin{bmatrix} 0 & 3 \\ 4 & 2 \end{bmatrix}$

   K. $\begin{bmatrix} 0 & -6 \\ -8 & 4 \end{bmatrix}$

39. The table below displays the value of the linear function $g(x)$ for different values of x.

x	−2	−1	0	1	2
$g(x)$	10	7	4	1	−2

Write an explicit formula for $g(x)$.

   A. $g(x) = -4x + 3$

   B. $g(x) = -4x + 4$

   C. $g(x) = -3x + 3$

   D. $g(x) = -3x + 4$

   E. $g(x) = -2x + 4$

40. A tire on a car rotates at 500 RPM (revolutions per minute) when the car is traveling at 50 km/hr (kilometers per hour). What is the circumference of the tire? Give your answer in meters.

F. $\dfrac{50{,}000}{2\pi}$

G. $\dfrac{50{,}000}{60 \times 2\pi}$

H. $\dfrac{50{,}000}{60}$

J. $\dfrac{10}{6}$

K. $\dfrac{10}{60 \times 2\pi}$

41. Given the equation, $\dfrac{2}{x-8} = \dfrac{3}{x}$, what is the value of x?

A. 16
B. 20
C. 24
D. 28
E. 32

42. Sophie is painting a wall in her living room red. She can cover 36 square feet with one gallon of paint. If the wall is 8 feet high and 15 feet long, how many gallons will she need to purchase if she can only purchase whole gallons of paint?

F. 2 gallons
G. 3 gallons
H. 4 gallons
J. 5 gallons
K. 6 gallons

43. If $g(x) = 3x + x + 5$, evaluate $g(2)$.

A. $g(2) = 8$
B. $g(2) = 9$
C. $g(2) = 13$
D. $g(2) = 17$
E. $g(2) = 19$

44. $\overline{AB}$ is tangent to Circle O. Find the length of $\overline{OB}$.

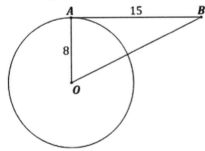

F. 13
G. 16
H. 17
J. 23
K. 64

45. The table below shows the average amount of rainfall Houston receives during the summer and autumn months.

Month	Rainfall (inches)
June	5.35
July	3.18
August	3.83
September	4.33
October	4.5
November	4.19

What percentage of rainfall in this timeframe is received during October?

- A. 13.5%
- B. 15.1%
- C. 16.9%
- D. 17.7%
- E. 18.38%

46. Use factoring to identify the zeroes of the function $f(x) = x^2 + 5x - 24$.

- F. −24
- G. −8 and 3
- H. −6 and 4
- J. 6 and −4
- K. 24

47. Which function has the same x-intercept as the function graphed below?

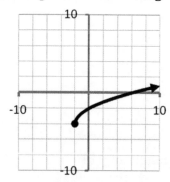

- A. $g(x) = -4x - 12$
- B. $g(x) = x^2 - 12x + 36$
- C. $g(x) = x^3 + 6x^2 - 2x - 2$
- D. $g(x) = \frac{6}{x-3}$
- E. $g(x) = x^2 - 12x - 36$

48. What is the constant of proportionality represented by the table below?

x	y
2	−8
5	−20
7	−28
10	−40
11	−44

    F. −12
    G. −8
    H. −6
    J. −4
    K. 4

49. The possible combinations of candy bars and packages of suckers that Amanda may purchase are represented by the graph shown below.

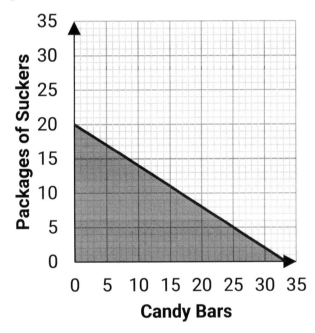

Which of the following inequalities represents the possible combinations of candy bars and packages of suckers that she may purchase?

    A. $y \leq -\frac{1}{2}x + \frac{40}{3}$
    B. $y \leq -\frac{2}{5}x + 20$
    C. $y \leq -\frac{3}{5}x + 20$
    D. $y \leq -\frac{5}{3}x + \frac{80}{3}$
    E. $y \leq -\frac{2}{3}x + \frac{80}{3}$

50. A local craft store specializes in selling marbles. To display their most popular sized marble, the store created a 3 ft × 2 ft × 6 in glass box and completely filled the box with 5,184 marbles. What is the density of marbles per cubic foot in the glass box?

F. 144 marbles/cubic foot
G. 864 marbles/cubic foot
H. 1,728 marbles/cubic foot
J. 15,522 marbles/cubic foot
K. None of the above.

51. Calculate the average rate of change of the function $f(x) = -3x + 1$, over the range from $x = 1$ to $x = 5$.

A. −4
B. −3
C. 3
D. 4
E. −4

52. Portia tosses a coin 1,000 times. Which of the following best represents the number of times she can expect to get tails?

F. 350
G. 400
H. 450
J. 500
K. 1000

53. The sides of quadrilateral $PQRS$ are tangent to the circle. What is the perimeter of quadrilateral $PQRS$?

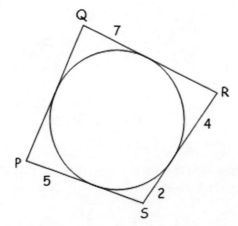

A. 36
B. 30
C. 24
D. 20
E. 18

54. James won a cash raffle prize. He paid taxes of 30% on the prize and had $14,000 remaining. How much was the original prize?

    F. $42,000

    G. $40,000

    H. $30,000

    J. $20,000

    K. $18,000

55. In $\triangle ABC$, $\cos A =$

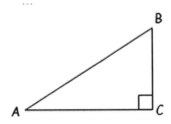

    A. $\dfrac{AC}{AB}$

    B. $\dfrac{AC}{BC}$

    C. $\dfrac{BC}{AC}$

    D. $\dfrac{BC}{AB}$

    E. None of the above.

56. A certain city covers 54.9 square miles of land and has a population of 382,578. What is the population density of the city?

    F. 126.9 persons/square mile

    G. 6,968.6 persons/square mile

    H. 21,003,532.2 persons/square mile

    J. 1,153,093,917.8 persons/square mile

    K. None of the above.

57. On Peter's homework assignment of a state map, $\frac{1}{2}$ inch represents 12 miles. If a distance is 84 miles, how many inches long will it be on Peter's map?

    A. 3

    B. 3.5

    C. 5

    D. 5.5

    E. 6

58. Which of the following numbers has the digit 3 in the hundredths place?

    F. 315

    G. 3.15

    H. 0.0315

    J. 0.00315

    K. 0.000315

59. A pump fills a cylindrical tank with water at a constant rate. The function $L(g) = 0.3g$ represents the water level of the tank (in feet) after g gallons are pumped into the tank. The function $w(t) = 1.2t$ represents the number of gallons that can be pumped into the tank in t minutes. Write a function $L(t)$ for the water level of the tank after t minutes.

    A. $L(t) = 0.25t$
    B. $L(t) = 0.36t$
    C. $L(t) = 0.9t$
    D. $L(t) = 3.6t$
    E. $L(t) = 4t$

60. As shown below, four congruent isosceles trapezoids are positioned such that they form an arch. Find x for the indicated angle.

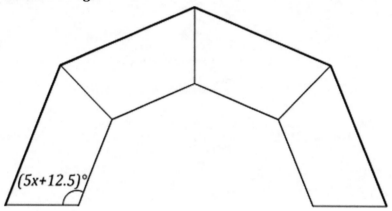

    F. $x = 11$
    G. $x = 20$
    H. $x = 24.5$
    J. $x = 135$
    K. The value of x cannot be determined from the information given.

Reading

Passage 1: Humanities: This passage is adapted from President Franklin D. Roosevelt's *State of the Union Address* in January of 1941.

Many subjects connected with our social economy call for immediate improvement. As examples:

We should bring more citizens under the
5 coverage of old-age pensions and unemployment insurance. We should widen the opportunities for adequate medical care. We should plan a better system by which persons deserving or needing gainful
10 employment may obtain it.

I have called for personal sacrifice. And I am assured of the willingness of almost all Americans to respond to that call. A part of the sacrifice means the payment of more
15 money in taxes. In my Budget Message I will recommend that a greater portion of this great defense program be paid for from taxation than we are paying for today. No person should try, or be allowed, to get rich
20 out of the program; and the principle of tax payments in accordance with ability to pay should be constantly before our eyes to guide our legislation. If the Congress maintains these principles, the voters, putting
25 patriotism ahead of pocketbooks, will give you their applause.

In the future days, which we seek to make secure, we look forward to a world founded upon four essential human freedoms. The
30 first is freedom of speech and expression— everywhere in the world. The second is freedom of every person to worship God in his own way—everywhere in the world. The third is freedom from want—which,
35 translated into world terms, means economic understandings which will secure to every nation a healthy peacetime life for its inhabitants—everywhere in the world. The fourth is freedom from fear—which,
40 translated into world terms, means a world-wide reduction of armaments to such a point and in such a thorough fashion that no nation will be in a position to commit an act of physical aggression against any neighbor—
45 anywhere in the world.

That is no vision of a distant millennium. It is a definite basis for a kind of world attainable in our own time and generation. That kind of world is the very antithesis of the
50 so-called new order of tyranny which the dictators seek to create with the crash of a bomb. To that new order we oppose the greater conception—the moral order. A good society is able to face schemes of world
55 domination and foreign revolutions alike without fear.

Since the beginning of our American history, we have been engaged in change—in a perpetual peaceful revolution—a revolution
60 which goes on steadily, quietly adjusting itself to changing conditions—without the concentration camp or the quick-lime in the ditch. The world order which we seek is the cooperation of free countries, working
65 together in a friendly, civilized society.

This nation has placed its destiny in the hands and heads and hearts of its millions of free men and women; and its faith in freedom under the guidance of God. Freedom means
70 the supremacy of human rights everywhere. Our support goes to those who struggle to gain those rights and keep them. Our strength is our unity of purpose. To that high concept there can be no end save victory.

1. Which statement best supports the idea that FDR believed that America is constantly evolving toward a better situation?

A. Since the beginning of our American history, we have been engaged in change—in a perpetual peaceful revolution—a revolution which goes on steadily, quietly adjusting itself to changing conditions—without the concentration camp or the quick-lime in the ditch.

B. This nation has placed its destiny in the hands and heads and hearts of its millions of free men and women; and its faith in freedom under the guidance of God.

C. To that new order we oppose the greater conception—the moral order. A good society is able to face schemes of world domination and foreign revolutions alike without fear.

D. The fourth is freedom from fear—which, translated into world terms, means a world-wide reduction of armaments to such a point and in such a thorough fashion that no nation will be in a position to commit an act of physical aggression against any neighbor—anywhere in the world.

2. In this text, FDR claims that raising taxes will result in a patriotic populace that will happily support the government. What might be one argument against this idea?

F. Americans are uninterested in pursuing freedom of any kind, and the four freedoms listed here are not considered important.

G. The average citizen already feels overburdened by taxes and feels the money is not being well-spent by the government.

H. Individuals will easily assent to the idea of a greater tax burden since it will naturally lead to a more prosperous state.

J. Patriots of all kinds are part of the natural makeup of America, and some will feel that the support of government is something that should be contemplated and debated.

3. What is a major theme that Roosevelt articulates in his speech?

A. It is important for all people to have access to the benefits of an old-age system that supports citizens when they can no longer work.

B. Patriotic people will feel the need to pay more taxes to the government in order to obtain certain benefits they would not be able to afford.

C. People who want to work should be able to find work without bias and without undue hardship.

D. There are four basic freedoms that are vital to the health of people: speech, worship, freedom from want, and freedom from fear.

4. The last sentence in this passage is, "<u>To that high concept there can be no end save victory.</u>" In the context of the preceding text, which of the following is the most precise meaning of the word "end"?

F. Death

G. Purpose

H. Outcome

J. Conclusion

5. FDR spoke of <u>"the so-called new order of tyranny which the dictators seek to create with the crash of a bomb."</u> In the context of this passage, which is the most accurate meaning of the word "order"?

    A. A command given by a military leader
    B. An authoritative decision or direction
    C. An arrangement of items in sequence
    D. A system of societal and world politics

6. When FDR spoke of <u>"personal sacrifice"</u>, which of these did he explicitly give as an example of it?

    F. Higher taxation
    G. Military service
    H. Arms reduction
    J. Four freedoms

7. FDR described America's constant engagement in change as <u>"a perpetual peaceful revolution...without the concentration camp or the quick-lime in the ditch."</u> In this description, we can infer his implicit reference to which war(s)?

    A. Revolutionary
    B. World War I
    C. World War II
    D. To all of them

8. FDR identified aspects of the social economy needing to be improved immediately. As evidence of this need, which example did he NOT cite in this passage?

    F. Expanding retirement benefits
    G. Expanding healthcare benefits
    H. Expanding draft by the military
    J. Expanding labor opportunities

9. As represented in this passage, the power and tone of FDR's speech are enhanced by which?

    A. Short, simple sentences
    B. Long, complex sentences
    C. Long, compound sentences
    D. (b), (c), complex-compound

10. What can readers infer from lines 15 - 24 of President Roosevelt's message?

    F. The President attempted to name every right in the 1st Amendment but failed.
    G. Roosevelt is more concerned about the people of other nations than American citizens.
    H. The President is uncertain on whether he can deliver on such a large promise.
    J. President Roosevelt is deeply concerned with individual rights and liberties.

Passage II: Literary Narrative: The following passage is adapted from Jack London's *The Call of the Wild* (1903).

Buck did not read the newspapers, or he would have known that trouble was brewing, not alone for himself, but for every tide-water dog, strong of muscle and with warm, long

5 hair, from Puget Sound to San Diego. Because men, groping in the Arctic darkness, had found a yellow metal, and because steamship and transportation companies were booming the find, thousands of men were rushing into
10 the Northland. These men wanted dogs, and the dogs they wanted were heavy dogs, with strong muscles by which to toil, and furry coats to protect them from the frost.

Buck lived at a big house in the sun-kissed
15 Santa Clara Valley. Judge Miller's place, it was called. It stood back from the road, half hidden among the trees, through which glimpses could be caught of the wide cool veranda that ran around its four sides. The
20 house was approached by gravelled driveways which wound about through wide-spreading lawns and under the interlacing boughs of tall poplars. At the rear things were on even a more spacious scale than at the
25 front. There were great stables, where a dozen grooms and boys held forth, rows of vine-clad servants' cottages, an endless and orderly array of outhouses, long grape arbors, green pastures, orchards, and berry patches.
30 Then there was the pumping plant for the artesian well, and the big cement tank where Judge Miller's boys took their morning plunge and kept cool in the hot afternoon.

And over this great demesne Buck ruled.
35 Here he was born, and here he had lived the four years of his life. It was true, there were other dogs, there could not but be other dogs on so vast a place, but they did not count. They came and went, resided in the populous
40 kennels, or lived obscurely in the recesses of the house after the fashion of Toots, the Japanese pug, or Ysabel, the Mexican hairless,—strange creatures that rarely put nose out of doors or set foot to ground. On the
45 other hand, there were the fox terriers, a score of them at least, who yelped fearful promises at Toots and Ysabel looking out of the windows at them and protected by a legion of housemaids armed with brooms and
50 mops.

But Buck was neither house-dog nor kennel-dog. The whole realm was his. He plunged into the swimming tank or went hunting with the Judge's sons; he escorted
55 Mollie and Alice, the Judge's daughters, on long twilight or early morning rambles; on wintry nights he lay at the Judge's feet before the roaring library fire; he carried the Judge's grandsons on his back, or rolled them in the
60 grass, and guarded their footsteps through wild adventures down to the fountain in the stable yard, and even beyond, where the paddocks were, and the berry patches. Among the terriers he stalked imperiously,
65 and Toots and Ysabel he utterly ignored, for he was king,—king over all creeping, crawling, flying things of Judge Miller's place, humans included.

His father, Elmo, a huge St. Bernard, had
70 been the Judge's inseparable companion, and Buck bid fair to follow in the way of his father. He was not so large,—he weighed only one hundred and forty pounds,—for his mother, Shep, had been a Scotch shepherd dog.
75 Nevertheless, one hundred and forty pounds, to which was added the dignity that comes of good living and universal respect, enabled him to carry himself in right royal fashion. During the four years since his puppyhood he
80 had lived the life of a sated aristocrat; he had a fine pride in himself, was even a trifle egotistical, as country gentlemen sometimes become because of their insular situation. But he had saved himself by not becoming a mere
85 pampered house-dog. Hunting and kindred outdoor delights had kept down the fat and hardened his muscles; and to him, as to the cold-tubbing races, the love of water had been a tonic and a health preserver.

90 And this was the manner of dog Buck was in the fall of 1897, when the Klondike strike dragged men from all the world into the frozen North. But Buck did not read the newspapers, and he did not know that
95 Manuel, one of the gardener's helpers, was an undesirable acquaintance. Manuel had one besetting sin. He loved to play Chinese lottery. Also, in his gambling, he had one besetting

230

weakness—faith in a system; and this made his damnation certain. For to play a system requires money, while the wages of a gardener's helper do not lap over the needs of a wife and numerous progenies.

The Judge was at a meeting of the Raisin Growers' Association, and the boys were busy organizing an athletic club, on the memorable night of Manuel's treachery. No one saw him and Buck go off through the orchard on what Buck imagined was merely a stroll. And with the exception of a solitary man, no one saw them arrive at the little flag station known as College Park. This man talked with Manuel, and money chinked between them.

11. What is the purpose of paragraphs 2-5?

A. To introduce all of the story's characters
B. To show Buck's personality
C. To introduce Buck
D. To show Buck's affection for Toots and Ysabel

12. Which sentence or phrase shows Buck's attitude about Judge Miller's place?

F. They came and went, resided in the populous kennels, or lived obscurely in the recesses of the house
G. The whole realm was his
H. He had a fine pride in himself
J. And to him, as to the cold-tubbing races, the love of water had been a tonic and a health preserver

13. The author uses the detail in paragraph 1 to

A. Describe Buck's life
B. Foreshadow Buck's story
C. Describe the story's setting
D. Introduce the story's villain

14. What is the significance of the Klondike strike in 1897?

F. It will lead to changes in Buck's life
G. It will cause more dogs to move to Judge Miller's place
H. It changed Elmo's life
J. It caused the Raisin Growers' Association to meet more frequently

15. The author organizes this selection mainly by

A. Describing Buck's life in the order in which it happened
B. Outlining Buck's history
C. Showing Buck's life and then showing a moment of change
D. Comparing Buck's life at Judge Miller's place to what came afterwards

16. Which answer choice best describes the purpose of the selection?

F. To set up a story by providing background information
G. To show Buck in a moment of heroism
H. To give details about the Klondike strike
J. To introduce all the dogs that live at Judge Miller's

17. This selection is part of a longer work. Based on the selection, what might be a theme of the larger work?

    A. Change

    B. Family

    C. Hard work

    D. Relationships

18. Which sentence from the passage foreshadows the rest of the story?

    F. And over this great demesne Buck ruled

    G. These men wanted dogs, and the dogs they wanted were heavy dogs, with strong muscles by which to toil, and furry coats to protect them from the frost

    H. His father, Elmo, a huge St. Bernard, had been the Judge's inseparable companion and Buck bid fair to follow in the way of his father

    J. But he had saved himself by not becoming a mere pampered house-dog

19. What is the most logical explanation for Manuel taking Buck away from Judge Miller's place?

    A. Manuel is taking the dog in order to find gold in the "frozen North."

    B. Buck will be trained to be a service dog for the Judge's daughters.

    C. Manuel needs the protection as he meets with the man at College Park.

    D. The dog will be used for hunting events.

20. Who is the narrator of this passage?

    F. Buck

    G. Mollie and Alice

    H. Judge Miller

    J. A non-participant narrator

Passage III: Natural Science: The following passage is adapted from Albert Einstein's paper on *Relativity: The Special and General Theory* (1916, revised 1924).

In order to attain the greatest possible clearness, let us return to our example of the railway carriage supposed to be travelling uniformly. We call its motion a uniform
5 translation ("uniform" because it is of constant velocity and direction, "translation" because although the carriage changes its position relative to the embankment yet it does not rotate in so doing). Let us imagine a
10 raven flying through the air in such a manner that its motion, as observed from the embankment, is uniform and in a straight line. If we were to observe the flying raven from the moving railway carriage, we should find
15 that the motion of the raven would be one of different velocity and direction, but that it would still be uniform and in a straight line. Expressed in an abstract manner we may say: If a mass m is moving uniformly in a straight
20 line with respect to a co-ordinate system K, then it will also be moving uniformly and in a straight line relative to a second co-ordinate system K1 provided that the latter is executing a uniform translatory motion with
25 respect to K. In accordance with the discussion contained in the preceding section, it follows that:

If K is a Galilean co-ordinate system, then every other co-ordinate system K' is a
30 Galilean one, when, in relation to K, it is in a condition of uniform motion of translation. Relative to K1 the mechanical laws of Galilei-Newton hold good exactly as they do with respect to K.

35 We advance a step farther in our generalization when we express the tenet

thus: If, relative to K, K1 is a uniformly moving co-ordinate system devoid of rotation, then natural phenomena run their course with respect to K1 according to exactly the same general laws as with respect to K. This statement is called the principle of relativity (in the restricted sense).

As long as one was convinced that all-natural phenomena were capable of representation with the help of classical mechanics, there was no need to doubt the validity of this principle of relativity...

Nevertheless, there are two general facts which at the outset speak very much in favor of the validity of the principle of relativity. Even though classical mechanics does not supply us with a sufficiently broad basis for the theoretical presentation of all physical phenomena, still we must grant it a considerable measure of "truth," since it supplies us with the actual motions of the heavenly bodies with a delicacy of detail little short of wonderful. The principle of relativity must therefore apply with great accuracy in the domain of mechanics. But that a principle of such broad generality should hold with such exactness in one domain of phenomena, and yet should be invalid for another, is a priori not very probable.

We now proceed to the second argument, to which, moreover, we shall return later. If the principle of relativity (in the restricted sense) does not hold, then the Galilean co-ordinate systems K, K1, K2, etc., which are moving uniformly relative to each other, will not be equivalent for the description of natural phenomena. In this case we should be constrained to believe that natural laws are capable of being formulated in a particularly simple manner, and of course only on condition that, from amongst all possible Galilean co-ordinate systems, we should have chosen one (K[0]) of a particular state of motion as our body of reference. We should then be justified (because of its merits for the description of natural phenomena) in calling this system "absolutely at rest," and all other Galilean systems K "in motion." If, for instance, our embankment were the system K[0] then our railway carriage would be a system K, relative to which less simple laws would hold than with respect to K[0]. This diminished simplicity would be due to the fact that the carriage K would be in motion (i.e. "really") with respect to K[0]. In the general laws of nature which have been formulated with reference to K, the magnitude and direction of the velocity of the carriage would necessarily play a part. We should expect, for instance, that the note emitted by an organ pipe placed with its axis parallel to the direction of travel would be different from that emitted if the axis of the pipe were placed perpendicular to this direction.

Now in virtue of its motion in an orbit round the sun, our earth is comparable with a railway carriage travelling with a velocity of about 30 kilometers per second. If the principle of relativity were not valid, we should therefore expect that the direction of motion of the Earth at any moment would enter into the laws of nature, and also that physical systems in their behavior would be dependent on the orientation in space with respect to the Earth. For owing to the alteration in direction of the velocity of revolution of the Earth in the course of a year, the Earth cannot be at rest relative to the hypothetical system K[0] throughout the whole year. However, the most careful observations have never revealed such anisotropic properties in terrestrial physical space, i.e. a physical non-equivalence of different directions. This is a very powerful argument in favor of the principle of relativity.

21. Which of the following choices best supports the claim of Einstein's theory of special relativity as accurate?

    A. the movement of the Earth around the sun
    B. Galilean co-ordinate systems and their application in classical mechanics
    C. the idea of chance in quantum mechanics
    D. the two different parts of relativity

22. What might be one question to ask to begin an argument against Einstein's theory of relativity?

    F. If relativity holds true, what does that say about the classical rules of motion?
    G. If relativity is valid, then why can it not explain all parts of the natural world, including the rules of quantum mechanics?
    H. If the natural laws concerning quantum mechanics are true, then shouldn't the classical rules of motion be suspect?
    J. If the natural laws formulated with reference to K are measurable, then wouldn't the magnitude and direction of the velocity of the carriage be important?

23. Which of the following choices provides the best meaning for the truth?

Even though classical mechanics does not supply us with a sufficiently broad basis for the theoretical presentation of all physical phenomena, still we must grant it a considerable measure of "truth," since it supplies us with the actual motions of the heavenly bodies with a delicacy of detail little short of wonderful.

    A. correctness regarding the abstract meaning of classical mechanics
    B. honesty regarding the movement of objects according to the rules of relativity
    C. validity regarding an understanding of the classical rules of motion
    D. exactness regarding the movement of small bodies on a coordinate plane

24. In lines 58-59, Einstein writes that classical mechanics describes astronomical movements with "a delicacy of detail little short of wonderful." In this context, what is the best synonym for the meaning of "delicacy"?

    F. A fragility
    G. A sensitivity
    H. A rare delight
    J. A soft texture

25. If a reader did not know the meaning of the phrase *a priori*, s/he could ascertain it from the sentence: "But that a principle of such broad generality should hold with such exactness in one domain of phenomena, and yet should be invalid for another, is a priori not very probable." Based on this context, to which of these is its meaning closest?

    A. Existing in the first place
    B. Having the highest priority
    C. Something happening after the fact
    D. General to specific/independently true

26. Einstein describes the detail with which classical mechanics describes celestial motions as "little short of wonderful." Rhetorically, this is most an example of which of these?

    F. Understatement
    G. Overstatement
    H. Amplification
    J. Metabasis

27. Within this passage, which of the following conclusions proposed by Einstein is predicated upon the condition that the principle of relativity is valid?

    A. "...then the Galilean co-ordinate systems K, K1, K2, etc., which are moving uniformly relative to each other, will not be equivalent for the description of natural phenomena."
    B. "...natural laws are capable of being formulated in a particularly simple manner, and...only on condition that...we...have chosen one...of a particular state of motion as our body of reference."
    C. "If, relative to K, K1 is a uniformly moving co-ordinate system devoid of rotation...then natural phenomena run their course with respect to K1 according to exactly the same general laws as with respect to K."
    D. "...we should therefore expect that the direction of motion of the earth at any moment would enter into the laws of nature, and also that physical systems in their behavior would be dependent on the orientation in space with respect to the earth."

28. What might Einstein mean when he writes that "we must grant it a considerable measure of "'truth,'" in paragraph five?

    F. correctness regarding the abstract meaning of classical mechanics
    G. honesty regarding the movement of objects according to the rules of relativity
    H. validity regarding an understanding of the classical rules of motion
    J. exactness regarding the movement of small bodies on a coordinate plane

29. Which of the following most accurately represents Einstein's use of claims and counterclaims in this passage?

    A. From one paragraph to the next, statements of claims and statements of counterclaims are presented alternately; the last two sentences summarize how these contrast.
    B. The first three paragraphs present a series of counterclaims; the following four present arguments that logically refute those counterclaims and then support his claims.
    C. The first five paragraphs mainly explain his claims; the last two state counterclaims, explaining results to expect if they were true; the last two sentences reassert his claims.
    D. Every paragraph begins by presenting a claim, then a counterclaim, then refutation of the counterclaim; and ends with repeating the original claim for emphasis.

30. Among the following, which sentence introduces evidence supporting Einstein's assertions?

    F. "This is very powerful argument in favor of the principle of relativity."
    G. "We now proceed to the second argument, to which, moreover, we shall return later."
    H. "Nevertheless, there are two general facts...in favor of the validity of the principle of relativity."
    J. "In order to attain the greatest possible clearness, let us return to our example of the railway carriage..."

Passage IV: Social Science

Passage A

Black History Month is unnecessary. In a place and time in which we overwhelmingly elected an African American president, we can and should move to a post-racial
5 approach to education. As Detroit Free Press columnist Rochelle Riley wrote in a February 1 column calling for an end to Black History Month, "I propose that, for the first time in American history, this country has reached a
10 point where we can stop celebrating separately, stop learning separately, stop being American separately."

In addition to being unnecessary, the idea that African American history should be
15 focused on in a given month suggests that it belongs in that month alone. It is important to instead incorporate African American history into what is taught every day as American history. It needs to be recreated as part of
20 mainstream thought and not as an optional,

often irrelevant, side note. We should focus efforts on pushing schools to diversify and broaden their curricula.

There are a number of other reasons to
25 abolish it: first, it has become a shallow commercial ritual that does not even succeed in its (limited and misguided) goal of focusing for one month on a sophisticated, intelligent appraisal of the contributions and
30 experiences of African Americans throughout history. Second, there is a paternalistic flavor to the mandated bestowing of a month in which to study African American history that is overcome if we instead assert the need for
35 a comprehensive curriculum. Third, the idea of Black History Month suggests that the knowledge imparted in that month is for African Americans only, rather than for all people.

Passage B

Black History Month is still an important observance. Despite the election of our first African American president being a huge achievement, education about African
5 American history is still unmet to a substantial degree. Black History Month is a powerful tool in working towards meeting that need. There is no reason to give up that tool now, and it can easily coexist with an
10 effort to develop a more comprehensive and inclusive yearly curriculum.

Having a month set aside for the study of African American history doesn't limit its study and celebration to that month; it
15 merely focuses complete attention on it for that month. There is absolutely no contradiction between having a set-aside month and having it be present in the curriculum the rest of the year.

20 Equally important is that the debate *itself* about the usefulness of Black History Month can, and should, remind parents that they can't necessarily count on schools to teach

African American history as thoroughly as
25 many parents would want.

Although Black History Month has, to an extent, become a shallow ritual, it doesn't have to be. Good teachers and good materials could make the February curriculum deeply
30 informative, thought-provoking, and inspiring. The range of material that can be covered is rich, varied, and full of limitless possibilities.

Finally, it is worthwhile to remind
35 ourselves and our children of the key events that happened during the month of February. In 1926, Woodson organized the first Black History Week to honor the birthdays of essential civil rights activists Abraham
40 Lincoln and Frederick Douglass. W. E. B. DuBois was born on February 23, 1868. The 15th Amendment, which granted African Americans the right to vote, was ratified on February 3, 1870. The first black US senator,
45 Hiram R. Revels, took his oath of office on February 25, 1870. The National Association

236

for the Advancement of Colored People
(NAACP) was founded on February 12, 1909.
Malcolm X was shot on February 21, 1965.

Questions 31 – 33 pertain to Passage A:

31. The author's primary purpose in Passage A is to:

    A. Argue that Black History Month should not be so commercial.
    B. Argue that Black History Month should be abolished.
    C. Argue that Black History Month should be maintained.
    D. Suggest that African American history should be taught in two months rather than just one.

32. It can be inferred that the term "post-racial" in the second sentence of Passage A refers to an approach that:

    F. treats race as the most important factor in determining an individual's experience.
    G. treats race as one factor, but not the most important, in determining an individual's experience.
    H. considers race after considering all other elements of a person's identity.
    J. is not based on or organized around concepts of race.

33. Which of the following does the author of Passage A not give as a reason for abolishing Black History Month?

    A. It has become a shallow ritual.
    B. There is a paternalistic feel to being granted one month of focus.
    C. It suggests that the month's education is only for African Americans.
    D. No one learns anything during the month.

Questions 34 – 36 pertain to Passage B:

34. Which event happened first?

    F. The passing of the 15th Amendment
    G. The birth of W.E.B.   DuBois
    H. The establishment of Black History Month
    J. The founding of the NAACP

35. Why does the author of Passage B believe that the debate itself about Black History Month can be useful?

    A. The people on opposing sides can come to an intelligent resolution about whether to keep it.
    B. African American history is discussed in the media when the debate is ongoing.
    C. The debate is a reminder to parents that they can't count on schools to teach their children about African American history.
    D. Black History Month doesn't have to be a shallow ritual.

36. What does the author of Passage B say about the range of material that can be taught during Black History Month?

 F. It is rich and varied.
 G. It is important.
 H. It is an unmet need.
 J. It is comprehensive.

Questions 37 – 40 pertain to both Passage A and Passage B:

37. The author of Passage A argues that celebrating Black History Month suggests that the study of African American history can and should be limited to one month of the year. What is the author of Passage B's response?

 A. Black History Month is still an important observance.
 B. Black History Month is a powerful tool in meeting the need for education about African American history.
 C. Having a month set aside for the study of African American history does not limit its study and celebration to that month.
 D. Black History Month does not have to be a shallow ritual.

38. From both passages, readers can infer that the authors: (similarity of the passages)

 F. voted for Barack Obama to become president.
 G. are well connected to the media.
 H. think that February is not the best time for Black History Month.
 J. are affiliated with an educational institution.

39. Which of the following statements is true?

 A. The author of Passage A thinks that it is important for students to learn about the achievements and experience of African Americans, while the author of Passage B does not think this is important.
 B. The author of Passage B thinks that it is important for students to learn about the achievements and experience of African Americans, while the author of Passage A does not think this is important.
 C. Neither author thinks that it is important for students to learn about the achievements and experience of African Americans.
 D. Both authors think that it is important for students to learn about the achievements and experience of African Americans.

40. Which individuals are described in either Passage A or Passage B as "essential civil rights activists?"

 F. Abraham Lincoln and Malcolm X
 G. Abraham Lincoln and W.E.B. DuBois
 H. Malcolm X and W.E.B. DuBois
 J. Abraham Lincoln and Frederick Douglass

Science

Blood consists of a liquid called *plasma*, in which many different types of blood cells are suspended. The plasma also contains many dissolved proteins. These proteins may be studied by subjecting the plasma to *electrophoresis*, in which it is subjected to an electric field, which pulls the proteins through a porous gel. Proteins typically have a negative charge on their surface, so they move toward the anode (positive electrode) in an electric field. The gel acts as a molecular sieve: it interferes with the movement, or *migration*, of the larger proteins more than the small ones, allowing the proteins to be separated on the basis of size. The further the proteins move during the experiment, the smaller they must be.

The experiment results in an *electropherogram*, such as the one shown in the figure below. This is a plot, or graph, of protein concentration versus migration, and corresponds to a graph of concentration versus size. Concentration is measured by passing light of a certain wavelength through the gel: proteins absorb the light, and the resulting *absorbance* measurement is proportional to protein concentration. Many major blood component proteins, such as albumin and several identified by Greek letters, have been discovered in this way. When disease is present, some component proteins may break down into smaller fragments. Others may aggregate, or clump together, to form larger fragments. This results in a change in the electropherogram: new species, corresponding to the aggregates or breakdown products, may be present, and the sizes of the normal peaks may be changed as the concentration of normal products is altered.

The Figure shows an electropherogram from a sick patient with an abnormal component in her blood (arrow). Peaks corresponding to some normal plasma proteins have been labeled.

Please examine the electropherogram and answer the following questions.

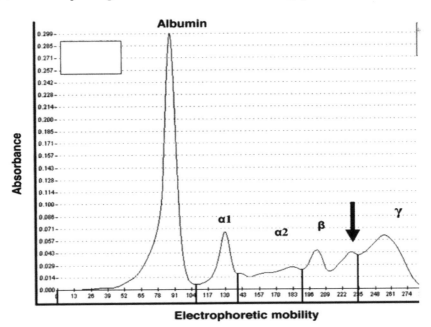

1. Which blood component protein is present in the greatest amounts in the plasma?

   A. Albumin
   B. $\alpha 1$
   C. $\alpha 2$
   D. β

2. Which of the following is the fastest-moving component in the electropherogram?

F. Albumin
G. $\alpha1$
H. $\alpha2$
J. γ

3. Which of the following statements is true about component $\alpha1$?

A. The molecules move through the gel faster than those of component $\alpha2$, but slower than Albumin.
B. The molecules are larger than albumin, but smaller than all the other components.
C. The molecules are smaller than albumin, but larger than all the other components.
D. It is not a protein.

4. Which of the components identified on the electropherogram is the smallest molecule?

F. Albumin
G. $\alpha1$
H. $\alpha2$
J. γ

5. Which of the following is true of the unknown component identified by the arrow?

A. The molecules are larger than the β component, but smaller than albumin
B. The molecules are larger than the β component, but smaller than the γ component.
C. The molecules move more slowly in the gel than all the other components except one.
D. The molecules move more rapidly in the gel than all the other components except one.

6. Which of the following may be true of the unknown component identified by the arrow?

F. It is formed of albumin molecules that have aggregated.
G. It is formed of $\alpha1$ molecules that have aggregated.
H. It is formed of $\alpha2$ molecules that have aggregated.
J. It is formed of γ molecules that have aggregated.

7. Which of the following may not be true of the unknown component identified by the arrow?

A. It is formed of albumin molecules that have broken down into fragments.
B. It is formed of $\alpha1$ molecules that have broken down into fragments.
C. It is formed of $\alpha2$ molecules that have broken down into fragments.
D. It is formed of γ molecules that have broken down into fragments.

8. The blood of healthy individuals does not contain the unknown component indicated by the arrow. The experiment therefore proves

F. The unknown component causes the patient's sickness.
G. The unknown component results from the patient's sickness.
H. The more of the unknown component there is, the sicker the patient will be.
J. None of the above.

In a study performed to determine the migration patterns of fish, 34,000 juvenile sablefish of the species *Anoplopoma fimbria* were tagged and released into waters of the eastern Gulf of Alaska during a twenty-year period. The tagged fish were all juveniles (less than 2 years of age), so that the age of the recovered fish could be determined from the date on the tag. This allowed age-specific movement patterns to be studied. Tagged fish were recovered from sites in the Bering Sea, throughout the Gulf of Alaska, and off the coast of British Columbia. The fish were recovered by commercial fishermen, with the results reported to the scientists performing the study. A total of 2011 tagged fish were recovered. It was found that fish spawned in coastal waters move to deeper waters when they are older. At the same time, they migrate north and west, across the Gulf of Alaska toward the Aleutian Islands. Eventually, they return to the eastern Gulf as adults.

The figure shows tag recoveries from sablefish tagged as juveniles by age (in years) and by depth (in meters) for all the areas in the study. The size of each circle is proportional to the number of recoveries. The range for each data point is 1 to 57 recoveries. The symbol x represents the median age.

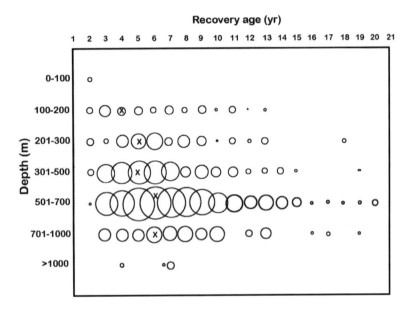

9. If a circle in the graph is twice the size (area) of another circle, this indicates that:
   A. It represents twice as many fish.
   B. The fish it represents were twice as old.
   C. Both A and B.
   D. None of the above.

10. The greatest number of tagged fish were recovered at depths of
   F. 101 – 200 m.
   G. 201 – 300 m.
   H. 301 – 500 m.
   J. 501 – 700 m.

11. What percentage of the released, tagged fish were recovered for this study?
   A. 2011
   B. 20
   C. 6
   D. Can't determine from the data given.

12. The median age of tagged fish recovered at depths between 301 and 500 meters is approximately

    F. 2 years.

    G. 5 years.

    H. 9 years.

    J. Data not shown.

13. Not all the tagged fish were recovered in this study. Which of the following reasons may be responsible for the losses?

    A. Some fish died during the study.

    B. The tags fell off some of the fish during the study.

    C. Some fish die as a result of being tagged.

    D. All of the above.

14. The largest fish are found at depths of

    F. 101 – 200 m.

    G. 201 – 300 m.

    H. 301 – 500 m.

    J. Can't determine from the data given.

15. Which of the following statements is supported by the data in the figure?

    A. Fish return to the eastern Gulf of Alaska to spawn.

    B. Sablefish move progressively deeper with age.

    C. Sablefish prefer cold waters.

    D. Younger fish swim faster than older ones.

16. The data indicate that sablefish may live as long as

    F. 10 years.

    G. 30 years.

    H. 20 years.

    J. 5 years.

Most particles studied by physicists are unstable. Given enough time, an unstable particle will break apart into two or more smaller particles or fragments. This event is called a decay. By carefully observing and logically classifying these decays according to some well-understood laws of nature, particle physicists have built a catalog of subatomic particles down to their most fundamental constituent parts.

Some particles, like the proton and electron, appear to be stable for very long times. They don't change into other particles, which is to say they don't decay. Most other particles have dominant decay modes. They decay into one combination of particles more often than into other combinations. Many particles also have rare decay modes. Someone who has the patience to watch a million or so decays, might see one of these rare combinations.

Two of the laws of nature that have been used to understand decays are *conservation of charge* and *conservation of energy*. Conservation of charge says that the net charge of all particles produced in a decay should equal the total charge of the original particle. Conservation of energy implies that the total mass of the resulting particles should not be greater than the mass of the original particle. Mass does not seem to be conserved in many decays until one accounts for the mass that is converted into the kinetic energy of the resulting particles as they move away from the original center of mass at some nonzero speed. Mass and energy can be measured with the same units: particle physicists use MeV (1.000 mega-electron volt = 1.602×10^{-13} joule = 1.783×10^{-30} kilogram).

At the most fundamental level, matter is thought to be made up of quarks and leptons. Quarks form the large baryons and mesons. There are six quarks named up (u), down (d), strange (s), charm (c), bottom (b), and top (t). (The last two are sometimes fancifully referred to as "beauty" and "truth.") Each comes in three "colors" and each has an antiparticle making 36 in all. The six quarks have been confirmed through indirect observations, but not isolated as individual particles.

Refer to the accompanying table of subatomic particles to answer the questions.

Table:

HADRONS - made of quarks

* BARYONS - made of three quarks or three anti-quarks
NUCLEONS - contain no strange quarks

PARTICLE	CHARGE	MASS(MeV)
proton	1	938.27231
anti-proton	-1	938.27231
neutron	0	939.56563
anti-neutron	0	939.56563

HYPERONS - contain one or more strange quarks

PARTICLE	CHARGE	MASS(MeV)
lambda	0	1115.684
anti-lambda	0	1115.684
positive sigma	1	1189.37
anti-positive sigma	-1	1189.37
neutral sigma	0	1192.55
anti-neutral sigma	0	1192.55
negative sigma	-1	1197.436
anti-negative sigma	1	1197.436
neutral xi	0	1314.9
anti-neutral xi	0	1314.9
negative xi	-1	1321.32
anti-negative xi	1	1321.32
negative omega	-1	1672.45
positive omega	1	1672.45

* MESONS - made of one quark and one anti-quark

PARTICLE	CHARGE	MASS(MeV)
positive pion	1	139.56995
negative pion	-1	139.56995
neutral pion	0	134.9764
positive kaon	1	493.677
negative kaon	-1	493.677
neutral kaon	0	497.672
anti-neutral kaon	0	497.672
eta	0	547.45

243

LEPTONS - elementary particles not made of quarks

PARTICLE	CHARGE	MASS(MeV)
positron	1	0.51099907
electron	-1	0.51099907
electron neutrino	0	0
electron anti-neutrino	0	0
positive muon	1	105.658389
negative muon	-1	105.658389
muon neutrino	0	0
muon anti-neutrino	0	0
positive tau	1	1777
negative tau	-1	1777
tau neutrino	0	0
tau anti-neutrino	0	0

17. **Which of the following particles has the greatest mass?**

    A. Muon
    B. Electron
    C. Proton
    D. Lambda

18. **Which of the following particles are made of quarks?**

    F. Neutrino
    G. Muon
    H. Proton
    J. None of these

19. **When a particle decays, the total charge on the resulting particles must always**

    A. be neutral.
    B. be equal to 0.
    C. satisfy the law of conservation of mass.
    D. be equal to the charge of the original particle.

20. **The most massive uncharged particles are found among the**

    F. Leptons.
    G. Mesons.
    H. Baryons.
    J. Hyperons.

21. **A lambda particle decays and one of the products is a proton. A second particle is also formed. Which of the following is the second particle?**

    A. Negative pion
    B. Positron
    C. Electron neutrino
    D. Neutron

22. A positive muon decays and one of the products is a positron. If a second particle is also formed, which of the following might it be?

   F. Proton

   G. Tau

   H. Neutrino

   J. Kaon

23. A negative omega particle decays into a lambda particle and a negative kaon. How much energy is released?

   A. 63.09 MeV

   B. 1115.68 MeV

   C. 493.68 MeV

   D. 1672.45 MeV

24. Tom weighs 60 kilograms. What is his mass in MeV?

   F. 6×10^{11}

   G. 33.65×10^{30}

   H. 60

   J. Cannot be determined

Pollutants typically enter seawater at *point sources*, such as sewage discharge pipes or factory waste outlets. Then, they may be spread over a wide area by wave action and currents. The rate of this dispersal depends upon a number of factors, including depth, temperature, and the speed of the currents. Chemical pollutants often attach themselves to small particles of sediment, so that studying the dispersal of sediment can help in understanding how pollution spreads.

In a study of this type, a team of scientists lowered screened collection vessels to various depths to collect particles of different sizes. This gave them an idea of the size distribution of particles at each depth. Figure A shows the results for six different sites (ND, NS, MD, MS, SD, and SS). The particle size is plotted in *phi* units, which is a logarithmic scale used to measure grain sizes of sand and gravel. The 0 point of the scale is a grain size of 1 millimeter, and an increase of 1 in phi number corresponds to a decrease in grain size by a factor of ½, so that 1 phi unit is a grain size of 0.5 mm, 2 phi units is 0.25 mm, and so on; in the other direction, -1 phi unit corresponds to a grain size of 2 mm and -2 phi units to 4 mm.

Grains of different size are carried at different rates by the currents in the water. The study also measured current speed and direction, pressure and temperature at different depths, and at different times of year. The results were used in a computer *modeling program* to predict the total transport of sediments both along the shore (north-south) and perpendicular to it (east-west). Figure B shows the program's calculation of the distance particles would have been transported during the study period. The abbreviation *mab* in the figure stands for *meters above bottom.*

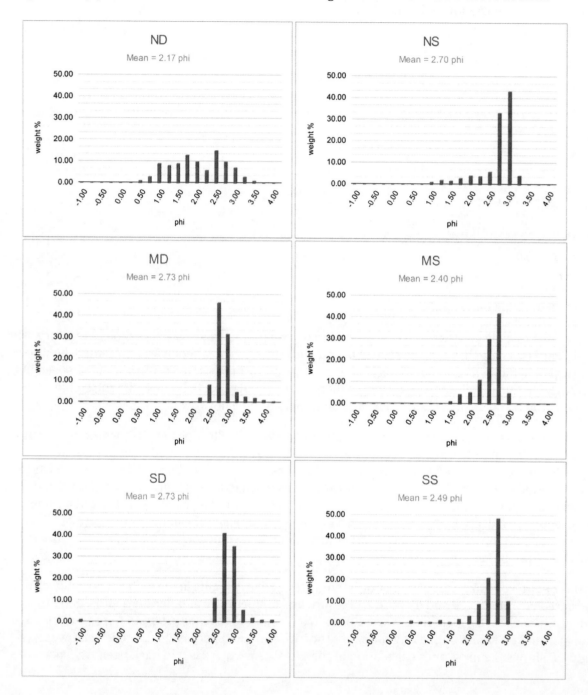

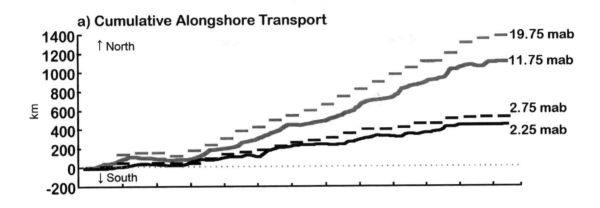

a) Cumulative Alongshore Transport

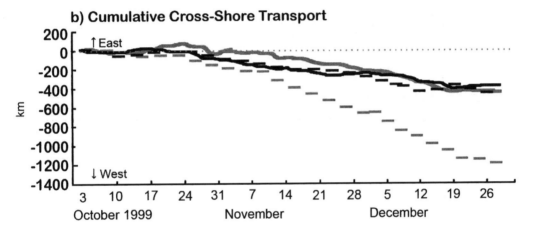

b) Cumulative Cross-Shore Transport

25. Which of the following sites was found to have the smallest average particle size?

  A. ND
  B. NS
  C. MD
  D. MS

26. With the exception of a few outliers, all of the phi values were in the range 1.0 to 4.0. This means that

  F. All particles studied were smaller than 0.5 mm.
  G. All particles studied were between 1.0 and 4.0 mm.
  H. No screens larger than 4.0 m were used in the study.
  J. All particles were larger than 0.5 mm.

27. For which site is it *least* true that the mean particle size represents the entire population?

  A. ND
  B. NS
  C. MD
  D. MS

28. What particle size corresponds to a phi value of -3?

F. 2mm
G. 0.5 mm
H. 0.0625 mm
J. 8 mm

29. In Figure B, the absolute value of the slope of the curves corresponds to

A. The speed of transport.
B. The size of the particles.
C. The phi value.
D. The depth.

30. The data indicates that along a NS axis

F. Transport is faster in deeper waters.
G. Transport is faster in shallower waters.
H. Transport is the same at all depths.
J. There is no correlation between transport speed and depth.

31. The data indicates that along the EW axis

A. Transport is faster in deeper waters.
B. Transport is faster in shallower waters.
C. Transport is the same at all depths.
D. There is no correlation between transport speed and depth.

32. Which of the following is closest to the overall direction of transport?

F. N
G. NW
H. NE
J. SE

Wind can provide a renewable source of energy. The energy of the wind is actually solar energy, as the sun warms the Earth's surface by varying amounts at different locations. This creates differential pressures as the warm air expands, and initiates air motions. High altitude airflows are similar to ocean currents, but near the surface, winds are affected by surface features.

Wind turbines capture this energy with a set of rotors that are set into rotation by the wind. The rotors are made of lightweight fiberglass or carbon fiber, and are held aloft on a tall tower. It is important to hold the blades high above the ground to avoid wind shear, a difference in airflow at different points along the rotor blades which can damage them. The blades rotate at about 40 rpm. Through a gearbox, they rotate a driveshaft at about 1500 rpm. The shaft, in turn, drives a generator.

The power P available from moving air is proportional to the cube of the wind velocity:

$$P = \frac{1}{2}pAv^3$$

where A is the cross section covered by the blades, P is the air density, and v is the air velocity. As the air passes through the rotor, it slows down. The turbine cannot take all the energy from the air, since then it would stop dead behind the rotor. Theoretically, the maximum efficiency that can be achieved is 59%. Figures A and B show a power curve for a 600-kilowatt (kW) wind turbine. To avoid damage from excessive winds, starting with wind speeds of 15 m/sec, the blades are adjusted to limit the power to 600 kW. For winds above 25 m/sec, the turbine is shut down.

One drawback of wind turbines has been the noise they make, but modern designs with slow-rotating blades are fairly quiet. Figure C shows the noise spectrum of a large turbine. The *x*-axis shows the frequency of sound in Hertz, and the *y*-axis shows the level of sound at each frequency. The total noise is 50 decibels (dB), which is less than the noise in a typical office.

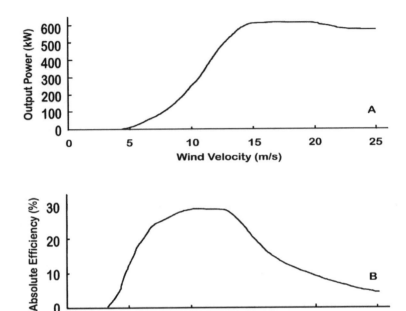

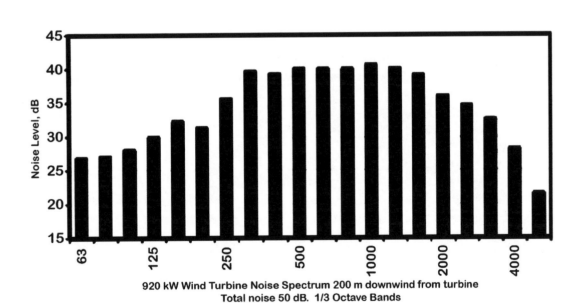

920 kW Wind Turbine Noise Spectrum 200 m downwind from turbine
Total noise 50 dB. 1/3 Octave Bands

33. What wind velocity provides the maximum efficiency for this turbine?

    A. 5 m/s

    B. 7 m/s

    C. 10 m/s

    D. 12 m/s

34. What wind velocity provides the maximum power output from this turbine?

    F. 5 m/s

    G. 7 m/s

    H. 10 m/s

    J. 15 m/s

35. Why does the curve in Figure A flatten for wind velocities greater than 15 m/sec?

    A. The generator runs less efficiently.

    B. The rotors are being trimmed to prevent damage.

    C. Surface turbulence makes the rotors turn more slowly.

    D. None of the above.

36. For wind speeds between 5 and 10 m/sec, we expect the curve in Figure A to increase

    F. Linearly

    G. Irregularly

    H. Exponentially

    J. Sinusoidally

37. An ideal wind turbine operates at 100% efficiency and generates 200 kW of power at a wind velocity of 6 m/sec. How much power will be available at a wind velocity of 12 m/sec?

    A. 400 kW

    B. 800 kW

    C. 1200 kW

    D. 1600 kW

38. A wind turbine operating at 50% efficiency generates 100 kW of power at a wind velocity of 6 m/sec. If it also works at 50% efficiency at winds of 12 m/sec, how much power will it generate?

    F. 400 kW

    G. 800 kW

    H. 1200 kW

    J. 1600 kW

39. Figure C shows that

    A. Most of the noise is at high frequencies.

    B. Most of the noise is at low frequencies.

    C. Most of the noise is at middle frequencies.

    D. The total noise is less than 40 dB.

40. The energy captured by wind turbines is created by

    F.   Surface features.

    G.   Carbon fiber materials.

    H.   A generator.

    J.   The sun.

Answer Key and Explanations

English

Question	Question	Question	Question	Question
1. A	16. F	31. C	46. J	61. B
2. J	17. B	32. J	47. B	62. J
3. C	18. H	33. B	48. H	63. A
4. J	19. B	34. J	49. B	64. F
5. D	20. J	35. A	50. H	65. C
6. G	21. A	36. H	51. A	66. G
7. D	22. G	37. C	52. F	67. D
8. J	23. D	38. J	53. B	68. F
9. D	24. J	39. A	54. G	69. C
10. G	25. B	40. G	55. D	70. G
11. D	26. J	41. A	56. H	71. B
12. G	27. A	42. H	57. J	72. J
13. A	28. J	43. B	58. H	73. A
14. J	29. C	44. G	59. B	74. H
15. C	30. F	45. D	60. J	75. D

1. A: Choice B is wrong because the comma is not necessary. Choice C is incorrect because the singular subject of *United States Coast Guard* needs the singular verb *was*. Choice D is incorrect because the future perfect verb tense is incorrect as the event was completed in the past.

2. J: This sentence adds no information to the passage that is not already in the surrounding sentences, and the sentence is unnecessary as a transition.

3. C: This is the best answer choice because the vague pronoun *It* has been replaced with a specific noun.

4. J: This is the best answer choice as it removes the unnecessary comma. Choice G incorrectly removes the infinitive signifier *to* from the sentence. Choice H changes *enforce* to *promote* which alters the author's meaning of the laws being upheld to the laws being advertised.

5. D: This is the correct choice because it correctly adds parallelism to the sentence with the additional infinitive signifier. Choice B makes *combat* plural which is unnecessary. Choice C adds a comma that is not needed in the sentence.

6. G: This is the best answer because it contains the same intent as the original sentence yet it is more concise than the original. Choice H is incorrect because of the dangling modifier. Choice J is incorrect because it is not only the Department of Homeland Security that considers the Coast Guard to be a federal law enforcement agency.

7. D: The problem with this sentence is a dangling modifier.

8. J: Sentence 10 basically provides a laundry list of things that Coast Guard members do on a daily basis. The only answer choice that introduces this effectively is J.

9. D: The correct word is *really* because this sentence calls for an adverb, not an adjective.

252

10. G: The purpose of this passage is to provide a brief history of the Coast Guard and a brief overview of their duties. As the answer choice notes, the author should use this sentence in a persuasive passage instead of an informative one in order to maintain the focus and the purpose of the passage.

11. D: The question deals with concise word choice and eliminating unnecessary language. The article "a" signifies one or single. So, it is sufficient to write "perform the following in a day."

12. G: This question also deals with concise word choice. If the Coast Guard is investigating a pollution incident, then it is understood that they have explored the incident as well.

13. A: Paragraph 3 gives information about what the Coast Guard does in an average day, but there is no indication as to where this very specific information comes from. Adding a line saying that the information came from the official Coast Guard Web site would add credibility.

14. J: The question asks for "the requirements for becoming a member of the US Coast Guard." Since the passage merely lists responsibilities of Coast Guard personnel and notes a key difference between them and the Navy, readers cannot be expected to see another purpose of the passage for the requirements of being US Coast Guard personnel.

15. C: This answer choice best sums up the information in this essay, and rounds out the writer's discussion about the organization as a whole. Answers A and B talk about the Coast Guard as a career, which isn't a theme in this essay. Answer D contradicts the information and ideas in the essay.

16. F: An island is a land mass that is surrounded by water at all points. In the following sentence, readers are told that New Zealand has "two large islands and a number of smaller ones." So, Choice G cannot be correct since it changes the meaning of New Zealand to being a single island. Choice H is wrong because the preposition *between* is for comparing two things, but the islands of New Zealand are being compared to "all the Pacific islands." Choice J is incorrect because the adjective *more* is the comparative degree which is used for comparing two things. Yet, the author is comparing New Zealand to "all the Pacific islands."

17. B: Although it is a simple combination, this connection of sentence 2 and sentence 3 is the one that remains grammatically correct, maintains the author's original intent, and is logical.

18. H: The error in this sentence is the unnecessary comma after *islands*. Choice G and J change out *number* for *amount*. Since the number of islands can be counted, the word *number* is still needed for this sentence.

19. B: Choice C is incorrect because the information about the migration occurring in the 15th century was deleted unnecessarily. Choice D is incorrect because it merely rearranges material. Choice B improves the sentence by removing the pronoun "it" and the direction of their travel which is understood to be southward.

20. J: This revision to the sentence is the best choice as it uses punctuation correctly and applies the correct use of verb tense.

21. A: Choices B and D incorrectly capitalize southward. Choice C incorrectly changes the verb tense to past perfect.

22. G: Although this statement is placed in the correct paragraph, the sentence should not be added at this point without further development in the sentence and paragraph.

23. D: This statement is the best choice as the revision connects to previous sentence on the difficult climate circumstances and maintains the author's original meaning with an active voice.

24. J: This is the best choice because it transitions correctly from sentence 9 to sentence 10 and maintains the author's original meaning.

25. B: With items in a series, a comma is needed after *shellfish* to separate each item correctly, and *shellfish* should not be capitalized.

26. J: With the other choices, there are no complete statements that come before the colon.

27. A: The adverb *markedly* does not need to be removed as it was in Choice C. As for Choice B and D, the adverb does not need to be moved because it is modifying the verb *disappeared* meaning that it became quite noticeable that the moa population was dropping and causing more tribal warfare.

28. J: Sentence 18 functions best in its current place as sentence 16 functions as a topic sentence on the sweet potato, and sentence 18 logically comes after sentence 17 stating how the sweet potato could grow in many areas and survive the winter months as well.

29. C: This revision is the best choice as the population is specified instead of a general "human population" which is already understood as the passage covers the settlement of the islands of New Zealand by Polynesian voyagers.

30. F: The author has stated that "the most important farmed crop in prehistoric New Zealand was the sweet potato." In the final paragraph, the author has shared how the sweet potato was relied upon for food at almost every point of the year and improved the population of people who lived on the islands. So, the addition of how the Maori people lived alongside their sweet potato farmlands is more evidence to support the topic sentence of this paragraph.

31. C: Choice B is incorrect because the present-perfect tense needs the past participle form for the verb, and *flew* is only the past form. Choice A and Choice D are incorrect because the future perfect tense points to an action that will take place at an appointed time in the future which is not accurate for this sentence structure.

32. J: The comma can be removed as this is not an appositive or absolute phrase. The piece following World War I is an adjective clause. So, the comma is not needed since it is not an introductory clause.

33. B: The other answer choices show a relationship between American pilots not having work because they gave up flying airplanes. The original sentences intend the opposite. Some American pilots returned from World War I without work to fly planes. So, they had to give up flying altogether and find other jobs.

34. J: Since the pilot has already been named in the sentence, the author does not need to capitalize *ace of aces*. Choice G is incorrect because the verb tense does not need to be changed. Choice H is not correct because the clause is non-essential to the sentence and needs to have commas to separate it from the rest of the sentence.

35. A: Choice B is not the best selection because *new* and *creative* are not exact synonyms. So, it is not redundant to say something is new and creative. Choice C is not the best choice because the verb *found* is sufficient and acceptable. Choice D is not the best choice because *things* has been exchanged for *tricks*. However, the following sentence highlights a pilot who transported news stories which is a service, not a stunt.

36. H: The issue being addressed with this sentence is a matter of a passive verb being exchanged for an active verb. Choice H is the best selection as it has a clear subject and an active voice verb.

37. C: Choice B is wrong because *big* and *news* are not coordinate adjectives in this context. Choice D is not the best choice because *broke* as a verb is being used correctly. The issue with this sentence is one of concise word choice. The previous sentence states that Jones used "his airplane to help get news across the country," and the following clause to the sentence in question states that Jones flew photos "to newspapers in different cities." Since it is understood within the larger context that Casey Jones is working with news stories, the author can write instead that "When an important story broke, Jones flew news photos to newspapers in different cities."

38. J: Choice G is not the best selection because the name of the pilot is essential information to know and should not be closed off with comma marks. Choice H is not the best selection because this sentence is starting a transition from Casey Jones to Roscoe Turner. So, a transition like "Another pilot" is needed for this sentence. Choice J is the best option because the words "another pilot" are not essential in the sentence structure and can be closed off with comma marks as readers learn that Roscoe Turner traveled "with a lion cub in his plane."

39. A: Choice B is incorrect because a colon cannot be used to separate two independent clauses unless what comes after the colon is an explanation of the preceding statement or a lengthy and formal quote. While the punctuation in Choice C is acceptable, the change from an active voice to a passive voice is not the best choice. Choice D is not correct because a comma is needed to separate the two independent clauses that are joined by a conjunction.

40. G: Choice H and Choice J are not the best revisions for this sentence because they set up an "either-or" and a contrast respectively which is not the original intent of the sentence. Choice G is the best selection as it provides context to the cost of an airplane ride without setting up a contrast.

41. A: Choice B is not correct because exchanging the colon for a comma would create a comma splice. Choice C is not correct because the quotation marks are not necessary as the word *barnstormers* is not being used in any special sense. Choice D is not correct because the author intends to convey an example that these barnstormers attempted the feat at one point, not regularly. So, it is not something that needs to be corrected.

42. H: The error in the sentence is an incorrect verb tense. Choice G is incorrect because *finally* creates a split modifier. Choice J is incorrect because the pronoun is a contraction, not the possessive pronoun.

43. B: This is the best choice because it correctly transitions from the sentence 15 to sentence 16 and maintains the original meaning of the author.

44. G: Point A is not the best choice because the previous and following sentences highlight how pilots had to resign from their flight hobby, not the accomplishments of famous pilots. Choice H and Choice J are not unacceptable places for the sentence, but Choice G is the best selection as the final sentence of the first paragraph suggests that examples will follow, and Mr. Lindbergh's feat is an example of a creative task for an airplane.

45. D: If the author wanted the purpose of the passage to focus on the American public's opinion on what the pilots should pursue after returning from WWI, then readers would need to be provided with reasons for their concerns about men and women pursuing careers in flight.

46. J: The need for revision with this sentence comes with the unnecessary adjective American. The passage understands that the American is already included since the sentence begins with "In Western society. The *individual self* should not be reduced to *individual* as it is a term used in psychology fields. In addition, Western is correct to be capitalized.

47. B: This is the best choice as there are multiple "Western societies," and the preposition among compares multiple options whereas the preposition "between" compares only two options.

48. H: In general, the first paragraph in an essay (of any length) introduces the discussion at hand or frames a particular debate. Most introductory paragraphs do not introduce extensive content. In this paragraph, there is no clear stance taken on either Buddhist or Western notions of the self, and so choices F and G are inappropriate. Choice H is a good answer because it stresses that the purpose of the first paragraph is to introduce a tension and not to make judgments one way or another. Choice J is inappropriate because "egolessness" is not discussed until the second paragraph. The best choice, then, is H.

49. B: This is the best choice as the revision selects a transition with the correct intent.

50. H: When using possessives for compounds, you need to be sure that the apostrophe works with the meaning of the sentence. This is the correct revision because the concerns of a person may be different from the concerns of a group. Choice G is incorrect because the pronoun *their* does not agree in number with the noun *individual*, and *group's* should not be deleted. Choice J is incorrect because the pronoun *their* does not agree in number with the noun *individual*.

51. A: The sentence is in the best position for the most logical organization. Moving it to the end of the paragraph (a) would be illogical because as it is now, it precedes the sentence "Buddhists who live in such societies....", which refers back to "In Western societies..." so reversing their order would make no sense. Moving it to the beginning of the paragraph (c) would interrupt the transition between the previous paragraph's last sentence, "...the struggles that Western Buddhists face" and the second paragraph's first sentence, "Central to Buddhist belief is the idea of 'egolessness.'" The latter sentence logically follows the former one. Not only would moving the quoted sentence interrupt this logical progression; it would moreover mention ego-toxicity prematurely—before it is introduced in the second paragraph's third sentence. The quoted sentence should not be removed entirely from the paragraph (d) as it further specifies ego-toxicity, introduced and defined in the previous sentence, as prevalent in Western societies; hence it provides essential information.

52. F: This question is easy to over think. In the second paragraph "egolessness" and "ego-toxicity" are defined and contrasted. The purpose of this paragraph, then, should mention this in some form. Choice F is good because it captures the fact that these terms are distinguished in the paragraph. Choice G is inappropriate because the paragraph only mentions the conflict that Buddhists feel— there is no judgment made on the conflict. Choices H and J are inappropriate because the paragraph does not praise one perspective over another.

53. B: This is the only revision of the phrase that uses proper grammar and punctuation.

54. G: This is the best choice as the pronouns agree with the introductory clause and the deletion of the first verb has made the sentence concise.

55. D: The original underlined portion has awkward phrasing that can be revised for clarity. Choice B is incorrect because the commas are not necessary. Choice C is not the best option because the awkward phrasing has not been revised.

56. H: This is the best choice because it is the most specific about how social action in an egoless manner has become more prevalent in secular institutions and movements.

57. J: Since the sentence ends with a period, it may not be phrased as a question, this is the correct revision.

58. H: In the first paragraph, the third sentence identifies increased tension in recent decades between individualism and collectivism in the West. This is developed in subsequent paragraphs by the discussion of ego-toxicity vs. egolessness reflecting individualism vs. collectivism. The second sentence (F) provides evidence supporting the first sentence, not a main idea. The fourth sentence (G) provides evidence supporting the third sentence. The first sentence (J) focuses only on Western emphasis of individualism over collectivism, not on the tension between the two that is a main idea on which the following paragraphs elaborate.

59. B: This passage is best characterized as persuasive because the author is making a point, arguing in its favor, and providing evidence to support it. Descriptive (A) text paints a vivid picture of a person, place, thing, scene, or situation by providing many specific sensory details to help readers imagine they are really experiencing it. Expository (C) prose provides factual information objectively without adding the author's opinions or seeking to convince readers of anything. Narrative (D) text tells readers a story.

60. J: The last sentence in each paragraph of this passage identifies "struggles", "caught between", "The struggle...continues"—all referring to a main conflict between individualism and collectivism—and the final sentence resolves it by stating that abandoning ego-toxicity enables compassionate caring for self and others. Hence none of these sentences identifies only half of this conflict, and the final sentence is not the only one to complete it (F). The first sentence of each paragraph does not identify this main conflict (G), (H); only the first sentence of the third paragraph does. In the first paragraph, the first sentence identifies Western emphasis of one over the other, not the conflict between them. In the second paragraph, the first sentence identifies the idea of "egolessness" central to Buddhist belief, not its conflict with ego-toxicity identified later in the paragraph. The final sentence does not simply reiterate the conflict (G) but resolves it.

61. B: The issue with this sentence is a comma that separates the subject from the verb. Choice C is not correct because the comma has not been removed and the preposition does not need to be changed. Choice D is not correct because the comma remains in the sentence, and the term *day and age* is an unnecessary change from *time*.

62. J: Choice G and Choice H are not the best options because the same piece of the original sentence is missing: "There have been many changes made to the game." Choice F is a nice revision, but is also removes an element from the sentence: "the essence remains the same." So, we are left with Choice J which does not remove a key part of the sentence or change the intent of the original. It merely revises the two original sentences to be combined.

63. A: Choice B is wrong because *worldwide* is one word and does not need to be hyphenated. Choice C is wrong because the present perfect verb tense does not need to be corrected because the worldwide appeal of basketball is something that started in the past and continues into the present. Choice D is not correct because the sport grew to become popular worldwide.

64. F: The capitalization in the sentence is correct as written.

65. C: The capitalization in this sentence is also correct as written, and the comma is needed after the name of the state.

66. G: Choice F is not the best option because the introduction is highlighting broad things that will be discussed in the body paragraphs. Choice H is not the best option because the focus of this paragraph is on the spread of the game after its invention and the development of organized basketball. Choice J is not the best option because new information should not be introduced in the new conclusion. So, Choice G is the best choice as it is a detail that follows directly after related information and is supporting information for this body paragraph.

67. D: The verb needs to agree with the subject in number. The verb in this sentence comes before the subject since the subject is two teams. Choice B is not the correct choice because what follows the semicolon is not an independent clause. Choice C is not the best choice because the comma and conjunction need an independent clause to separate the sentence.

68. F: Choice G and Choice J are not correct because the simple past is needed for this sentence, not the past perfect.

69. C: This writing is best characterized as an exposition or explanation of how basketball began.

70. G: The error with this sentence is the failure to add a comma after the year. Choice H is incorrect because the capitalization is correct in the original sentence. Choice J is not correct because a comma is needed, not a semicolon.

71. B: The correction to this sentence can be a revision of redundancy since basketball is already understood to be a sport. So, the best answer choice is Choice B which removes the redundancy.

72. J: The error in the sentence is with the contraction *it's*. The author should replace it with the possessive pronoun *its*.

73. A: Choice B is not correct because there is no error with describing the kind of fun that is characteristic of the sport. Choice C is wrong because a comma is needed in this situation, not a colon. Choice D is incorrect because the verb tense is correct as the event started in the past and continues into the present.

74. H: Switching sentences 11 and 12 improves the organization and clarity of paragraph 3.

75. D: This is the best choice because the question asks the influence of the YMCA on multiple sports, and this passage only addresses basketball and its invention at the YMCA.

Mathematics

Question	Question	Question	Question	Question
1. C	13. C	25. D	37. B	49. C
2. G	14. J	26. G	38. H	50. H
3. E	15. D	27. C	39. D	51. B
4. J	16. F	28. G	40. J	52. J
5. C	17. E	29. C	41. C	53. A
6. H	18. J	30. H	42. H	54. J
7. B	19. A	31. D	43. C	55. A
8. K	20. G	32. F	44. H	56. G
9. C	21. C	33. C	45. D	57. B
10. H	22. H	34. D	46. G	58. H
11. C	23. A	35. G	47. B	59. B
12. F	24. G	36. J	48. J	60. G

1. C: One strategy is to draw polygons with fewer sides and look for a pattern in the number of the polygons' diagonals.

Polygon	Sides	Diagonals	Δ Diagonals
	3	0	-
	4	2	2
	5	5	3
	6	9	4

A quadrilateral has two more diagonals than a triangle, a pentagon has three more diagonals than a quadrilateral, and a hexagon has four more diagonals than a pentagon. Continue this pattern to find that a dodecagon has 54 diagonals.

2. G: The product is equal to $-14i^2$. Since $i^2 = -1$, the product can be rewritten as $(-14)(-1)$, or 14.

3. E: If $\frac{1}{4}$ inch represents 8 miles, then 1 inch represents $4 \times 8 = 32$ miles. Two inches represents $2 \times 32 = 64$ inches. Since $\frac{1}{8}$ is half of $\frac{1}{4}$, we can take half of 8 to find that $\frac{1}{8}$ inch represents 4 miles. Then $2\frac{1}{8}$ inches represents $64 + 4 = 68$ miles.

4. J: When a number is raised to a power, you multiply the number by itself by the number of times of the power. For example, $2^3 = 2 \times 2 \times 2 = 8$. A number raised to the power of 0 is always equal to 1. So, 6^0 is the smallest number shown. Similarly, for the other numbers:

$$9 = 9; 10^1 = 10; 4^2 = 4 \times 4 = 16$$

Since $1 < 8 < 9 < 10 < 16$, we can write the order as $6^0, 2^3, 9, 10^1, 4^2$.

5. D: The volume of the box is the product of $\sqrt{3}$, $2\sqrt{5}$, and 4. To multiply two or more square root radicals, multiply the coefficients and then multiply the radicands.

$$\sqrt{3} \times 2\sqrt{5} \times 4 = 8\sqrt{3}\sqrt{5} = 8\sqrt{15}$$

Then, simplify the radicand if possible by factoring out any squares. Since 15 cannot be factored into any square factors, it cannot be simplified further.

6. H: If Abe goes 3 miles in one hour, he goes half of that or $1\frac{1}{2}$ miles in half an hour. Similarly, Beatriz can go half of 4, or 2 miles, in half an hour. Subtract to find that Beatriz can run $2 - 1\frac{1}{2} = \frac{1}{2}$ mile more than Abe.

7. C: To determine the scale factor of the dilation, compare the coordinates of $\Delta J'K'L'$ to the coordinates of ΔJKL. J is at $(-2, -3)$ and J' is at $(-4, -6)$, which means that the coordinates of J were multiplied by a scale factor of 2 to get the coordinates of J'. K is at $(1, 3)$ and K' is at $(2, 6)$. L is at $(4, -1)$ and L' is at $(8, -2)$. The coordinates of K and L were also multiplied by a scale factor of 2 to get to the coordinates of K' and L'. Therefore, the scale factor of the dilation is 2.

8. H: The expression can be written as $(x - 3)(x - 3)$. Distribution gives $x^2 - 3x - 3x + 9$. Combining like terms gives $x^2 - 6x + 9$.

9. B: Data is said to be positively skewed when there are more lower values, indicating data that is skewed right. An approximately normal distribution shows an increase in frequency, followed by a decrease in frequency, of approximately the same rate, following a general bell curve.

10. K: Since the two triangles have all three corresponding pairs of sides and corresponding pairs of angles marked congruent, then the two triangles are congruent. Similar triangles are the same shape but not necessarily the same size; they have congruent angles. All congruent triangles are similar triangles, so the correct choice is that the triangles are both similar and congruent. An equilateral triangle has three congruent sides and angles measuring 60° each, so these triangles are not equilateral.

11. C: The cost of the ticket is constant and represents the value of the y-intercept. The cost per ride is variable and represents the slope. Therefore, the expression that could be used to find the total amount spent is $30 + 3.50x$, where x represents the number of rides.

12. F: Statements G, H, and J all infer non-quantitative issues that are not presented in the matrix. Smith does have more students than Tan, but since the reasons for this are not presented in the matrix, we cannot conclude anything about those reasons.

13. C: Since rectangle $ABCD$ is centered at the origin and $\overline{AC}$ passes through the origin, any dilation of rectangle $ABCD$ will leave that line unchanged. Since A has the coordinates $(-3, -4)$ and C has the coordinates $(3, 4)$, the slope of $\overline{AC} = \frac{4-(-4)}{3-(-3)} = \frac{8}{6} = \frac{4}{3}$. When rectangle $ABCD$ is dilated by a scale

260

factor of $\frac{1}{2}$ to create image $A'B'C'D'$, A' has the coordinates $(-1.5, -2)$ and C' has the coordinates $(1.5, 2)$. The slope of $\overline{A'C'} = \frac{2-(-2)}{1.5-(-1.5)} = \frac{4}{3}$. Therefore, the slope of $\overline{A'C'}$ is the same as the slope of $\overline{AC}$.

14. J: When the dress is marked down by 20%, the cost of the dress is 80% of its original price; thus, the reduced price of the dress can be written as $\frac{80}{100}x$, or $\frac{4}{5}x$, where x is the original price. When discounted an extra 25%, the dress costs 75% of the reduced price, or $\frac{75}{100}\left(\frac{4}{5}x\right)$, or $\frac{3}{4}\left(\frac{4}{5}x\right)$, which simplifies to $\frac{3}{5}x$. So the final price of the dress is three-fifths of the original price.

15. D: The equation may be solved for x by first subtracting b from both sides of the equation. Doing so gives $ax = c - b$. Dividing both sides of the equation by a gives $x = \frac{c-b}{a}$.

16. F: Note that Anna's route creates a right triangle. One leg is 8 blocks, the other leg is 6 blocks, and the straight-line distance to school is the hypotenuse. Use the Pythagorean Theorem to calculate the answer: $8^2 + 6^2 = x^2$, so $64 + 36 = x^2$, or $100 = x^2$. We take the root of each side to find that $x = 10$, so the school is 10 blocks from Anna's house.

17. E: Segment $\overline{AD} = 48$. Because the length of $\overline{CD}$ is 2 times the length of $\overline{AB}$ let $\overline{AB} = \overline{BC} = x$ and let $\overline{CD} = 2x$. Thus the total length of $\overline{AD} = \overline{AB} + \overline{BC} + \overline{CD} = x + x + 2x = 4x = 48$. We divide both sides by 4 to find that $x = 12$. To find the length of $\overline{BD}$, we add $\overline{BC} + \overline{CD} = x + 2x = 3x$. Since $x = 12$, we multiply 3×12 to find that $\overline{BD} = 36$.

18. J: First, add the two straight 150-yard portions. Also, note that the distance for the two semi-circles put together is the circumference of a circle. Since the circumference of a circle is π times the diameter, the length of the circular portion of the track is simply 30π. Then, add this to the length of the two straight portions of the track:

$$\text{Length} = 30\pi + (2 \times 150) = 394.25$$

Choice J is the closest to this calculated answer.

19. A: Matrices can be added or subtracted only if they have the same dimensions. Since both are 2×2 matrices, each position of the resulting matrix is the sum of the values of each matrix at the corresponding positions:

$$\begin{bmatrix} 4 & 2 \\ 7 & 12 \end{bmatrix} + \begin{bmatrix} -1 & 15 \\ 3 & -5 \end{bmatrix} = \begin{bmatrix} 4+(-1) & 2+15 \\ 7+3 & 12+(-5) \end{bmatrix} = \begin{bmatrix} 3 & 17 \\ 10 & 7 \end{bmatrix}$$

20. G: To solve for the percentage, set up a ratio: $\frac{36}{81} = \frac{x}{100}$. Cross-multiply: $81x = 3600$. Solve by dividing both sides by 81: $x \cong 44$.

21. C: Using the method of elimination to solve the system of linear equations, multiply each term in the top equation by -2 and each term in the bottom equation 5. Doing so produces two new equations with x-terms that will add to 0.

$$\begin{cases} -10x - 18y = 14 \\ 10x - 20y = 100 \end{cases}$$

The sum of $-10x - 18y = 14$ and $10x - 20y = 100$ may be written as $-38y = 114$. Solve this equation for y.

$$-38y = 114$$
$$y = -3$$

Substitute the y-value of -3 into the top, original equation, and solve for x.

$$5x + 9(-3) = -7$$
$$5x - 27 = -7$$
$$5x = 20$$
$$x = 4$$

Thus, the solution to the system of equations is $x = 4$, $y = -3$.

22. H: The average is found by adding the four prices and then dividing by 4.

$$\frac{18.00 + 18.50 + 19.99 + 15.39}{4} = \frac{71.88}{4} = 17.97$$

So, the average price is $17.97.

23. A: Multiply the terms of the complex binomials using the FOIL method. To use the FOIL method, multiply the First terms, the Outer terms, the Inner terms, and the Last terms, then add all the products together.

$$(3 - 6i)(5 + 4i)$$

$$15 + 12i - 30i - 24i^2$$

Next, replace i^2 with -1.

$$15 + 12i - 30i - 24(-1)$$

$$15 + 12i - 30i + 24$$

Finally, combine like terms.

$$39 - 18i$$

24. G: The volume of the cylinder is the amount of grain that the farmer will be able to store in the silo. The formula for the volume of a cylinder is $V = \pi r^2 h$, where r is the radius and h is the height. The cylinder has a diameter of 8 m. So, the radius is half of the diameter or 4 m. The height is 24 m. So, your equation becomes $V = \pi(4 \text{ m})^2(24 \text{ m}) = 384\pi \text{ m}^3$.

25. D: The general form of the interest exponential is $A(t) = P(1 + r)^t$, where P is the initial principal, r the interest rate (as a decimal), and t the number of interest yield periods after the initial investment. P is $315 in this case, which means that is the initial amount put into the account. Furthermore, the exponential function $b(t) = 315(1.05)^t$ equals 315 when $t = 0$. Therefore, John initially put $315 into the bank account.

26. G: Based on the location of the 34°, the 14 ft section is the adjacent leg and the ramp length is the hypotenuse of the right triangle. Therefore, in order to solve for x, it needs to be set up as

$\cos 34° = \frac{adjacent\ leg}{hypotenuse}$ or $\cos 34° = \frac{14}{x}$. The value of x is found using the calculation $x = \frac{14}{\cos 34°}$. Answer F incorrectly set up the equation as $\cos 34° = \frac{x}{14}$. Answer H incorrectly used $\tan 34° = \frac{14}{x}$. Answer J incorrectly used $\sin 34° = \frac{14}{x}$.

27. C: To find the temperature in degrees Fahrenheit, plug 20 into the formula for degrees Celsius and solve.

$$°F = \left(\frac{9}{5}\right)(20) + 32 = 36 + 32 = 68$$

Therefore, the temperature in degrees Fahrenheit is 68°.

28. G: We can write the width as w and the length as $w + 14$. The perimeter of a rectangle is twice the length plus twice the height, so we can write it as: $2(w + 14) + 2w = 92$. This simplifies to $2w + 28 + 2w = 92$, or $4w + 28 = 92$. We subtract 28 from each side: $4w = 64$. Finally, we divide each side by 4 to find that $w = 16$.

29. C: To find the probability that a student is enrolled at TAMU or that a student prefers lattes, the addition rule needs to be used. The addition rule adds the probabilities of two independent events and subtracts the probability that both events are true to avoid double counting. The probability may be written as $P(A\ or\ B) = \frac{750}{1,650} + \frac{675}{1,650} - \frac{350}{1,650}$, which simplifies to $P(A\ or\ B) = \frac{1,075}{1,650} \approx 65\%$. Therefore, the probability is approximately 65%.

30. H: The linear function $s(h) = 27h + 720$ starts at 720 when $h = 0$ and increases by 27 every time h increases by 1. Therefore, for every hour after 40, the librarian earns $27, so his salary is $27 per hour.

31. D: Since he does not replace the first card, the events are dependent. The sample space will decrease by 1 for the second draw because there will be one less card to choose. Thus, the probability may be written as $P(A\ and\ B) = \frac{13}{52} \times \frac{13}{51}$, or $P(A\ and\ B) = \frac{169}{2652} = \frac{13}{204}$.

32. F: The number of bacteria forms a geometric sequence: 100, 200, 400, 800, 1,600, etc. Notice that, if you ignore the two zeroes, these numbers are all powers of 2 (i.e. $2^0, 2^1, 2^2, 2^3, 2^4$, etc.). In other words, they are all 100 multiplied by a power of 2, so the sequence can be written as an exponential function of the form $y = 100 \times 2^n$. However, since this sequence begins with an exponent of 0 on the first day, rather than 1, and an exponent of 1 on the second day rather than 2, you need to subtract 1 from n to get the correct power. Thus, the function $b(n) = 100 \times 2^{n-1}$ represents the number of bacteria on the nth day.

33. C: The number of students who chose either turkey or egg salad is $45 + 15 = 60$. Adding the number of campers yields a total of 180, so we can write the fraction $\frac{60}{180} = \frac{1}{3}$, or approximately 33%.

34. K: The ratio indicates the number of people who chose veggie (60) to the number of people who chose turkey (45). Write the ratio $60 : 45$ and then reduce it by dividing both parts by 15 so that it becomes $4 : 3$.

35. B: An arc is a piece of a circle. In the figure, $\overset{\frown}{AB}$ is the piece of the circle that starts at point A and ends at point B. In general, an arc length s is given by $s = \theta r$, where r is the radius of the circle containing the arc and θ is the angle created by radii drawn to the endpoints of the arc. In a unit circle, the length of an arc is simply the measure of the angle (in radians). Therefore, the arc length of $\widehat{AB}$ is equal to the measure of $\angle AOB$, so its length is $\frac{\pi}{3}$.

Alternatively, we can solve using the angle and circumference. We know that the arc length is the fraction of the circle corresponding with the angle. For instance, if an angle was $\frac{\pi}{2}$, we divide this by the measure of the full circle (2π radians) to find that the arc length is $\frac{\pi}{2} \div 2\pi = \frac{\pi}{2} \times \frac{1}{2\pi} = \frac{1}{4}$ of the circumference of the circle. So, in this case, we find that the fraction of the circle is $\frac{\pi}{3} \div 2\pi = \frac{\pi}{3} \times \frac{1}{2\pi} = \frac{1}{6}$. The circumference of the circle is $C = 2\pi r$, and since the radius is 1, the circumference is simply 2π. Multiplying this by the fraction yields $\frac{2\pi}{1} \times \frac{1}{6} = \frac{\pi}{3}$. Therefore, solving using the angle and circumference also results in an arc length of $\frac{\pi}{3}$.

36. J: Standard form for complex numbers requires the denominator be completely real, that is, to have no imaginary part. When dividing complex numbers, $\frac{a+bi}{c+di}$, first multiply by a fraction equal to 1, written to make the product of the denominators completely real. This is accomplished by using the conjugate of the denominator over itself: $\frac{c-di}{c-di}$. Then, FOIL both numerator and denominator, and combine like terms and simplify, remembering that $i^2 = -1$:

$$\frac{15 - 5i}{4 - 2i} \times \frac{4 + 2i}{4 + 2i} = \frac{60 + 30i - 20i - 10i^2}{16 + 8i - 8i - 4i^2} = \frac{60 + 10i + 10}{16 + 4} = \frac{70 + 10i}{20} = \frac{10(7 + i)}{10(2)} = \frac{7 + i}{2}$$

37. B: The expected value is equal to the sum of the product of the probabilities of the rolls and the amount he will win or lose. The probability of rolling a 1 or 2 is $\frac{2}{6}$. The probability of rolling a 3 is $\frac{1}{6}$. The probability of rolling any other number is $\frac{3}{6}$. Since he will win \$5.00 if he rolls a 1 or 2, lose \$1.00 if he rolls a 3, and lose \$2.50 if he rolls any other number, the expected value is $\left(5 \times \frac{2}{6}\right) + \left(-1 \times \frac{1}{6}\right) + \left(-2.50 \times \frac{3}{6}\right)$, which equals 0.25. Thus, he can expect to win \$0.25 after one roll and $(50 \times \$0.25)$, or \$12.50, after 50 rolls.

38. H: When subtracting A from B, the difference matrix can be written as $\begin{bmatrix} 1 - 1 & -3 - (-3) \\ -4 - (-4) & 2 - (-2) \end{bmatrix}$, which reduces to $\begin{bmatrix} 0 & 0 \\ 0 & 4 \end{bmatrix}$.

39. D: Linear functions can be written in the form $g(x) = mx + b$. To determine the value of the slope, m, notice that $g(x)$ decreases by 3 every time x increases by 1: when x goes from 0 to 1, the value of the function goes from 4 to 1; and when x goes from 1 to 2, the function goes from 1 to -2. Since $g(x)$ decreases by 3, the slope is -3, so the function is $g(x) = -3x + b$.

Next, calculate the value of the y-intercept, b. The y-intercept is the value of y, or in this case $g(x)$, when $x = 0$. From the table, you can tell that $g(0) = 4$. Thus, the function is $g(x) = -3x + 4$.

40. J: It is not necessary to use the circle formula to solve the problem. Note that 50 km/hr matches with 50,000 meters per hour. You have the car's revolutions per minute, and the answer must be given in meters. So, the speed must be converted to meters per minute. This matches with a speed of $\frac{50,000}{60}$ meters per minute. The reason is that there are 60 minutes in an hour. In any given minute, the car travels at $\frac{50,000}{60}$ meters/min. The tires rotate 500 times around. So, this is 500 times its circumference. This matches with $\frac{50,000}{60 \times 500} = \frac{10}{6}$ meters per revolution. This is the circumference of the tire.

41. C: To solve the equation, cross-multiply: $2(x) = 3(x - 8)$. Multiply through to obtain: $2x = 3x - 24$. Combine like terms by subtracting $3x$ from each side to obtain: $-x = -24$, or $x = 24$.

42. H: Start by determining the area Sophie needs to paint. The area of a rectangle can be calculated by multiplying the length by the width.

$$A = l \times w = 15 \times 8 = 120$$

Therefore, she needs to cover 120 square feet of wall with paint. Since one gallon of paint can cover 36 square feet, divide 120 by 36 to determine how many gallons of paint she needs.

$$120 \div 36 = 3\frac{1}{3}$$

Sophie needs $3\frac{1}{3}$ gallons of paint to cover the room, but she needs to purchase 4 gallons since she can only purchase whole gallons of paint. 3 gallons would not be enough to cover the whole wall.

43. C: To evaluate $g(2)$, substitute 2 for every occurrence of x in the equation $g(x) = 3x + x + 5$. Then simplify the result using order of operations.

$$g(2) = 3(2) + (2) + 5$$
$$g(2) = 6 + 2 + 5$$
$$g(2) = 13$$

44. H: Since $\overline{AB}$ is tangent to Circle O, then $\overline{AB}$ forms a right angle with radius $\overline{AO}$. $\triangle AOB$ is then a right triangle, so the Pythagorean Theorem can be used to find the measure of $\overline{OB}$. Therefore, $(\overline{OB})^2 = 8^2 + 15^2 = 64 + 225 = 289$. Take the square root of both sides, to find that $\overline{OB} = 17$.

45. D: Begin by calculating the total rainfall in the summer and autumn months by adding all the values together. The total rainfall is 25.38 inches. Then, create a ratio comparing the rainfall in October to the total rainfall. The ratio $\frac{4.5}{25.38}$ represents the fraction of rainfall received during October. Convert the ratio to a percentage by dividing the numerator by the denominator and then multiplying by 100: $\frac{4.5}{25.38} \approx 0.177 = 17.7\%$. Therefore, about 17.7% of the rain fell during October.

46. G: The zeroes of a function are the domain values where the function equals 0. So, in this case, the zeroes are the values of x for which $f(x) = 0$. To find the zeroes of the function, set up an equation and then solve it for x. The first step is to factor the quadratic expression.

$$f(x) = 0$$
$$x^2 + 5x - 24 = 0$$
$$(x + 8)(x - 3) = 0$$

When the coefficient of x^2 is 1, factor the quadratic into a product of binomials $(x + a)(x + b)$, where a and b are chosen so their product is the constant term in the quadratic (including sign), and their sum is the coefficient of the linear term in the quadratic (the x-term). Then use the zero-product rule to solve the result. Using the factorization of f, write two equations and solve them both for x.

$$x + 8 = 0 \quad \text{or} \quad x - 3 = 0$$
$$x = -8 \qquad \qquad x = 3$$

47. B: The x-intercept of a function is the point where the line passes through the x-axis. Since the graph passes through the x-axis at $(6, 0)$, its x-intercept is 6. To determine which function has the same x-intercept, substitute 6 for x into each function and see if the result is zero. Start with choice A, $g(x) = -4x - 12$.

$$-4(6) - 12 = -24 - 12$$
$$= -36$$

Since the result is not 6, the x-intercept is not 6. Next try choice B, $g(x) = x^2 - 12x + 36$.

$$(6)^2 - 12(6) + 36 = 36 - 72 + 36$$
$$= 0$$

Thus, the function $g(x) = x^2 - 12x + 36$ has the same x-intercept as the graphed function.

48. J: The constant of proportionality is equal to the slope. Using the points, $(2, -8)$ and $(5, -20)$, the slope may be written as $\frac{-20-(-8)}{5-2}$, which equals $\frac{-12}{3}$ or -4.

49. C: The y-intercept of the inequality is 20. The slope can be determined by calculating the ratio of the change in y-values per change in corresponding x-values. Choose any two points to calculate the slope. For example, the points $(0,20)$ and $(25,5)$ can be used.

$$m = \frac{y_2 - y_1}{x_2 - x_1} = \frac{5 - 20}{25 - 0} = \frac{-15}{25} = -\frac{3}{5}$$

Therefore, the slope is -0.6. Write the inequality in slope-intercept form. Use the less than or equal to sign ($\leq$) because the line is solid and the graph is shaded below the line.

$$y \leq -\frac{3}{5}x + 20.$$

50. H: To determine the density of marbles per cubic foot, the calculation takes the number of marbles in the box divided by the volume of the box. The dimensions of the box are 3 ft $\times$ 2 ft $\times$ 6 in. Since the dimensions are not all in the same unit, 6 in is converted into 0.5 ft. The volume of the box then becomes 3 ft $\times$ 2 ft $\times$ 0.5 ft $= 3$ ft^3. The density of marbles per cubic foot is then calculated as $\frac{5,184 \text{ marbles}}{3 \text{ ft}^3} = 1,728 \frac{\text{marbles}}{\text{ft}^3}$. Answer F incorrectly calculated the volume of the box by failing to convert 6 in to feet and multiplied $3 \times 2 \times 6$ to get 36 ft^3. Answer G incorrectly divided the number of marbles only by the area of the bottom of the box (3 ft $\times$ 2 ft). Answer J incorrectly multiplied the number of marbles by the volume of the box.

51. B: The average rate of change of a function $f(x)$ from x_1 to x_2 is given by $\frac{f(x_2)-f(x_1)}{x_2-x_1}$. This formula is the same as the one for slope, rewritten in the context of functions. If $x_1 = 1$ and $x_2 = 5$, the average rate of the given function is given by expression below:

$$\frac{f(x_2) - f(x_1)}{x_2 - x_1} = \frac{f(5) - f(1)}{5 - 1}$$

Calculate the values of $f(1)$ and $f(5)$:

$$f(1) = -3(1) + 1 = -2$$
$$f(5) = -3(5) + 1 = -14$$

Then substitute these values into the expression for the average rate of change and simplify the result:

$$\frac{f(5) - f(1)}{5 - 1} = \frac{(-14) - (-2)}{5 - 1}$$
$$= \frac{-12}{4}$$
$$= -3$$

52. J: The theoretical probability of getting tails is $\frac{1}{2}$. Thus, she can expect to get a total of $\frac{1}{2} \times 1{,}000$ tails, or 500 tails.

53. A: For any point outside a circle, there are exactly two lines tangent to the circle passing through that point. Further, the lengths of these line segments from the point to the circle are equal. In this problem, the two segments extending from Q both have a length of 7. The two segments extending from R have a length of 4. The two segments extending from S have a length of 2. The two segments extending from P have a length of 5. Therefore, the perimeter of quadrilateral $PQRS$ can be calculated as $7 + 7 + 4 + 4 + 2 + 2 + 5 + 5 = 36$. The perimeter of the quadrilateral is 36.

54. J: If James paid 30% of the prize in taxes, this means he has 70% left. If 70% of the original prize is \$14,000, we can set up the equation: $0.7x = 14{,}000$. We divide both sides by 0.7 to find that $x = 20{,}000$, so James originally won \$20,000.

55. A: The cosine function is represented by the ratio $\frac{adjacent\ leg}{hypotenuse}$. In $\triangle ABC$, the adjacent leg to $\angle A$ is $\overline{AC}$ and the hypotenuse is $\overline{AB}$. Therefore, $\cos A = \frac{\overline{AC}}{\overline{AB}}$. Answer B is $\cot A$. Answer C is $\tan A$. Answer D is $\sin A$.

56. G: Population density is calculated by taking the population of a city and dividing that value by the square miles of land in the city. For this city, the population density is calculated as $\frac{382{,}578\ persons}{54.9\ square\ miles} = 6{,}968.6$ persons/square mile. Answer F incorrectly calculated the population density by dividing 382,578 by 54.9^2. Answer H incorrectly multiplied the population by the land area. Answer J incorrectly multiplied the population by the 54.9^2.

57. B: Since we are given a conversion factor, begin by setting up conversion fractions. We know that $\frac{1}{2}$ inch $= 12$ miles, and we are looking for how many inches would represent 84 miles. Set up the following conversion fraction.

$$\frac{\frac{1}{2}\ inch}{12\ miles} = \frac{x\ inches}{84\ miles}$$

Since the units are lined up properly, we can ignore them for the moment, cross multiply the values, and solve for x.

$$\frac{1}{2} \times 84 = 12x$$
$$42 = 12x$$
$$3.5 = x$$

Since $x = 3.5$, a distance of 84 miles would be represented by 3.5 inches on the map.

58. H: Remember that starting at the decimal point and going right, the place values are tenths, hundredths, thousandths and so on. Thus, the decimal 0.0315 has the three in the hundredths place.

59. B: The first function $L(g)$ gives the water level after g gallons are pumped into the tank. The second function $w(t)$ gives the number of gallons pumped into the tank after t minutes, which the first function calls g. Consequently, we can have L act on w: the composition of the functions $L\big(w(t)\big)$ is the water level of the tank after t minutes. Calculate $L\big(w(t)\big)$.

$$L\big(w(t)\big) = 0.3 \times w(t)$$
$$= 0.3 \times 1.2t$$
$$= 0.36t$$

Thus, the function $L(t) = 0.36t$ represents the water level of the tank after t minutes.

60. G: If the touching edges of the trapezoids are extended, they meet at a point on the horizontal. Using this information and the following geometric relationships, solve for x:

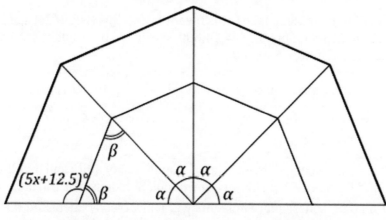

$$4\alpha = 180° \quad \alpha + 2\beta = 180° \quad (5x + 12.5)° + \beta = 180°$$
$$\alpha = 45° \qquad \beta = \frac{135°}{2} \qquad (5x + 12.5)° = 112.5°$$
$$\beta = 67.5° \qquad\qquad 5x = 100$$
$$x = 20$$

Reading

Question	Question	Question	Question
1. A	11. C	21. A	31. B
2. G	12. G	22. G	32. J
3. D	13. B	23. C	33. D
4. H	14. F	24. G	34. G
5. D	15. C	25. D	35. C
6. F	16. F	26. F	36. F
7. D	17. A	27. C	37. C
8. H	18. G	28. H	38. J
9. D	19. A	29. C	39. D
10. J	20. J	30. H	40. J

1. A: Lines 31-34: "Since the beginning of our American history, we have been engaged in change—in a perpetual peaceful revolution—a revolution which goes on steadily, quietly adjusting itself to changing conditions—without the concentration camp or the quick-lime in the ditch."

This is the only statement listed here that directly supports the idea that FDR thought that America is constantly moving toward a better way of life.

2. G: The average citizen already feels overburdened by taxes and feels the money is not being well-spent by the government. The argument that needs to be evaluated is that people will be happy to give more money in taxes to the government. It would be safe to raise the counterargument that the general population may already believe they are paying enough in taxes and don't think the government is spending that money wisely. Not everyone will be happy to give more to the government to spend. Choices F and J do not address the question. Choice H actually agrees with FDR's premise.

3. D: There are four basic freedoms that are vital to the health of people: speech, worship, freedom from want, and freedom from fear. This speech is typically referred to as the "Four Freedoms" speech. In it, FDR articulates the basic freedoms he believes in. These freedoms are the central focus of the speech, since it supports the other ideas that he is focusing on (i.e., social issues). Choice A is a detail in the speech, Choice B is not articulated, and Choice C is not in the speech.

4. H: FDR spoke of freedom, defining it in the previous paragraph as "the supremacy of human rights everywhere." This is the "high concept" he refers to in the following paragraph/sentence. In this context, the "end" of victory does not mean death (F). It does not precisely mean purpose (G), as in the common phrase "a means to an end" (a way of achieving a purpose): he was not saying victory was the only purpose of the concept, but rather that this concept could have no other outcome (H) or result than victory. "End" can also mean conclusion (J), i.e., the termination or finishing of something, which does not fit the meaning in this context quite as precisely as (H) because it does not imply cause and effect as "outcome" does.

5. D: After describing the four freedoms he identified, FDR said the vision of a world founded on those freedoms was "no vision of a distant millennium" but "a definite basis for a kind of world attainable in our own time and generation. That kind of world is the very antithesis of the so-called new order of tyranny..." referring to the "order" that dictators wanted to impose, to which "we oppose the greater conception—the moral order." He further described the "cooperation of free countries, working together in a friendly, civilized society" as the "world order which we seek". This context establishes that "order" more nearly means a system of societal and world politics (D) rather than a military leader's command (A); an authoritative decision or direction (B), e.g., a court order or a doctor's order; or an arrangement in sequence (C), e.g., alphabetical, numerical, or chronological order.

6. F: In lines 8 – 10 FDR said, "A part of the sacrifice means the payment of more money in taxes" for "a greater portion of this great defense program".

While he called for taxpayers to support the military, in this passage he did not equate personal sacrifice with serving in the military (G). While he described worldwide arms reduction (H), he did not equate this with personal sacrifice, but with the fourth freedom: freedom from fear. The four freedoms (J) he identified were "essential human freedoms", i.e., things all human beings had rights to, not examples of personal sacrifice.

7. D: FDR implicitly referred to the American Revolutionary War (A) by contrasting it with the process of continual change which he characterized as America's ongoing *"perpetual peaceful revolution"*. He continued a pattern of implicit contrast by further characterizing this peaceful revolution as adjusting to change "without the concentration camp or the quick-lime in the ditch." Concentration camps were established by the Nazis during World War II as part of the Holocaust; quicklime was used in trenches during World War I (B), when trench warfare was widely practiced. In World War II (C), soldiers dug more individual foxholes than trenches (though there were some); but quicklime was also used by Nazis in mass graves of people they murdered and on the floors of train cattle cars transporting people to concentration camps, labor camps, and death camps.

8. H: In this passage there is no mention of expanding the draft of citizens into military service. As examples of aspects of the social economy needing "immediate improvement", FDR cited, "We should bring more citizens under the coverage of old-age pensions...." (F); "We should widen the opportunities for adequate medical care" (G); and "We should plan a better system by which persons deserving or needing gainful employment may obtain it" (J).

9. D: In this passage, FDR did include some simple sentences, but they are typically not short (A). The shortest sentences in the passage have six and seven words respectively and are the only ones that short. The structure used most frequently is the complex sentence; these are typically long (B). He also included some long compound sentences (C); and some long complex-compound sentences (D).

10. J: Choice F is incorrect because while the President does name some of the rights that come under the first amendment, he is not merely reciting or trying to paraphrase the first amendment. Although President Roosevelt uses the phrase "everywhere in the world" several times, readers should also acknowledge that "everywhere in the world" includes the United States of America and neither the world or America are emphasized as being more important than the other. In addition, the President says that he Americans are seeking to make the world more secure, and he asserts that this can be achieved when all people around the world enjoy the same freedoms as Americans. So, Choice G is not the best choice. Choice H is also not the best choice because while the task is challenging and immense, the President does not seem to be wavering or doubtful on his hope for that dream.

11. C: The correct answer choice is C because paragraphs 2-5 introduce Buck and the setting in which he lives. The paragraphs accomplish this introduction by giving many detailed facts, such as the detail in paragraph 5 about the times he escorted Mollie and Alice on walks. Choice A is incorrect because two new characters, Manuel and the stranger, are introduced in paragraphs 7 and 8. While aspects of paragraphs 2-5 show Buck's personality, choice B is incorrect because the paragraphs also give other details about Buck, such as information about his parents and appearance. Choice D is incorrect because Toots and Ysabel are only mentioned in paragraphs 3 and 4. Furthermore, paragraph 4 says that he utterly ignored Toots and Ysabel, not that he is affectionate towards them.

12. G: The correct answer is choice G because the sentence indicates that Buck felt as if he owned or ruled over Judge Miller's place. The word *realm* indicates that the sentence is referring to everything. Choice F is incorrect because it talks about other dogs that came and went but does not show Buck's attitude towards them or Judge Miller's place. Choice H is incorrect because it shows Buck's opinion of himself but not his opinion of Judge Miller's place. Choice F is incorrect because it describes something that Buck enjoys, but does not give his attitude about the house and grounds at Judge Miller's.

13. B: The correct answer is choice B because details in the passage foreshadow what might happen to Buck. Phrases like "trouble was brewing" or "these men wanted dogs" indicate that Buck might be heading for trouble. Choice A is incorrect because the paragraph does not give details about Buck's life; later paragraphs give those details. Choice C is incorrect because the paragraph does not give setting details. Setting details about Buck's current situation are given in later paragraphs. Choice D is incorrect because the paragraph does not describe any characters other than Buck; it does not indicate that Buck is the villain.

14. F: Choice F is the correct answer because the Klondike strike has caused people to look for dogs like Buck. Although paragraph 1 does not directly mention the Klondike strike, the reader can infer from paragraph 6 that the events discussed refer to the Klondike strike. Choice G is incorrect because paragraph 3 makes it clear that dogs came and went even before the Klondike strike. Choice H is incorrect because Elmo is Buck's father but not a main character in the story. Choice J is incorrect because the passage does not draw a connection between the Klondike strike and the frequency of the Raisin Growers' Association's meetings.

15. C: Choice C is correct because the first part of the passage mostly describes Buck's life, but the passage ends in a moment of change when the stranger wraps a piece of rope around Buck's neck. Choice A is incorrect because the passage does not describe a sequence of events as they happen. Instead the passage gives an overview of how Buck lived before the moment of change. Although part of the passage describes Buck's history, the passage also describes the moment in which his life changes, making choice B incorrect. Choice D is incorrect because the passage only describes life at Judge Miller's place but doesn't describe what came afterwards.

16. F: The correct answer is choice F because most of the passage provides background information about Buck's life and personality. Choice G is incorrect because the passage does not describe any moments in which Buck is acting heroic; instead, it describes Buck's regular interactions with the other people and animals at Judge Miller's place. Choice H is incorrect because the passage only briefly mentions the Klondike strike. The majority of the passage describes Buck's life. Choice J is incorrect because the other dogs are described in paragraphs 3 and 4. The rest of the passage focuses on Buck.

17. A: The best answer is choice A because the passage begins by setting up Buck's life and then showing a moment where his life is about to change drastically. Choice B is incorrect because only paragraph 5 refers to family; this is not a big enough portion of the passage to imply that the larger selection is about family. Although Buck might need to work hard in the future, choice C is incorrect because the passage does not have that many clues about upcoming hard work. Choice C is incorrect because the passage does not spend time showing that Buck strongly values relationships. The end of the passage indicates that Buck is about to experience a moment of change.

18. G: The correct answer is choice G because the sentence talks about how the men want dogs; the sentence foreshadows that Buck may be the type of dog that the men want. Choice F is incorrect because it refers to Buck's attitude around Judge Miller's place but does not hint at what might be coming next. Although part of the sentence indicates that Buck hopes to follow in Elmo's footsteps, the rest of the sentence simply describes Buck's father. Choice G better foreshadows what's going to happen in the story because it more closely relates to the events in paragraph 7 and 8. Choice J is incorrect because the sentence describes Buck's personality and interests without giving clues about what's going to happen next.

19. A: At the beginning of the passage, the author explains that "every tide-water dog, strong of muscle and with warm, long hair, from Puget Sound to San Diego" were being taken to the North to help find the "yellow metal." Since, the value of gold is so high, it is the most likely explanation that Manuel took Buck in order for Manuel to pay off his debts from gambling.

20. J: In these paragraphs, the narrator oversees all of the events and explains the situation to readers in detail. So, of the choices that you have, Choice J is the best selection.

21. A: Only this choice provides support for the idea of special relativity. Choice B is used in the explanation, but does not provide support on its own. Choice C is actually part of a counterargument to relativity. Choice D only indicates that there are two sections, and does not provide any support.

22. G: If relativity is valid, then why can it not explain all parts of the natural world, including the rules of quantum mechanics? Only this choice deals closely with an argument against relativity. The classical laws of motion are in agreement with relativity. Choice C. does not pose an argument against relativity and Choice D. focuses on asking a detailed question about the thought experiment, not the entire theory.

23. C: The word "truth" was quoted because Einstein was referring to the understanding of the laws of motion we had before relativity, which did indeed seem to provide the correct answers for a great deal of physics questions. However, according to the other sentences around this word, we can conclude that it does not refer to an absolute truth because relativity turns classical ideas on their heads.

24. B: Corresponding to the noun "delicacy", one meaning of the adjective "delicate" is fragile (a) or easily damaged. This meaning is not supported by the context. As it modifies "detail", delicacy here refers to how sensitively and specifically classical mechanics describes the movements of stars, planets, etc. Another meaning of a delicacy is an expensive and/or rare delight (c), especially regarding food; e.g., caviar is considered a delicacy. This meaning makes no sense in this context. Delicacy can also refer to soft texture (d), e.g., the delicacy of a lace fabric. This meaning does not relate to the subject matter.

25. D: *A priori* is Latin, meaning literally "from the one before". In the context of Einstein's discussion, he means that because the principle of relativity can be generalized so broadly across domains, its applying so precisely in one domain predicts it would apply with comparable accuracy in another domain; and therefore, that its being valid for one domain but not another is not very likely. It is *a priori* not very likely when considering this application of a general principle to a specific domain, and this unlikeliness is logically true/valid independent of observation or experience.

26. A: The quoted phrase is most an example of understatement. To emphasize through reversal how exquisite he found the detail provided by classical mechanics, Einstein downplayed it by describing it as less than wonderful, but only a little less. He further qualified this by not writing "*nothing* short of wonderful", but "*little* short of wonderful", making it comparative rather than absolute. An example of overstatement (b) or hyperbole in this case would be something like "the most wonderful ever seen", "too wonderful to be believed", etc. Amplification (c) is repeating a word/phrase but with added details or expanded description for emphasis; e.g., "...it supplies us with the actual motions of the heavenly bodies with a delicacy of detail—a delicacy of detail so fine that it can only be perceived as wonderful." Metabasis (d) is a transitional summary that recapitulates what was said previously and predicts what will be said next, to clarify and organize discourse.

27. C: As Einstein indicated in the sentence following this one, "This statement is called the principle of relativity (in the restricted sense)." The statements in (A), (B), and (D) are all conclusions predicated upon the condition that this principle were NOT true: (A) begins with "If the principle of relativity (in the restricted sense) does not hold," continuing with the "then" clause quoted. (B) continues from (A), saying, "In this case we should be constrained to believe that..." finishing with the clause quoted. (D) is prefaced by, "If the principle of relativity were not valid" and continues with the clause quoted.

28. H: validity regarding an understanding of the classical rules of motion. The word "truth" was quoted because Einstein was referring to the understanding of the laws of motion we had before relativity, which did indeed seem to provide the correct answers for a great deal of physics questions. However, according to the other sentences around this word, we can conclude that it does not refer to an absolute truth because relativity turns classical ideas on their heads.

29. C: Of the first five paragraphs, the first four are completely positive in Einstein's assertions and explanations of his claims; the fifth is also mainly positive, with only a hint of counterclaim in its last sentence refuted to emphasize the claim's validity ("But that [this] principle...should hold...in one domain...and yet...be invalid for another, is a priori not very probable."). The last two paragraphs present counterclaims, introduced by "If the principle of relativity does not hold..." and similar clauses, followed by "then..." conclusions illustrating the logically necessary yet improbable results of such counterclaims.

30. H: Einstein's identification of "two general facts" introduces two arguments wherein he explains reasoning to support the principle of relativity. (F) is the last sentence in the excerpted passage, summarizing rather than introducing his preceding evidence. (G) introduces the second of his two "arguments" or "general facts" rather than introducing both of them. (J) is the first sentence in the excerpted passage, but it is obvious from the clause "let us return to our example" that he is revisiting an example he introduced in a previous part of his paper not included in this excerpt; hence he was not introducing new evidence there, but rather reusing previously introduced evidence to make additional points.

31. B: The entire passage makes the argument that Black History Month should be abolished, offering various reasons why this is the best course of action.

32. J: The context of the sentence suggests that post-racial refers to an approach in which race is not a useful or positive organizing principle.

33. D: The author of Passage A never suggests that people do not learn about African American history during Black History Month.

34. G: Passage B states that W.E.B. DuBois was born in 1868; his birth was therefore the first of the identified events.

35. C: The author points out in paragraph 3 of Passage B that the debate about how to meet the need to teach children about African American history can remind parents that this need is not yet fully met.

36. F: In paragraph 4, the author of Passage B states that the material available is rich and varied.

37. C: The author of Passage B points out that just because there is a month focused on African American history, this doesn't mean that African American history must be ignored for the rest of the year.

38. J: Choice F is not the best choice because while the authors seem to be supportive of the President, there is not enough information in the passages to draw that conclusion. Choice G is wrong because the author of Passage A merely quotes an article, and the author of Passage B makes no mention of the media. Choice H suggests that the authors would be supportive of Black History Month if it were moved to another month. However, the author of Passage A wants to remove the recognition of Black History Month, not merely change the dates. Instead, Choice J is the best option because both authors agree that revisions to curriculum in the education system are necessary to improve the understanding of black history.

39. D: Clearly both authors think it is important for students to learn about the achievements and experience of African Americans; their debate is whether observing Black History Month is the best way to achieve this goal.

40. J: The last paragraph of Passage 2 states that Abraham Lincoln and Frederick Douglass were essential civil rights activists.

Science

Question	Question	Question	Question
1. A	11. C	21. A	31. B
2. J	12. G	22. H	32. G
3. C	13. D	23. A	33. C
4. J	14. J	24. G	34. J
5. D	15. B	25. C	35. B
6. J	16. H	26. J	36. H
7. D	17. D	27. A	37. D
8. J	18. H	28. J	38. G
9. A	19. D	29. A	39. C
10. J	20. J	30. G	40. J

1. A: The peak for albumin is the highest in the electropherogram, so the concentration of albumin is higher than that of any other component.

2. J: The peak for component γ is furthest from the origin along the mobility axis, indicating that it has moved the furthest during the experiment.

3. C: The peak for component $\alpha 1$ lies to the right of that for albumin, indicating greater mobility, and to the left of all the other peaks, indicating lesser mobility than the components represented by those peaks. Since small molecules move faster than large ones, $\alpha 1$ must be smaller than albumin and larger than the other components.

4. J: The peak for component γ is the fastest, indicating that γ is the smallest component seen on the electropherogram.

5. D: The peak for the unknown lies between those for γ and β, indicating an intermediate size. It has moved more rapidly than all components except for component γ.

6. J: If the unknown is an aggregate, it must be larger than the components that have clumped together to form it, not smaller.

7. D: If the unknown is a breakdown product, it must be smaller than the components that have broken down to form it, not larger.

8. J: The experiment shows only that this patient's blood contains an unknown component. It does not demonstrate that the component causes the patient's disease, or that it results from it. It may be unrelated. Further experiments are required to fully characterize the relationship between the component and the illness.

9. A: As stated in the text, the size of each circle is proportional to the number of recoveries.

10. J: The graph shows that the largest number of circles, and the largest circles as well, are at this depth. Since the size of the circles is proportional to the number of fish recovered, the greatest numbers of these fish were at these depths.

11. C: 2011 fish were recovered out of 34,000 released. The percentage is given by $P = 100 \times \frac{2,011}{34,000} = 6\%$.

12. G: The median age at each depth is shown by the X symbols on the plot. For this depth, the symbol lines up approximately with the mark corresponding to 5 years on the upper axis of the graph.

13. D: Although not specifically described in the text, all of the reasons stated may occur, reducing the recovery of tagged fish. The conclusions of the study must assume that the fraction of fish recovered (sample) are representative of the population as a whole.

14. J: The chart describes the age of the fish, but does not provide any information concerning their size.

15. B: The median age of the populations recovered at each depth is shown by the X symbol on the plot, and corresponds to progressively older fish at greater depths. Although some of the other statements are true, they are not supported by the data in the figure.

16. H: The right-most symbol on the plot shows that some 20-year old fish were recovered at depths of 501-700 meters. No older fish were recovered in this study.

17. D: The table shows that the lambda particle has a mass of over 1115 MeV

18. H: Protons and other nucleons are baryons, which are made of quarks. The other choices are all leptons, which are not.

19. D: To satisfy the law of conservation of charge, the net charge of all the particles produced in a decay must equal that of the original particle. Note that while conservation of mass applies to the decay, it does not pertain to charge.

20. J: The most massive particles of neutral charge are the Xi particles, with a mass of 1314.9 MeV.

21. A: The lambda particle has no charge. The proton has a charge of +1. To satisfy the law of conservation of charge, the other particle must have a charge of -1. The negative pion is the only choice that satisfies that condition.

22. H: The mass of the muon is 105.65 MeV. That of the positron is 0.65 MeV. To satisfy the law of conservation of mass, the mass of the positron plus that of the other resulting particles cannot add up to more than 105.65 MeV. Among the choices given, only the neutrino is small enough to satisfy that condition.

23. A: To satisfy the law of conservation of mass, the mass difference between the original particle and its decay products is released as knetic energy. Since the omega particle has a mass of 1672.45 MeV, and the kaon and lambda particles have masses of 493.68 and 1115.68 MeV, respectively, the difference is 63.09 MeV.

24. G: One MeV is equivalent to 1.783×10^{-30} kilogram, so that

$$60\text{kg} = \frac{60}{1.783 \times 10^{-30}} \text{ MeV} = 33.65 \times 10^{30}$$

25. C: Of the sites listed, the phi value for site MD, 2.73 phi, is the largest value. The text explains how phi varies inversely with particle size, so these are the smallest particles.

26. J: According to the definition of phi supplied in the text, the range 1.0 to 4.0 phi units corresponds to particle sizes in the range 0.06 to 0.5 mm.

27. A: At all of the sites except site ND, the particle size distributions are tightly centered around a well-defined modal value. At site ND, the distribution is spread out over a broader range, and there is no well-defined central value.

28. J: Each unit of added phi value in the negative direction corresponds to a doubling of the particle size, so that -1 corresponds to 2mm, -2 to 4 mm, and -3 to 8 mm.

29. A: The curves represent the distance traveled, and they approximate a straight line. The slope of the line represents the speed of travel. Although the curve in part (b) has a negative slope, the absolute value of that slope will be a positive value, representing speed of transport towards the west.

30. G: The steepest slopes correspond to the greatest values of mab, or meters above bottom. These are the shallowest waters.

31. B: The steepest slopes correspond to the greatest values of mab, or meters above bottom. These are the shallowest waters. Although the slopes are negative in this plot, it is the magnitude of the slope that indicates the speed of transport. Here, the negative value simply indicates that the sediments drift toward the west, not the east.

32.G: The upper graph shows transport toward the north. The lower graph shows transport toward the west. If these two are combined, overall transport will be toward the NW.

33. C: The efficiency curve in part B of the figure has a clear maximum value at a wind velocity of 10 m/s.

34. J: The power curve in part A of the figure increases with increasing wind velocity, until a plateau is reached at 15 m/s and above.

35. B: The text explains that for wind velocities above 15 m/s, the rotor blades are trimmed to protect the equipment. Above 25 m/s, the turbine must be shut down.

36. H: Power increases with the cube of wind velocity. This is an exponential function.

37. D: The power increases with the cube, or third power, of wind velocity, v. If the wind velocity is doubled, the power output will be proportional to the third power of the new wind velocity v'. But if v' = 2v, then

$$v'^3 = (2v)^3 = 8v^3$$

and the new power output is 8 times greater than the original output, or 1600 kW.

38. G: See question 37. Since this generator operates at 50% efficiency, only half of the theoretical power is available.

39. C: The longest bars in the histogram correspond to the middle frequencies, from about 300 to 2000 Hz.

40. J: The text explains that winds originate from differential warming of the earth's surface by the sun. It is this energy that is captured by a wind turbine.

How to Overcome Test Anxiety

Just the thought of taking a test is enough to make most people a little nervous. A test is an important event that can have a long-term impact on your future, so it's important to take it seriously and it's natural to feel anxious about performing well. But just because anxiety is normal, that doesn't mean that it's helpful in test taking, or that you should simply accept it as part of your life. Anxiety can have a variety of effects. These effects can be mild, like making you feel slightly nervous, or severe, like blocking your ability to focus or remember even a simple detail.

If you experience test anxiety—whether severe or mild—it's important to know how to beat it. To discover this, first you need to understand what causes test anxiety.

Causes of Test Anxiety

While we often think of anxiety as an uncontrollable emotional state, it can actually be caused by simple, practical things. One of the most common causes of test anxiety is that a person does not feel adequately prepared for their test. This feeling can be the result of many different issues such as poor study habits or lack of organization, but the most common culprit is time management. Starting to study too late, failing to organize your study time to cover all of the material, or being distracted while you study will mean that you're not well prepared for the test. This may lead to cramming the night before, which will cause you to be physically and mentally exhausted for the test. Poor time management also contributes to feelings of stress, fear, and hopelessness as you realize you are not well prepared but don't know what to do about it.

Other times, test anxiety is not related to your preparation for the test but comes from unresolved fear. This may be a past failure on a test, or poor performance on tests in general. It may come from comparing yourself to others who seem to be performing better or from the stress of living up to expectations. Anxiety may be driven by fears of the future—how failure on this test would affect your educational and career goals. These fears are often completely irrational, but they can still negatively impact your test performance.

Elements of Test Anxiety

As mentioned earlier, test anxiety is considered to be an emotional state, but it has physical and mental components as well. Sometimes you may not even realize that you are suffering from test anxiety until you notice the physical symptoms. These can include trembling hands, rapid heartbeat, sweating, nausea, and tense muscles. Extreme anxiety may lead to fainting or vomiting. Obviously, any of these symptoms can have a negative impact on testing. It is important to recognize them as soon as they begin to occur so that you can address the problem before it damages your performance.

The mental components of test anxiety include trouble focusing and inability to remember learned information. During a test, your mind is on high alert, which can help you recall information and stay focused for an extended period of time. However, anxiety interferes with your mind's natural processes, causing you to blank out, even on the questions you know well. The strain of testing during anxiety makes it difficult to stay focused, especially on a test that may take several hours. Extreme anxiety can take a huge mental toll, making it difficult not only to recall test information but even to understand the test questions or pull your thoughts together.

278

Effects of Test Anxiety

Test anxiety is like a disease—if left untreated, it will get progressively worse. Anxiety leads to poor performance, and this reinforces the feelings of fear and failure, which in turn lead to poor performances on subsequent tests. It can grow from a mild nervousness to a crippling condition. If allowed to progress, test anxiety can have a big impact on your schooling, and consequently on your future.

Test anxiety can spread to other parts of your life. Anxiety on tests can become anxiety in any stressful situation, and blanking on a test can turn into panicking in a job situation. But fortunately, you don't have to let anxiety rule your testing and determine your grades. There are a number of relatively simple steps you can take to move past anxiety and function normally on a test and in the rest of life.

Physical Steps for Beating Test Anxiety

While test anxiety is a serious problem, the good news is that it can be overcome. It doesn't have to control your ability to think and remember information. While it may take time, you can begin taking steps today to beat anxiety.

Just as your first hint that you may be struggling with anxiety comes from the physical symptoms, the first step to treating it is also physical. Rest is crucial for having a clear, strong mind. If you are tired, it is much easier to give in to anxiety. But if you establish good sleep habits, your body and mind will be ready to perform optimally, without the strain of exhaustion. Additionally, sleeping well helps you to retain information better, so you're more likely to recall the answers when you see the test questions.

Getting good sleep means more than going to bed on time. It's important to allow your brain time to relax. Take study breaks from time to time so it doesn't get overworked, and don't study right before bed. Take time to rest your mind before trying to rest your body, or you may find it difficult to fall asleep.

Along with sleep, other aspects of physical health are important in preparing for a test. Good nutrition is vital for good brain function. Sugary foods and drinks may give a burst of energy but this burst is followed by a crash, both physically and emotionally. Instead, fuel your body with protein and vitamin-rich foods.

Also, drink plenty of water. Dehydration can lead to headaches and exhaustion, especially if your brain is already under stress from the rigors of the test. Particularly if your test is a long one, drink water during the breaks. And if possible, take an energy-boosting snack to eat between sections.

Along with sleep and diet, a third important part of physical health is exercise. Maintaining a steady workout schedule is helpful, but even taking 5-minute study breaks to walk can help get your blood pumping faster and clear your head. Exercise also releases endorphins, which contribute to a positive feeling and can help combat test anxiety.

When you nurture your physical health, you are also contributing to your mental health. If your body is healthy, your mind is much more likely to be healthy as well. So take time to rest, nourish your body with healthy food and water, and get moving as much as possible. Taking these physical steps will make you stronger and more able to take the mental steps necessary to overcome test anxiety.

Mental Steps for Beating Test Anxiety

Working on the mental side of test anxiety can be more challenging, but as with the physical side, there are clear steps you can take to overcome it. As mentioned earlier, test anxiety often stems from lack of preparation, so the obvious solution is to prepare for the test. Effective studying may be the most important weapon you have for beating test anxiety, but you can and should employ several other mental tools to combat fear.

First, boost your confidence by reminding yourself of past success—tests or projects that you aced. If you're putting as much effort into preparing for this test as you did for those, there's no reason you should expect to fail here. Work hard to prepare; then trust your preparation.

Second, surround yourself with encouraging people. It can be helpful to find a study group, but be sure that the people you're around will encourage a positive attitude. If you spend time with others who are anxious or cynical, this will only contribute to your own anxiety. Look for others who are motivated to study hard from a desire to succeed, not from a fear of failure.

Third, reward yourself. A test is physically and mentally tiring, even without anxiety, and it can be helpful to have something to look forward to. Plan an activity following the test, regardless of the outcome, such as going to a movie or getting ice cream.

When you are taking the test, if you find yourself beginning to feel anxious, remind yourself that you know the material. Visualize successfully completing the test. Then take a few deep, relaxing breaths and return to it. Work through the questions carefully but with confidence, knowing that you are capable of succeeding.

Developing a healthy mental approach to test taking will also aid in other areas of life. Test anxiety affects more than just the actual test—it can be damaging to your mental health and even contribute to depression. It's important to beat test anxiety before it becomes a problem for more than testing.

Study Strategy

Being prepared for the test is necessary to combat anxiety, but what does being prepared look like? You may study for hours on end and still not feel prepared. What you need is a strategy for test prep. The next few pages outline our recommended steps to help you plan out and conquer the challenge of preparation.

STEP 1: SCOPE OUT THE TEST

Learn everything you can about the format (multiple choice, essay, etc.) and what will be on the test. Gather any study materials, course outlines, or sample exams that may be available. Not only will this help you to prepare, but knowing what to expect can help to alleviate test anxiety.

STEP 2: MAP OUT THE MATERIAL

Look through the textbook or study guide and make note of how many chapters or sections it has. Then divide these over the time you have. For example, if a book has 15 chapters and you have five days to study, you need to cover three chapters each day. Even better, if you have the time, leave an extra day at the end for overall review after you have gone through the material in depth.

If time is limited, you may need to prioritize the material. Look through it and make note of which sections you think you already have a good grasp on, and which need review. While you are studying, skim quickly through the familiar sections and take more time on the challenging parts.

Write out your plan so you don't get lost as you go. Having a written plan also helps you feel more in control of the study, so anxiety is less likely to arise from feeling overwhelmed at the amount to cover.

STEP 3: GATHER YOUR TOOLS

Decide what study method works best for you. Do you prefer to highlight in the book as you study and then go back over the highlighted portions? Or do you type out notes of the important information? Or is it helpful to make flashcards that you can carry with you? Assemble the pens, index cards, highlighters, post-it notes, and any other materials you may need so you won't be distracted by getting up to find things while you study.

If you're having a hard time retaining the information or organizing your notes, experiment with different methods. For example, try color-coding by subject with colored pens, highlighters, or post-it notes. If you learn better by hearing, try recording yourself reading your notes so you can listen while in the car, working out, or simply sitting at your desk. Ask a friend to quiz you from your flashcards, or try teaching someone the material to solidify it in your mind.

STEP 4: CREATE YOUR ENVIRONMENT

It's important to avoid distractions while you study. This includes both the obvious distractions like visitors and the subtle distractions like an uncomfortable chair (or a too-comfortable couch that makes you want to fall asleep). Set up the best study environment possible: good lighting and a comfortable work area. If background music helps you focus, you may want to turn it on, but otherwise keep the room quiet. If you are using a computer to take notes, be sure you don't have any other windows open, especially applications like social media, games, or anything else that could distract you. Silence your phone and turn off notifications. Be sure to keep water close by so you stay hydrated while you study (but avoid unhealthy drinks and snacks).

Also, take into account the best time of day to study. Are you freshest first thing in the morning? Try to set aside some time then to work through the material. Is your mind clearer in the afternoon or evening? Schedule your study session then. Another method is to study at the same time of day that you will take the test, so that your brain gets used to working on the material at that time and will be ready to focus at test time.

STEP 5: STUDY!

Once you have done all the study preparation, it's time to settle into the actual studying. Sit down, take a few moments to settle your mind so you can focus, and begin to follow your study plan. Don't give in to distractions or let yourself procrastinate. This is your time to prepare so you'll be ready to fearlessly approach the test. Make the most of the time and stay focused.

Of course, you don't want to burn out. If you study too long you may find that you're not retaining the information very well. Take regular study breaks. For example, taking five minutes out of every hour to walk briskly, breathing deeply and swinging your arms, can help your mind stay fresh.

As you get to the end of each chapter or section, it's a good idea to do a quick review. Remind yourself of what you learned and work on any difficult parts. When you feel that you've mastered the material, move on to the next part. At the end of your study session, briefly skim through your notes again.

But while review is helpful, cramming last minute is NOT. If at all possible, work ahead so that you won't need to fit all your study into the last day. Cramming overloads your brain with more information than it can process and retain, and your tired mind may struggle to recall even previously learned information when it is overwhelmed with last-minute study. Also, the urgent nature of cramming and the stress placed on your brain contribute to anxiety. You'll be more likely to go to the test feeling unprepared and having trouble thinking clearly.

So don't cram, and don't stay up late before the test, even just to review your notes at a leisurely pace. Your brain needs rest more than it needs to go over the information again. In fact, plan to finish your studies by noon or early afternoon the day before the test. Give your brain the rest of the day to relax or focus on other things, and get a good night's sleep. Then you will be fresh for the test and better able to recall what you've studied.

STEP 6: TAKE A PRACTICE TEST

Many courses offer sample tests, either online or in the study materials. This is an excellent resource to check whether you have mastered the material, as well as to prepare for the test format and environment.

Check the test format ahead of time: the number of questions, the type (multiple choice, free response, etc.), and the time limit. Then create a plan for working through them. For example, if you have 30 minutes to take a 60-question test, your limit is 30 seconds per question. Spend less time on the questions you know well so that you can take more time on the difficult ones.

If you have time to take several practice tests, take the first one open book, with no time limit. Work through the questions at your own pace and make sure you fully understand them. Gradually work up to taking a test under test conditions: sit at a desk with all study materials put away and set a timer. Pace yourself to make sure you finish the test with time to spare and go back to check your answers if you have time.

After each test, check your answers. On the questions you missed, be sure you understand why you missed them. Did you misread the question (tests can use tricky wording)? Did you forget the information? Or was it something you hadn't learned? Go back and study any shaky areas that the practice tests reveal.

Taking these tests not only helps with your grade, but also aids in combating test anxiety. If you're already used to the test conditions, you're less likely to worry about it, and working through tests until you're scoring well gives you a confidence boost. Go through the practice tests until you feel comfortable, and then you can go into the test knowing that you're ready for it.

Test Tips

On test day, you should be confident, knowing that you've prepared well and are ready to answer the questions. But aside from preparation, there are several test day strategies you can employ to maximize your performance.

First, as stated before, get a good night's sleep the night before the test (and for several nights before that, if possible). Go into the test with a fresh, alert mind rather than staying up late to study.

Try not to change too much about your normal routine on the day of the test. It's important to eat a nutritious breakfast, but if you normally don't eat breakfast at all, consider eating just a protein bar. If you're a coffee drinker, go ahead and have your normal coffee. Just make sure you time it so that the caffeine doesn't wear off right in the middle of your test. Avoid sugary beverages, and drink enough water to stay hydrated but not so much that you need a restroom break 10 minutes into the test. If your test isn't first thing in the morning, consider going for a walk or doing a light workout before the test to get your blood flowing.

Allow yourself enough time to get ready, and leave for the test with plenty of time to spare so you won't have the anxiety of scrambling to arrive in time. Another reason to be early is to select a good seat. It's helpful to sit away from doors and windows, which can be distracting. Find a good seat, get out your supplies, and settle your mind before the test begins.

When the test begins, start by going over the instructions carefully, even if you already know what to expect. Make sure you avoid any careless mistakes by following the directions.

Then begin working through the questions, pacing yourself as you've practiced. If you're not sure on an answer, don't spend too much time on it, and don't let it shake your confidence. Either skip it and come back later, or eliminate as many wrong answers as possible and guess among the remaining ones. Don't dwell on these questions as you continue—put them out of your mind and focus on what lies ahead.

Be sure to read all of the answer choices, even if you're sure the first one is the right answer. Sometimes you'll find a better one if you keep reading. But don't second-guess yourself if you do immediately know the answer. Your gut instinct is usually right. Don't let test anxiety rob you of the information you know.

If you have time at the end of the test (and if the test format allows), go back and review your answers. Be cautious about changing any, since your first instinct tends to be correct, but make sure you didn't misread any of the questions or accidentally mark the wrong answer choice. Look over any you skipped and make an educated guess.

At the end, leave the test feeling confident. You've done your best, so don't waste time worrying about your performance or wishing you could change anything. Instead, celebrate the successful completion of this test. And finally, use this test to learn how to deal with anxiety even better next time.

> **Review Video: Test Anxiety**
> Visit mometrix.com/academy and enter code: 100340

Important Qualification

Not all anxiety is created equal. If your test anxiety is causing major issues in your life beyond the classroom or testing center, or if you are experiencing troubling physical symptoms related to your anxiety, it may be a sign of a serious physiological or psychological condition. If this sounds like your situation, we strongly encourage you to seek professional help.

Additional Bonus Material

Due to our efforts to try to keep this book to a manageable length, we've created a link that will give you access to all of your additional bonus material:

mometrix.com/bonus948/preact